Royal Festival Hall
on the South Bank

The World's Best Writers, Artists and Orchestras come to the Royal Festival Hall and Hayward Gallery - Why Don't You?

Join the **Royal Festival Hall** and **Hayward Gallery.** For just £8 you will receive a monthly diary and advanced booking for all events

To join, call the Membership Department on **0171 921 0655** or send a cheque payable to:

South Bank Centre
Membership Department
Royal Festival Hall
FREEPOST
London SE1 8BR

GRANTA 58, SUMMER 1997

EDITOR Ian Jack
DEPUTY EDITOR Robert Winder
MANAGING EDITOR Claire Wrathall
ASSISTANT EDITOR Karen Whitfield

CONTRIBUTING EDITORS Neil Belton, Pete de Bolla, Frances Coady,
Ursula Doyle, Will Hobson, Liz Jobey, Blake Morrison, Andrew O'Hagan

Granta, 2–3 Hanover Yard, Noel Road, London N1 8BE
TEL (0171) 704 9776, FAX (0171) 704 0474
SUBSCRIPTIONS (0171) 704 0470

FINANCE Geoffrey Gordon
ASSOCIATE PUBLISHER Sally Lewis
SALES David Hooper
PUBLICITY Claire Paterson, Rebecca Linsley
SUBSCRIPTIONS John Kirkby, Mark Williams
PUBLISHING ASSISTANT Jack Arthurs
TO ADVERTISE CONTACT Jenny Shramenko 0171 704 9776

Granta US, 1755 Broadway, 5th Floor, New York, NY 10019-3780, USA

PUBLISHER Rea S. Hederman

SUBSCRIPTION DETAILS: a one-year subscription (four issues) costs £24.95 (UK),
£32.95 (rest of Europe) and £39.95 (rest of the world).

Granta is printed in the United States of America. The paper used in this publication
meets the minimum requirements of American National Standard for Information
Sciences—Permanence of Paper for Printed Library Materials, ANSI Z39.48-1984. ∞

Cover design by The Senate
Cover photograph: Elliot Kaufman Collection/Corbis-Bettmann

ISBN 0 903141 07 8

JOHN
BANVILLE
Sex, lies and betrayal:
the secret history of
British treason.
THE
UNTOUCHABLE
Extracted in Granta 56: 'What Happened to Us?'
PICADOR
AVAILABLE NOW IN HARDBACK

Two rarely performed masterpieces from the nation's theatre company

RSC
ROYAL
SHAKESPEARE
COMPANY
Sponsored by
ALLIED
DOMECQ

CAMINO REAL
by Tennessee Williams

Tennessee Williams' dreamlike play where heroic and romantic figures come face to face with their lost youth.

'A triumph...irresistible revival...wonderful scenes of lust, betrayal, confession and the author's most exultant poetry of frustration and despair' OBSERVER

'Camino Real emerges as Williams' great 'lost' play... the acting is first rate' GUARDIAN

PLAYING IN REPERTOIRE UNTIL 19 AUGUST

FOR A FREE LEAFLET WITH FULL DETAILS
CALL 01789 205301

Little Eyolf
by Henrik Ibsen
in a translation by Michael Meyer

Little Eyolf is an exceptionally powerful and poignant drama about family relationships. Its frankness about sex and marriage is startling.

'The RSC in top form' DAILY TELEGRAPH

'Great drama...a production of stunning power' INDEPENDENT

PLAYING IN REPERTOIRE UNTIL 23 AUGUST

These productions are sponsored by

ALLIED DOMECQ

Swan Theatre, Stratford-upon-Avon
Box Office 01789 295623

A M B I T I O N

Aspirational & Inspirational

£5.99

£5.99

£4.99

£6.99

EDITORIAL: THE MEMOIR

The memoir is possibly the most natural of the forms available to writers. A first-person narrative based on real life, it arises easily out of our everyday conversation, being the form we use for jokes, gossip and the anecdotes that lubricate both our daily chatter ('You'll never believe what happened to me the other day') and our working habits ('Tell us a little bit about yourself'). It is almost certainly—in the what-I-did-in-the-holidays school essay—the first written form we attempt. It is the form we use in letters and postcards, or on the telephone; the way we narrate big events or private worries to anyone willing to listen. It is the preferred form of our dreams and the way we compare notes with our own hopes, tracing the extent to which life has given us what we wanted, or refused us what we once aspired to. Unaffected, idiomatic, apparently artless, it doesn't even seem to require what the world would call real work. It releases writers from the mental effort of having to make things up and dignifies them by announcing, categorically, that they are telling the truth.

In the very first sentence of his remarkable memoir *The Confessions* (published two centuries ago, in 1781) Jean-Jacques Rousseau emphasized that he was embarking on a project—self-revelation—which had no precedent and would have no imitator. He might have been correct in seeing himself as the origin of the species (St Augustine's memoir is primarily a religious argument). But on the latter point he could hardly have been more wrong. His proud, almost boastful plea for sympathy was barely in print before Wordsworth, in *The Prelude*, was making a romantic virtue of childhood memories as he measured the growth of a poetic sensibility. And then Mill and Ruskin started using self-criticism as a model for social philosophy. So by the time Joyce was writing *A Portrait of the Artist as a Young Man*, Gosse was publishing *Father and Son*, and Virginia Woolf was refining her perceptions in *A Room of One's Own*, the memoir was a popular and respectable literary form. Elements of autobiography had already become, in Goethe, Dickens, Proust and Tolstoy, one of the decisive inspirations for fiction. The great European drive towards the liberation of the individual consciousness was leading writers and readers alike to honour and support the whole idea of self-examination. Nabokov, Mary McCarthy, V. S. Pritchett, Orwell, Ackerley, Naipaul . . . the memoir became one of the most likeable products of any substantial literary career.

Recent times have seen a marked shift of emphasis, however. The memoir is no longer the prerogative of senior writers, public notables and adventurers, of—to put it loosely—the rich and famous. It is not even the preserve of those mid-range politicians who for years have recorded their unmemorable exploits in volumes with titles like 'Nothing Ventured'. The list is long, but books such as *Wild Swans* (Jung Chang), *Fever Pitch* (Nick Hornby), *This Boy's Life* (Tobias Wolff), *And when did you last see your father?* (Blake Morrison), *Angela's Ashes* (Frank McCourt) and *The Kiss* (Kathryn Harrison) have made unsung lives the very stuff of autobiography. In a new twist the memoir became not a late, personal flourish in an accomplished career, but the very first step in a writer's life. Suddenly, we could read about childhoods recollected not in tranquillity but from close range, with feeling. They deservedly gripped large audiences and in the process kindled in publishers a keen desire for follow-ups. Not all of the contrived sequels have been as fine or resonant as the models they have in their sights, but that is inevitable: for every wild swan, there are bound to be a few tame coots. The result, though, is that bookshops now groan with confessions: criminals and addicts, abuse victims and sports fans, war heroes and domestic saints (or sinners) queue up to get their lives off their chests. These days, the non-fiction shelf sometimes looks like a spillover from the self-help department, putting one in mind of nothing so much as Stephen Sondheim's lines from *West Side Story*:

> My father is a bastard,
> My ma's an SOB.
> My grandpa's always plastered,
> My grandma pushes tea.
> My sister wears a moustache,
> My brother wears a dress—
> Goodness gracious! That's why I'm a mess.

This vogue for what we might call the kitchen-sink memoir may yet prove to be something more than a passing fad. It is driven along by powerful forces. This is, after all, the Freudian century, and our daily vocabulary has been thoroughly invaded by the assumptions of psychoanalysis—a fact we confirm whenever we use words like repressed, displaced, anal or latent. We know—don't we?—that the truth lies within, that our personalities were formed by childhood experiences, most of them subconscious (another key word). We presume that the path to wisdom and happiness lies through the promotion of self-awareness. Memoirs simultaneously serve and confirm this, as do many of the cultural habits of the modern world: the chat-show culture, the colossal emphasis on self-help and self-improvement. It is axiomatic, these days, that our selves, like our bodies, require regular exercise; and even in a secular age it turns out that confession is the recommended therapeutic procedure. As a result, some modern memoirs are proud of their taboo-busting candour, not seeming to recognize that candour is itself almost a genre, that even if we brag about our most embarrassing feats we are signalling a keen pride in our frankness. But it is true that many of the unwritten limits on self-expression have been lifted. It is now more than possible to speak confidently about matters that once would have been thought impossibly intimate; indeed it seems unnaturally coy or immature not to. There was a time when it would have been difficult to write straightforwardly about, say, masturbation. Now, there'd be a fat publisher's advance on offer to anyone who could sincerely claim never to have had a go.

Other forces converge. We live in individualistic times. Right-wing thinkers insist that we get on our bikes, paddle our own canoes, make our own beds and lie in them. Their left-wing colleagues, emphasizing that the personal is political, stress that our private experiences—our racial make-up and sexuality, our ambitions—are honourable (the key word is 'valid') and deserve acknowledgement. Both sides encourage us, as it were, to help ourselves. In this sense, the memoir is a rebellion against the evasive, self-deprecating instincts of modernism, which holds most truths, and certainly most selves, to be unknowable. It is also a revolt against the recent dominion of biographers, against the occasionally arrogant ease with which complicated lives can be reduced to simple or sensational case studies. The memoir powerfully asserts the sturdy resilience of individual experience. We sing ourselves. We want, therefore we are.

All of which suggests to some critics that the memoir is a decadent, second-division genre which needs to be taken down a peg. This cannot be true. There are fine memoirs as well as lousy ones, just as as there are fine and lousy novels. It was noticeable, when the spring publication of Kathryn Harrison's *The Kiss*—the story of her incestuous relationship with her father—sparked off a little firestorm of controversy in New York, that the critical voices raised against autobiography tended to use the term 'memoir' to mean memoirs written in bad faith—self-justifying, narcissistic whinges. Yet they did not seem, when they spoke of 'the novel', to be referring to Jeffrey

Archer or Jackie Collins. It is difficult to argue for a strict hierarchy of forms: the lines are blurred and overlapping.

But there are, nevertheless, reasons to be fearful. The present fashion for memoirs does suggest the presence of something like a cult of authenticity, a suspicion of purely imaginative endeavours. We want things to be grand; but more than previously we also require them to be true. It has long been the case that the literature of fancy—science fiction, for example—has occupied a low rung on the ladder of literary approval. And there has, in the Anglo-Saxon world at any rate, always been a marked fondness for biography, if only because biography conforms so well—chronicles of real lives, told from cradle to grave—to the procedures of old-fashioned novels, procedures often neglected nowadays. But memoirs, significantly, offer something biographies rarely manage: a happy ending. The heroes and heroines of memoirs do not often leap in front of trains or poison themselves; they rarely fall on their swords or get washed overboard. There is in all memoirs a conservative tone, a knowing sense of storms safely passed, of terrors successfully overcome.

Perhaps this alone explains the seemingly insatiable taste for authentic, verifiable experience which leads publishers, and the public, to prefer authors to books. As Doris Lessing notes in her forthcoming autobiography *Walking in the Shade*, the question that has pursued her throughout her novelist's life is: 'Is it autobiographical?' And she comments on the relief that spreads across readers' faces when she can answer yes, the puzzled alarm that greets a curt no. Last year the Booker Prize-winning novelist Roddy Doyle published a pointed and affecting novel called *The Woman Who Walked into Doors*. It told the story of a battered wife. Unlike any of his previous works it was published to polite, slightly perplexed reviews and then silence. If Doyle had been able to proclaim, truthfully, that he was himself a battered wife—if his book had been by Molly Doyle, a black-eyed woman from Belfast—then we can be sure it would have been granted wall-to-wall television coverage and amazing space in the newspapers. Poor bruised Molly would have been a sensation on the chat-show circuit, telling it how it was, with that famous Irish sense of humour to make it extra poignant. As it was, the book was greeted with bafflement: as if it had been a pointless enterprise or, worse, as if the author had no right to intrude, even imaginatively, on such delicate territory. It ought at least to give us pause that the reflexes of our cultural machinery are so thoroughly weighted in favour of the first-person testimonial, and so against imaginary excursions. As has been pointed out, if Tennyson wrote *In Memoriam* today, it would almost certainly have to be presented as part of a 'Gay Encounters' series.

This issue of *Granta* explores the many uses of memoir. Doris Lessing looks back, with the steadiest eye, on the time she came to London, with a small child, £150 and—as they say in novel blurbs—a suitcase full of hopes. Paul Auster considers the chores he undertook to subsidize his dangerous and addictive writing habit. J. M. Coetzee recalls his lonely, frightened time in what others kept calling the happiest days of his life. George Steiner watches the Tyrolean rain drip over his earliest encounters with the guiding principles of scholarship. And Nell Stroud describes the family crisis that helped propel her towards a hard life under the circus top.

These are all fine writers who have written fine works. Do they help us arrive at even a tentative idea of what constitutes a memoir? Is it merely an autobiography in which the author doesn't need to check the facts? A partial autobiography, an impressionistic fragment? As it stands, the memoir is free to make up its own rules. Many novels are imaginary memoirs, first-person narratives by invented characters (what is *Lolita* but the memoir of Humbert Humbert?). So it is fair enough that the best modern memoirs should, in their way, read like novels. J. M. Coetzee's reflection *Boyhood* is presented in the third person, an intriguing gambit which suggests the barely bridgeable distance between the author and the boy he once was.

But if no formal distinction exists either way, then the defining question to be asked of memoirs concerns nothing less than the degree of truthfulness they seem to manifest. This is where today's eager appetite for self-consciousness seems contradictory. How can we enjoy memoirs, believing them to be true, when nothing, as everyone knows, is so unreliable as memory? Memoirs make a virtue of seeming unadorned, unvarnished; but the first and most unforgettable thing we learn about memory is that it is fallible. Memories, we now know, can be buried, lost, blocked, repressed, even recovered. We remember what suits us, what we have been reminded of; and there is almost no limit to what we can forget. Only those who keep faithful diaries will know what they were doing at this time, on this day, a year ago. The rest of us recall only the most intense moments, and even these tend to have been mythologized by repetition into well-wrought chapters in the story of our lives. To this extent, memoirs

11

Robert Winder

really can claim to be modern novels, all the way down to the presence of an unreliable narrator.

Not to every extent, however. In London there is an annual get-together in a smart hotel to award a prize for non-fiction. Each year the smoked salmon and noisettes of lamb are eaten beneath a large banner which proclaims: ALL THE BEST STORIES ARE TRUE. It's a cunning slogan; it makes you think. But not for very long. It only takes a moment or two to come up with a formidable list of untrue stories that can claim to have truly formed the furniture of our minds: Adam and Eve, Oedipus, Achilles, Odysseus, Noah's Ark, the birth of Christ (forgive me), the Knights of the Round Table, Hamlet, Little Red Riding Hood, Frankenstein, Dracula, the Hare and the Tortoise, Alice in Wonderland . . . the list grows longer with every mouthful.

It might be, though, that the most serious consequences of this burst of memory-gazing is being felt by non-fiction. In giving a higher priority to what we remember than to what can be found out, in putting feelings before facts, memoirs subtly demote research. In his Wigan Pier diary, Orwell recorded a woman he passed in a squalid alley; in the book itself, the woman features as a bitter face glimpsed from the window of a passing train. Which is the truer vision? The fabricated version generates a more intense flash of sympathy for the woman and her hard life, but is it truly more intense—or just simpler, more melodramatic? The lives in memoirs often have clean lines, like touched-up photographs. They glow in the dark. But does the pursuit of dramatic effects enhance the truth, or bend it?

ROBERT WINDER

Sampāti

' Why
do
you
cry? '
' I
flew
too
high.
Un-
done,
all
see
me
fall. '

In the last issue of Granta, the poem by Vikram Seth, printed correctly above, was published with an epigraph and a footnote added by the editor and not authorized by the writer.

Hayward Gallery
on the South Bank | London

RHAPSODIES IN BLACK
ART OF THE HARLEM RENAISSANCE

19 June - 17 August

A special week of talks and literature events coincides
with this major exhibition from 21 June - 28 June.

For a free brochure, ring
0171 921 0734 - Exhibitions
0171 921 0906 - Talks

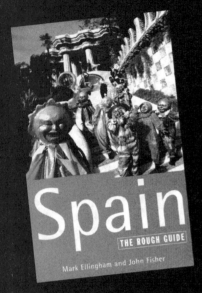
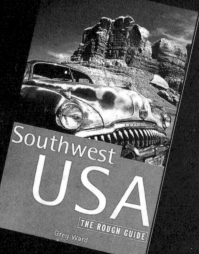

PAUL AUSTER
THE MONEY CHRONICLES

Shipping out

In my late twenties and early thirties, I went through a period of several years when everything I touched turned to failure. My marriage ended in divorce, my work as a writer foundered, and I was overwhelmed by money problems. I'm not just talking about an occasional shortfall or some periodic belt-tightenings—but a constant, grinding, almost suffocating lack of money that poisoned my soul and kept me in a never-ending state of panic.

There was no one to blame but myself. My relationship with money had always been flawed, enigmatic, full of contradictory impulses, and now I was paying the price for refusing to take a clear-cut stand on the matter. All along my only ambition had been to write. I had known that as early as sixteen or seventeen years old, and I had never deluded myself into thinking I could make a living at it. Becoming a writer is not a 'career decision' like becoming a doctor or a policeman. You don't choose it so much as get chosen, and once you accept the fact that you're not fit for anything else, you have to be prepared to walk a long, hard road for the rest of your days. Unless you turn out to be a favourite of the gods (and woe to the man who banks on that), your work will never bring in enough to support you, and if you mean to have a roof over your head and not starve to death, you must resign yourself to doing other work to pay the bills. I understood all that. I was prepared for it. I had no complaints. In that respect, I was immensely lucky. I didn't particularly want anything in the way of material goods, and the prospect of being poor didn't frighten me. All I wanted was a chance to do the work I felt I had it in me to do.

Most writers lead double lives. They earn good money at legitimate professions and carve out time for their writing as best they can: early in the morning, late at night, weekends, vacations. My problem was that I had no interest in leading a double life. It's not that I wasn't willing to work, but the idea of punching a clock at some nine-to-five job left me cold, utterly devoid of enthusiasm. I was in my early twenties, and I felt too young to settle down, too full of other plans to waste my time earning

PAUL AUSTER IN 1967, AGED TWENTY

17

more money than I either wanted or needed. As far as finances went, I just wanted to get by. Life was cheap in those days, and with no responsibility for anyone but myself, I figured I could scrape along on an annual income of roughly three thousand dollars.

Little by little I learned how to improvise, trained myself how to roll with the punches. During my last two years at Columbia I took any number of odd freelance jobs, gradually developing a taste for the kind of literary hack work that would keep me going until I was thirty—and which ultimately led to my downfall. There was a certain romance in it, I suppose, a need to affirm myself as an outsider and prove that I could make it on my own without kowtowing to anyone else's idea of what constituted the good life. My life would be good if and only if I stuck to my guns and refused to give in. Art was holy, and to follow its call meant making any sacrifice that was demanded of you, maintaining your purity of purpose to the bitter end.

Knowing French helped. It was hardly a rarefied skill, but I was good enough at it to have some translation jobs tossed my way. Art writings, for example, and an exceptionally tedious document from the French Embassy about the reorganization of its staff that droned on for more than a hundred pages. I also tutored a high-school girl one spring, travelling across town every Saturday morning to talk to her about poetry, and another time I was collared by a friend (for no pay) to stand on an outdoor podium with Jean Genet and translate his speech in defence of the Black Panthers. Genet walked around with a red flower tucked behind his ear and rarely stopped smiling the whole time he was on the Columbia campus. New York seemed to make him happy, and he handled the attention he received that day with great poise. One night not long after that I bumped into an acquaintance in the West End, the old student watering-hole on Broadway and 114th Street. He told me that he had just started working for a pornography publisher, and if I wanted to try my hand at writing a dirty book, the price was fifteen hundred dollars per novel. I was more than willing to have a go at it, but my inspiration petered out after twenty or thirty pages. There were just so many ways to describe that one thing, I discovered, and my stock of synonyms soon dried up. I started writing book reviews instead—for a shoddily put together publication aimed at students. Sensing that the magazine wasn't going to add up to much, I signed my articles with a pseudonym, just to keep things interesting. Quinn was the name I chose for myself, Paul Quinn. The pay, I remember, was twenty-five dollars per review.

That I wound up working on an oil tanker for several months was largely a matter of chance. You can't work on a ship without a Merchant Seaman's card, and you can't obtain a Merchant Seaman's card without a job on a ship. Unless you know someone who can break through the circle for you, it's impossible to get in. The someone who did it for me was my mother's second husband, Norman Schiff. My mother had remarried about a year after her divorce from my father, and by 1970 my stepfather and I had been fast friends for nearly five years. An excellent man with a generous heart, he had consistently stood behind me and supported my vague, impractical ambitions. His early death in 1982 (at age fifty-five) remains one of the great sorrows of my life, but back then as I was finishing up my year of graduate work and preparing to leave school, his health was still reasonably good. He practised law, mostly as a labour negotiator, and among his many clients at the time was the Esso Seaman's Union, for whom he worked as legal counsel. That was how the idea got planted in my head. I asked him if he could swing me a job on one of the Esso tankers, and he said he would handle it. And without further ado, that was precisely what he did.

The *Esso Florence* was one of the oldest tankers in the fleet, a pipsqueak relic from a bygone age. Put a two-door Chevy next to a stretch limousine, and you'll have some idea of how it compared to the supertankers they build today. Already in service during World War II, my ship had logged untold thousands of watery miles by the time I set foot on it. There were enough beds on board to accommodate a hundred men, but only thirty-three of us were needed to take care of the work that had to be done. That meant that each person had his own cabin—an enormous benefit when you considered how much time we had to spend together.

19

With other jobs you get to go home at night, but we were boxed in with each other twenty-four hours a day. Every time you looked up, the same faces were there. We worked together, lived together, and ate together, and without the chance for some genuine privacy, the routine would have been intolerable.

We shuttled between the Atlantic coast and the Gulf of Mexico, loading and unloading airplane fuel at various refineries along the way: Charleston, South Carolina; Tampa, Florida; Galveston, Texas. My initial responsibilities were mopping floors and making beds, first for the crew and then for the officers. The technical term for the position was utility man, but in plain language the job was a combination of janitor, garbage collector and chambermaid. I can't say I was thrilled to be scrubbing toilets and picking up dirty socks, but once I got the hang of it, the work turned out to be incredibly easy. In less than a week, I had polished my custodial skills to such a point that it took me only two or two-and-a-half hours to finish my chores for the day. That left me with abundant quantities of free time, most of which I spent alone in my cabin. I read books, I wrote, I did everything I had done before—but more productively, somehow, with better powers of concentration now that there was so little to distract me. In many ways, it felt like an almost ideal existence, a perfect life.

Then, after a month or two of this blissful regimen, I was 'bumped' into the galley. The ship rarely travelled more than five days between ports, and nearly everywhere we docked, some crew members would get off, and others would get on. The jobs for the fresh arrivals were doled out according to seniority. It was a strict pecking order, and the longer you had worked for the company, the more say you had in what you were given. As a low man on the totem pole, I had no say at all. If an old-timer wanted my job, he had only to ask for it, and it was his. After my long run of good luck, the boom finally fell somewhere in Texas.

The job of messman quadrupled my hours and made my life altogether more eventful. My responsibilities now included serving three meals a day to the crew (about twenty men), washing dishes by hand, cleaning the mess hall and writing out the menus for the steward, who was generally too drunk to bother with them himself. My breaks were short—no more than an hour or two between meals—and yet in spite of having to work much harder than before, my income actually shrank. On the old job, there had been plenty of time for me to put in an extra hour or two in the evenings, scraping and painting in the boiler room, for example, or refurbishing rusty spots on deck, and those volunteer jobs had padded my pay cheque quite nicely. Still, in spite of the disadvantages, I found working in the mess hall more of a challenge than mopping floors had been. It was a public job, so to speak, and in addition to all the hustling around that was now required of me, I had to stay on my toes as far as the men were concerned. That, finally, was my most important task: to learn how to handle the griping and rough-tempered complaints, to fend off insults, to give as good as I got.

The crew was a fairly grimy, ill-mannered bunch. Most of the men lived in Texas and Louisiana, and apart from a handful of Chicanos, one or two blacks, and the odd foreigner who cropped up now and then, the dominant tone on board was white, redneck and blue collar. A jocular atmosphere prevailed, replete with funny stories and dirty jokes and much talk about guns and cars, but there were deep, smouldering currents of racism in many of those men, and I made a point of choosing my friends carefully. To hear one of your co-workers defend South African apartheid as you sat with him over a cup of coffee ('they know how to treat niggers down there') doesn't bring much joy to the soul, and if I found myself hanging out mostly with the dark-skinned and Spanish-speaking men around me, there was a good reason for it. As a New York Jew with a college degree, I was an entirely alien specimen on that ship, a man from Mars. It would have been easy to make up stories about myself, but I had no interest in doing that. If someone asked me what my religion was or where I came from, I told him. If he didn't like it, I figured that was his problem. I wasn't going to hide who I was or pretend to be someone else just to avoid trouble. As it happened, I had only one awkward run-in the whole time I was there. One of the men started calling me Sammy whenever I walked by. He seemed to think it was funny, but as I failed to see any humour in the epithet, I told him to stop it. He did it again the next day, and once again I told him to stop it. When he did it again the day after that, I understood that polite words were not going to be enough. I grabbed hold of his shirt, slammed him against the wall, and very calmly told him that if he ever called me that again, I would kill him. It shocked me to hear myself talk like that. I was not someone who trafficked in violence, and I had never made that kind of threat to anyone, but for that one brief instant, a demon took possession of my soul. Luckily, my willingness to fight was enough to defuse the fight before it began. My tormentor threw up his hands in a gesture of peace. 'It was just a joke,' he said, 'just a joke,' and that was the end of it. As time went on, we actually became friends.

I loved being out on the water, surrounded by nothing but sky and light, the immensity of the vacant air. Seagulls accompanied us wherever we went, circling overhead as they waited for buckets of garbage to be dumped overboard. Hour after hour, they would hover patiently just above the ship, scarcely beating their wings until the scraps went flying, at which point they would plunge frantically into the foam, calling out to each other like drunks at a football game. Few pleasures can match the spectacle of that foam, of sitting at the stern of a large ship and staring into the white, churning tumult of the wake below. There is something hypnotic about it, and on still days the sense of well-being that washes through you can be overpowering. On the other hand, rough weather also holds its charms. As summer melted away, and we headed into autumn, the inclemencies multiplied, bringing down some wild winds and pelting rains, and at those moments the ship felt no more safe or solid than a child's paper boat. Tankers have been known to crack in half, and all it takes is one wrong wave to do the job. The worst stretch, I remember, occurred when we were off Cape Hatteras in late September or early October, a twelve- or fifteen-hour period of flipping and flopping through a tropical storm. The captain stayed up all night at the wheel, and even after the worst of it was over and the steward instructed me to carry the captain his breakfast the next morning, I was nearly blown overboard when I stepped on to the bridge with my tray. The rain might have stopped, but the wind speed was still at gale force.

For all that, working on the *Esso Florence* had little to do with high-seas adventure. The tanker was essentially a floating factory, and rather than introduce me to some exotic swashbuckling life, it taught me to think of myself as an industrial labourer. I was one of millions now, an insect toiling beside countless other insects, and every task I performed was part of the great, grinding enterprise of American capitalism. Petroleum was the primary source of wealth, the raw material that fuelled the profit-machine and kept it running, and I was glad to be where I was, grateful to have landed in the belly of the beast. The refineries where we loaded and unloaded our cargo were enormous, hellish structures, labyrinthine networks of hissing pipes and towers of flame, and to walk through one of them at night was to feel that you were living in your own worst dream. Most of all, I will never forget the fish, the hundreds of dead, iridescent fish floating on the rank, oil-saturated water around the refinery docks. That was the standard welcoming committee, the sight that greeted us every time the tugboats pulled us into another port. The ugliness was so universal, so deeply connected to the business of making money and the power that money bestowed on the ones who made it—even to the point of disfiguring the landscape, of turning the natural world inside out—that I began to develop a grudging respect for it. Get to the bottom of things, I told myself, and this was how the world looked.

Whenever we docked somewhere, I made it my business to leave the ship and spend some time ashore. I had never been south of the Mason–Dixon Line, and those brief jaunts on to solid ground took me to places that felt a lot less familiar or understandable than anything I'd met up with in Paris or Dublin. The South was a different country, a separate American universe from the one I'd known in the North. Most of the time, I tagged along with one or two of my shipmates, going the rounds with them as they visited their customary haunts. If Baytown, Texas, stands out with particular clarity, that was because we spent more time there than anywhere else. I found it a sad, crumbling little place. Along the main drag, a row of once-elegant movie theatres had been turned into Baptist churches, and instead of announcing the titles of the latest Hollywood films, the marquees now sported fiery quotations from the Bible. More often than not, we wound up in sailors' bars on the back streets of broken-down neighbourhoods.

23

All of them were essentially the same: squalid, low-life joints; dim drinking holes; dank corners of oblivion. Everything was always bare inside. Not a single picture on the walls, not one touch of publican warmth. At most there was a quarter-a-rack pool table, a jukebox stuffed with country-and-western songs, and a drink menu that consisted of just one drink: beer.

Once, when the ship was in a Houston dry dock for some minor repairs, I spent the afternoon in a skid-row bar with a Danish oiler named Teddy, a wild man who laughed at the slightest provocation and spoke English with an accent so thick that I scarcely understood a word he said. Walking down the street in the blinding Texas sun, we crossed paths with a drunken couple. It was still early in the day, but this man and woman were already so soused, so entrenched in their inebriation, they must have been going at the booze since dawn. They wobbled along the sidewalk with their arms round each other, listing this way and that, their heads rolling, their knees buckling, and yet both with enough energy left to be engaged in a nasty, foul-mouthed quarrel. From the sound of their voices, I gathered they'd been at it for years—a pair of bickering stumblebums in search of their next drink, forever repeating the same lines to each other, forever shuffling through the same old song and dance. As it turned out, they wound up in the bar where Teddy and I had chosen to while away the afternoon, and because I was not more than ten feet away from them, I was in a perfect position to observe the following little drama:

The man leaned forward and barked out at the woman across the table. 'Darlene,' he said, in a drawling, besotted voice, 'get me another beer.'

Darlene had been nodding off just then, and it took her a good long moment to open her eyes and bring the man into focus. Another long moment ticked by, and then she finally said, 'What?'

'Get me a beer,' the man repeated. 'On the double.'

Darlene was waking up now, and a lovely, fuck-you sassiness suddenly brightened her face. She was clearly in no mood to be pushed around.

'Get it yourself, Charlie,' she snapped back at him. 'I ain't your slave, you know.'

'Damn it, woman,' Charlie said. 'You're my wife, ain't you?

What the hell did I marry you for? Get me the goddamn beer!'

Darlene let out a loud, histrionic sigh. You could tell she was up to something, but her intentions were still obscure. 'OK, darling,' she said, putting on the voice of a meek, simpering wife, 'I'll get it for you,' and then stood up from the table and staggered over to the bar.

Charlie sat there with a grin on his face, gloating over his small, manly victory. He was the boss, all right, and no one was going to tell him different. If you wanted to know who wore the pants in that family, just talk to him.

A minute later, Darlene returned to the table with a fresh bottle of Bud. 'Here's your beer, Charlie,' she said, and then, with one quick flick of the wrist, proceeded to dump the contents of the bottle on to her husband's head. Bubbles foamed up in his hair and eyebrows; rivulets of amber liquid streamed down his face. Charlie made a lunge for her, but he was too drunk to get very close. Darlene threw her head back and burst out laughing. 'How do you like your beer, Charlie?' she said. 'How do you like your fucking beer?'

Of all the scenes I witnessed in those bars, nothing quite matched the bleak comedy of Charlie's baptism, but for overall oddness, a plunge into the deepest heart of the grotesque, I would have to single out Big Mary's Place in Tampa, Florida. This was a large, brightly lit emporium that catered to the whims of dock hands and sailors, and it had been in business for many years. Among its features were half a dozen pool tables, a long mahogany bar, inordinately high ceilings, and live entertainment in the form of quasi-naked go-go dancers. These girls were the cornerstone of the operation, the element that set Big Mary's Place apart from other establishments of its kind—and one look told you that they weren't hired for their beauty, nor for their ability to dance. The sole criterion was size. The bigger the better was how Big Mary put it, and the bigger you got, the more money you were paid. The effect was quite disturbing. It was a freak show of flesh, a cavalcade of bouncing white blubber, and with four girls dancing on the platform behind the bar at once, the act resembled a casting call for the lead role in *Moby-Dick*. Each girl was a continent unto herself, a mass of quivering lard decked out

25

in a string bikini, and as one shift replaced another, the assault on the eyes was unrelenting. I have no memory of how I got there, but I distinctly recall that my companions that night were two of the gentler souls from the ship (Martinez, a family man from Texas, and Donnie, a seventeen-year-old boy from Baton Rouge) and that they were both just as flummoxed as I was. I can still see them sitting across from me with their mouths hanging open, doing everything they could not to laugh from embarrassment. At one point, Big Mary herself came over and sat down with us at our table. A splendid dirigible of a woman dressed in an orange pants suit and wearing a ring on every finger, she wanted to know if we were having a good time. When we assured her that we were, she waved to one of the girls at the bar. 'Barbara,' she yelled, belting out the word in a brassy, three-pack-a-day voice, 'get your fat butt over here!' Barbara came, all smiles and good humour, laughing as Big Mary poked her in the stomach and pinched the ample rolls bulging from her hips. 'She was a scrawny one at first,' Mary explained, 'but I've fattened her up pretty good. Ain't that so, Barbara?' she said, cackling like some mad scientist who's just pulled off a successful experiment, and Barbara couldn't have agreed with her more. As I listened to them talk, it suddenly occurred to me that I had it all wrong. I hadn't gone to sea. I'd run off and joined the circus.

In the end, the months I spent on that ship felt like years. Time passes in a different way when you're out on the water, and given that the bulk of what I experienced was utterly new to me, and given that I was constantly on my guard because of that, I managed to crowd an astonishing number of impressions and memories into a relatively small sliver of my life. Even now, I don't fully understand what I was hoping to prove by shipping out like that. To keep myself off balance, I suppose. Or, very simply, just to see if I could hold my own in a world I didn't belong to. In that respect, I don't think I failed. I can't say what I accomplished during those months, but at the same time I'm certain I didn't fail.

I received my discharge papers in Charleston. The company provided airfare home, but you could pocket the money if you wanted to and make your own travel arrangements. I chose to keep the money. The trip by milk train took twenty-four hours, and I rode back with a fellow crew member from New York, Juan Castillo. Juan was in his late forties or early fifties, a squat, lumpy man with a big head and a face that looked like something pieced together with the skins and pulps of nineteen mashed potatoes. He had just walked off an oil tanker for the last time, and in appreciation of his twenty-five years of service to the company, Esso had given him a gold watch. I don't know how many times Juan pulled that watch out of his pocket and looked at it during the long ride home, but every time he did, he would shake his head for a few seconds and then burst out laughing. At one point the ticket collector stopped to talk to us during one of his strolls down the aisle of the car. He looked very natty in his uniform, I remember, a black Southern gentleman of the old school. In a haughty, somewhat condescending manner, he opened the conversation by asking: 'You boys going up north to work in the steel mills?'

We must have been a curious pair, Juan and I. I recall that I was wearing a beat-up leather jacket at the time, but other than that I can't see myself, have no sense of what I looked like or what other people saw when they looked at me. The ticket collector's question is the only clue I have. Juan had taken pictures of his shipmates to put in the family album at home, and I remember standing on the deck and looking into the camera for him as he clicked the shutter. He promised to send me a copy of the photo, but he never did.

Journey to Gaul

In the three-and-a-half years I lived in France, I had any number of jobs, bounced from one part-time gig to another, freelanced until I was blue in the face. When I didn't have work, I was looking for work. When I had work, I was thinking about how to find more. Even at the best of times, I rarely earned enough to feel secure, and yet in spite of one or two close calls, I managed to avoid total ruin. It was, as they say, a hand-to-mouth existence. Through it all, I wrote steadily, and if much of what I wrote was discarded (mostly prose), a fair chunk of it (mostly poems and translations) was not. For better or worse, by the time I returned to New York in July 1974, the idea of not writing was inconceivable to me.

Most of the work I landed came through friends or the friends of friends or the friends of friends of friends. Living in a foreign country restricts your opportunities, and unless you know some people who are willing to help you, it is next to impossible to get started. Not only will doors not open when you knock on them, but you won't even know where to look for those doors in the first place. I was lucky enough to have some allies, and at one time or another they all moved small mountains on my behalf.

At one point, I was steered to the Paris bureau of the *New York Times*. I can't remember who was responsible for the connection, but an editor named Josette Lazar began throwing translations my way whenever she could: articles for the Sunday *Book Review*, op-ed pieces by Sartre and Foucault, this and that. One summer, when my money was at low ebb again, she finagled a position for me as the night-time switchboard operator at the *Times* office. The phone didn't ring very often, and mostly I just sat at a desk, working on poems or reading books. One night, however, there was a frantic call from a reporter stationed somewhere in Europe. 'Sinyavsky's defected,' she said. 'What should I do?' I had no idea what she should do, but since none of the editors was around at that hour, I figured I had to tell her something. 'Follow the story,' I said. 'Go where you have to go, do what you have to do, but stick with the story, come hell or high water.' She thanked me profusely for the advice and then hung up.

Few of these jobs paid well, but they all brought in something, and if I didn't always have great stocks of food in my refrigerator, I was rarely without a pack of cigarettes in my pocket. Still, I couldn't have sustained myself on odds and ends alone. I needed another source of income to pay the bills, and as luck would have it I found one. To put it more accurately, it found me. For the first two years I spent in Paris, it was the difference between eating and not eating.

The story goes back to 1967. During an earlier stay as a student, an American friend had introduced me to a woman I will call Madame X. Her husband, Monsieur X, was a well-known film producer of the old style (epics, extravaganzas, a maker of deals), and it was through her that I started working for him. The first opportunity arose just a few months after I arrived. There was no telephone in the apartment I had rented, which was still the case with many Paris apartments in 1971, and there were only two ways of contacting me: by *pneumatique*, a rapid, intra-city telegram sent through the post office, or by coming to the apartment and knocking on the door. One morning, not long after I had woken up, Madame X knocked on the door. 'How would you like to earn a hundred dollars today?' she said. The job seemed simple enough: read a movie script, then write out a six- or seven-page summary. The only constraint was time. A potential backer of the film was waiting on a yacht somewhere in the Mediterranean, and the outline had to be delivered to him within forty-eight hours.

Madame X was a flamboyant, stormy character, the first larger-than-life woman I had ever met. Mexican by birth, married since the age of eighteen or nineteen, the mother of a boy just a few years younger than I was, she lived her own independent life, drifting in and out of her husband's orbit in ways I was still too unsophisticated to understand. Artistic by temperament, she dabbled by turns at painting and writing, showing talent in both fields but with too little discipline or concentration to take those talents very far. Her true gift was encouraging others, and she surrounded herself with artists and would-be artists of all ages, hobnobbing with the known and the unknown as both a colleague and a patroness. Wherever she went, she was the centre of attention, the gorgeous, soulful woman with the long black hair and the hooded cloaks and the clattering Mexican jewellery— moody, generous, loyal, her head full of dreams. Somehow or other, I had made it on to her list, and because I was young and just starting out, she counted me among those friends who needed looking after, the poor and struggling ones who required an occasional helping hand.

There were others, too, of course, and a couple of them were invited along with me that morning to earn the same round figure that I had been promised. A hundred dollars sounds like pocket change today, but back then it represented more than half a month's rent, and I was in no position to turn down a sum of that magnitude. The work was to be done at the Xs' apartment, an immense, palatial establishment in the sixteenth arrondissement with untold numbers of high-ceilinged rooms. The starting time was set for eleven o'clock, and I showed up with half an hour to spare.

I had met each of my co-workers before. One of them was an American in his mid-twenties, a fey, unemployed pianist who walked around in women's high heels and had recently spent time in a hospital with a collapsed lung. The other was a Frenchman with decades of film experience, mostly as a second-unit director. Among his credits were the chariot scenes in *Ben-Hur* and the desert scenes in *Lawrence of Arabia*, but since those days of wealth and success, he had fallen on hard times: nervous breakdowns, periods of confinement in mental wards, no work. He and the pianist were major reclamation projects for Madame X, and throwing me together with them was just one example of how she operated. No matter how good her intentions were, they were invariably undermined by complex, impractical schemes, a desire to kill too many birds with a single stone. Rescuing one person is hard enough, but to think you can save the whole world all at once is to ask for disappointment.

So there we were, the most mismatched trio ever assembled, gathered around the gigantic table in the dining room of the Xs' gigantic apartment. The script in question was also gigantic. A work of nearly three hundred pages (three times the length of the normal script), it looked like the telephone book of a large city. Because the Frenchman was the only one with any professional knowledge of the movies, the pianist and I deferred to him and allowed him to take charge of the discussion. The first thing he did was pull out a sheet of blank paper and begin jotting down the names of actors—Frank Sinatra, Dean Martin, Sammy Davis, Jnr, followed by six or seven others. When he was finished, he slapped his hands on the table with great satisfaction. 'You see this piece of paper?' he asked. The pianist and I nodded our heads. 'Believe it or not, this little piece of paper is worth ten million dollars.' He patted the list once or twice and then pushed it aside. 'Ten, maybe twelve million dollars.' He spoke with the utmost conviction, betraying not the slightest hint of humour or irony. After a brief pause, he opened the manuscript to the first page. 'Well,' he said, 'are we ready to begin?'

Almost immediately, he became excited. On the second or third line of the first page, he noticed that the name of one of the characters began with a letter Z. 'Aha,' he said. 'Z. This is very important. Pay close attention, my friends. This is going to be a political film. Mark my words.'

Z was the title of a film by Costa-Gavras, a popular hit two years earlier. That film had most assuredly been about politics, but the screenplay we had been asked to summarize was not. It was an action-thriller about smuggling. Largely set in the Sahara desert, it featured trucks, motorcycles, and guns, several gangs of warring bad guys, and a number of spectacular explosions. The only thing that set it apart from a thousand other movies was its length.

We had been at work for approximately a minute and a half, and already the pianist had lost interest. He stared down at the table and snickered to himself as the Frenchman rambled on, lurching from one bit of nonsense to another. Suddenly, without any transition or preamble, the poor man started talking about David Lean, recalling several philosophical discussions he'd had with the director fifteen years earlier. Then, just as abruptly, he broke off from his reminiscences, stood up from the table, and walked around the room, straightening the pictures on the walls. When he was finished with that task, he announced that he was going to the kitchen to look for a cup of coffee. The pianist shrugged. 'I think I'll go play the piano,' he said, and just like that, he was gone as well.

As I waited for them to return, I started reading the script. I couldn't think of anything else to do, and by the time it dawned on me that neither one of them would be coming back, I had worked my way through most of it. Eventually, one of Monsieur X's associates drifted into the room. He was a youngish, good-natured American who also happened to be Madame X's special friend (the complexities of the household were fathomless), and he instructed me to finish the job on my own, guaranteeing that if I managed to produce an acceptable piece of work by seven o'clock, all three of the hundred-dollar payments would be mine. I told him I would do my best. Before I hustled out of there and went home to my typewriter, he gave me an excellent bit of advice. 'Just remember,' he said. 'This is the movies, not Shakespeare. Make it as vulgar as you can.'

I wound up writing the synopsis in the extravagant, overheated language of Hollywood coming attractions. If they wanted vulgar, I would give them vulgar. I had sat through enough movie trailers to know what they sounded like, and by dredging up every hackneyed phrase I could think of, by piling one excess on top of another, I boiled the story down to seven pages of frantic, non-stop action, a bloodbath wrought in pulsing, Technicolor prose. I finished typing at six-thirty. An hour later, a chauffeur-driven car arrived downstairs to take me and my girlfriend to the restaurant where Monsieur and Madame X had invited us for dinner. The moment we got there, I was supposed to deliver the pages to him in person.

Monsieur X was a small, enigmatic man in his mid to late fifties. Of Russian-Jewish origin, he spoke several languages with equal fluency, often shifting from French to English to Spanish in the course of a single conversation, but always with the same cumbersome accent, as if in the end he didn't feel at home in any of them. He had been producing movies for over thirty years, and in a career of countless ups and downs, he had backed good films and bad films, big films and small films, art films and trash films. Some had made piles of money for him, others had put him miserably in debt. I had crossed paths with him only a few times before that night, but he had always struck me as a lugubrious person, a man who played things close to the vest—shrewd, hidden, unknowable. Even as he talked to you, you sensed that he was thinking about something else, working out some mysterious calculations that might or might not have had anything to do with what he was saying. It's not that they didn't, but at the same time it would have been wrong to assume that they did.

That night in the restaurant, he was noticeably edgy when I arrived. A potentially lucrative deal hinged on the work of one of his wife's arty friends, and he was anything but optimistic. I had barely settled into my seat when he asked to see the pages I had written. As the rest of us made small talk around the table, Monsieur sat hunched in silence, reading through my florid, slam-bang paragraphs. Little by little, a smile began to form on his lips. He started nodding to himself as he turned the pages, and once or twice he was even heard to mutter the word 'good' under his breath. He didn't look up, however. Not until he'd come to the last sentence did he finally raise his head and give me the verdict.

'Excellent,' he said. 'This is just what I wanted.' The relief in his voice was almost palpable.

Madame X said something about how she'd told him so, and he confessed that he'd had his doubts. 'I thought it would be too literary,' he said. 'But this is good. This is just right.'

He became very effusive after that. We were in a large, gaudy restaurant in Montmartre, and he immediately started snapping his fingers for the flower girl. She came scurrying over to our table, and Monsieur X bought a dozen roses, which he handed to my girlfriend as an impromptu gift. Then he reached into his breast pocket, pulled out his chequebook, and wrote me a cheque for three hundred dollars. It was the first cheque I had ever seen from a Swiss bank.

I was glad to have delivered the goods under pressure, glad to have earned my three hundred bucks, glad to have been roped into the absurd events of that day, but once we left the restaurant and I returned to my apartment on the rue Jacques Mawas, I assumed that the story was over. It never once crossed my mind that Monsieur X might have further plans for me. One afternoon the following week, however, as I sat at my table working on a poem, I was interrupted by a loud knock on the door. It was one of Monsieur X's gofers, an elderly gentleman I'd seen lurking about the house on my visits there, but I had never had the pleasure of talking to him. He wasted no time in getting to the point. Are you Paul Auster? he asked. When I told him I was, he informed me that Monsieur X wanted to see me. When? I asked. Right now, he said. There's a taxi waiting downstairs.

It was a little like being arrested by the secret police. I suppose I could have refused the invitation, but the cloak-and-dagger atmosphere made me curious, and I decided to go along to see what was up. In the cab, I asked my chaperone why I had been summoned like this, but the old man merely shrugged. Monsieur X had told him to bring me back to the house, and that was what he was doing. His job was to follow orders, not ask questions. I therefore remained in the dark, and as I mulled over

33

the question myself, the only answer I could think of was that Monsieur X was no longer satisfied with the work I had done for him. By the time I walked into his apartment, I was fully expecting him to ask me for the money back.

He was dressed in a paisley smoking jacket with satin lapels, and as he entered the room where I'd been told to wait for him, I noticed that he was rubbing his hands together. I had no idea what that gesture meant.

'Last week,' he said, 'you do good works for me. Now I want to make package deal.'

That explained the hands. It was the gesture of a man ready to do business, and all of a sudden, on the strength of that dashed-off, tongue-in-cheek manuscript I'd concocted for him the other day, it looked as though I was about to be in business with Monsieur X. He had at least two jobs for me right away, and if all went well with those, the implication was that others would follow. I needed the money and accepted, but not without a certain wariness. I was stepping into a realm I didn't understand, and unless I kept my wits about me, I realized that strange things could be in store for me. I don't know how or why I knew that, but I did. When Monsieur X started talking about giving me a role in one of his upcoming movies, a swashbuckling adventure story for which I would need fencing and riding lessons, I held my ground. 'We'll see,' I said. 'The fact is, I'm not much interested in acting.'

Apparently, the man on the yacht had liked my synopsis just as much as Monsieur X had. Now he wanted to take things to the next level and was commissioning a translation of the screenplay from French into English. That was the first job. The second job was somewhat less cut and dried. Madame X was at work on a play, Monsieur X told me, and he had agreed to finance a production at a theatre in London next season. The piece was about Quetzalcoatl, the mythical plumed serpent, and since much of it was written in verse, and since much of that verse was written in Spanish, he wanted me to turn it into English and make sure that the drama was in playable shape. Fine, I said, and that was how we left it. I did both jobs, everyone was satisfied, and two or three months later Madame X's play was performed in London. It was a vanity production, of course, but the reviews were good, and all in all the play was quite well received. A British publisher happened to attend one of the performances, and he was so impressed by what he'd seen that he proposed to Madame X that she turn the play into a prose narrative, which he would then publish as a book.

That was where things started getting sticky between me and Monsieur X. Madame X didn't have it in her to write the book on her own, and he believed that I was the one person on earth capable of helping her. I might have accepted the job under different circumstances, but since he also wanted me to go to Mexico to do the work, I told him I wasn't interested. Why the book had to be written in Mexico was never made clear to me. Research, local colour, something along those lines, I'm not sure. I was fond of Madame X, but being thrown together with her for an unspecified length of time struck me as less than a good idea. I didn't even have to think about Monsieur X's offer. I turned him down on the spot, figuring that would close the matter once and for all. Events proved me wrong. True indifference has power, I learned, and my refusal to take the job irritated Monsieur X and got under his skin. He wasn't in the habit of having people say no to him, and he became hell-bent on changing my mind. Over the next several months, he launched an all-out campaign to wear down my resistance, besieging me with letters, telegrams and promises of ever greater sums of money. In the end, I reluctantly gave in. As with every other bad decision I've made in my life, I acted against my better judgement, allowing secondary considerations to interfere with the clarity of my instincts. In this case, what tipped the balance was money. I was having a hard time of it just then, desperately falling behind in my struggle to remain solvent, and Monsieur X's offer had grown so large, would eliminate so many of my problems at once, that I talked myself into accepting the wisdom of compromise. I thought I was being clever. Once I had climbed down from my high horse, I laid out my conditions in the toughest terms I could think of. I would go to Mexico for exactly one month, I told him—no more, no less—and I wanted full payment in cash before I left Paris. It was the first time I had ever negotiated for anything, but I was determined to protect myself, and I refused to yield on any of these points. Monsieur X was less than thrilled with my intractability, but he understood that I'd gone as far as I would go and gave in to my demands. The same day I left for Mexico, I deposited twenty-five one-hundred-dollar bills in my bank account. Whatever happened in the next month, at least I wouldn't be broke when I returned.

I was expecting things to go wrong, but not quite to the degree that they did. Without rehashing the whole complicated business (the man who threatened to kill me, the schizophrenic girl who thought I was a Hindu god, the drunken, suicidal misery that permeated every household I entered), the thirty days I spent in Mexico were among the grimmest, most unsettling of my life. Madame X had already been there for a couple of weeks when I arrived, and I quickly learned that she was in no shape to work on the book. Her boyfriend had just left her, and this love drama had plunged her into the throes of an acute despair. It's not that I blamed her for her feelings, but she was so distraught, so distracted by her suffering, that the book was the last thing she wanted to think about. What was I supposed to do? I tried to get her started, but she simply wasn't interested. Every time we took a stab at it, the conversation would quickly veer off on to other subjects. Again and again, she broke down and cried. Again and again, we got nowhere. After several of these attempts, I understood that the only reason she was bothering to make an effort was because of me. She knew that I was being paid to help her, and she didn't want to let me down, didn't want to admit that I had come all this way for nothing.

That was the essential flaw in the arrangement. To assume that a book can be written by a person who is not a writer is already a murky proposition, but granting that such a thing is possible, and granting that the person who wants to write the book has someone else to help with the writing of it, perhaps the two of them, with much hard work and dedication, can arrive at an acceptable result. On the other hand, if the person who is not a writer does not want to write a book, of what use is the someone else? Such was the quandary I found myself in. I was willing to help Madame X write her book but I couldn't help her unless she wanted to write it, and if she didn't want to, there was nothing I could do but sit around and wait until she did.

So there I sat, biding my time in the little village of Tepotzolán, hoping that Madame X would wake up one morning and discover that she had a new outlook on life. I was staying with Madame X's brother (whose unhappy marriage to an American woman was on its last legs), and I filled my days with aimless walks around the dusty town, stepping over mangy dogs and batting flies out of my face and accepting invitations to drink beers with the local drunks. My room was in a stucco outbuilding on the brother's property, and I slept under a muslin netting to guard against the tarantulas and mosquitoes. The crazy girl kept showing up with one of her friends, a Central American Hare Krishna with a shaved head and orange robes, and boredom ate away at me like some tropical disease. I wrote one or two short poems, but otherwise I languished, unable to think, bogged down by a persistent, nameless anxiety.

When I finally returned to Paris, Monsieur X arranged to meet me in the lobby of a hotel on the Champs-Elysées. I can't remember why he chose that place, but I think it had something to do with another appointment he'd scheduled there before mine, strictly a matter of convenience. In any case, we didn't talk in the hotel. The instant I showed up, he led me outside again and pointed to his car, which was waiting for us just in front of the entrance. It was a tan Jaguar with leather upholstery, and the man behind the wheel was dressed in a white shirt. 'We'll talk in there,' Monsieur X said. 'It's more private.' We climbed into the back seat, the driver started up the engine, and the car pulled away from the curb. 'Just drive around,' Monsieur X said to the chauffeur. I suddenly felt as if I had landed in a gangster movie.

Most of the story was known by then, but he wanted me to give him a full report, an autopsy of the failure. I did my best to describe what had happened, expressing more than once how sorry I was that things hadn't worked out, but with Madame X's heart no longer in the book, I said, there wasn't much I could do to motivate her. Monsieur X seemed to accept all this with great calm. As far as I could tell, he wasn't angry, not even especially

Paul Auster

disappointed. Just when I thought the interview was about to end, however, he brought up the subject of my payment. Since nothing had been accomplished, he said, it seemed only right that I should give him back the money, didn't it? No, I said, it didn't seem right at all. A deal is a deal, and I had gone to Mexico in good faith and had kept up my end of the bargain. No one had ever suggested that I write the book *for* Madame X. I was supposed to write it *with* her, and if she didn't want to do the work, it wasn't my job to force her to do it. That was precisely why I'd asked for the money in advance. I was afraid that something like this would happen, and I needed to know that I would be paid for my time—no matter how things turned out.

He saw the logic of my argument, but that didn't mean he was willing to back down. All right, he said, keep the money, but if you want to go on working for me, you'll have to do some more jobs to square the account. In other words, instead of asking me to return the money in cash, he wanted me to give it back in labour. I told him that was unacceptable. Our account was square, I said, I wasn't in debt to him, and if he wanted to hire me for other jobs, he would have to pay me what those jobs were worth. Needless to say, that was unacceptable to him. I thought you wanted a part in the movie, he said. I never said that, I answered. Because if you do, he continued, we'll have to clear up this business first. Once again I told him there was nothing to clear up. All right, he said, if that's how you feel about it, then we have nothing to say to each other any more. And with that remark he turned away from me and told the driver to stop the car.

We had been riding around for about half an hour by then, slowly drifting toward the outer fringes of Paris, and the neighbourhood where the car had stopped was unfamiliar to me. It was a cold January night, and I had no idea where I was, but the conversation was over, and there was nothing for me to do but say goodbye to him and get out of the car. If I remember correctly, we didn't even shake hands. I stepped out on to the sidewalk, shut the door, and the car drove off. And that was the end of my career in the movies.

Action Baseball

Moving out of New York was the first step in a long series of miscalculations. My wife and I figured we could live on less money in the country, but the plain fact was that we couldn't. Car expenses, heating expenses, house repairs, and paediatrician's bills ate up whatever advantage we thought we had gained, and before long we were working so hard just to make ends meet that there was no time left for anything else. In the past, I had always managed to keep a few hours to myself every day, to push on with my poems and writing projects after spending the first part of the day working for money. Now, as our need for money rose, there was less time available to me for my own work. I started missing a day, then two days, then a week, and after a while I lost my rhythm as a writer. When I did manage to find some time for myself, I was too tense to write very well. Months went by, and every piece of paper I touched with my pen wound up in the garbage.

By the end of 1977, I was already feeling trapped, desperate to find a solution. I had spent my whole life avoiding the subject of money and now, suddenly, I could think of nothing else. I dreamed of miraculous reversals, lottery millions falling down from the sky, outrageous get-rich-quick schemes. Even the ads on matchbook covers began to hold a certain fascination. 'Make Money Growing Worms in Your Basement.' Now that I lived in a house with a basement, don't think I wasn't tempted.

My old way of doing things had led to disaster, and I was ripe for new ideas, a new way of tackling the dilemma that had dogged me from the start: how to reconcile the needs of the body with the needs of the soul. The terms of the equation were still the same: time on the one hand, money on the other. I had gambled on being able to manage both, but after ten years of trying to feed first one mouth, then two mouths, and then three mouths, I had finally lost.

In early December, a friend came up from the city to visit for a few days. We had known each other since college, and he too had turned into a struggling writer—yet one more Columbia graduate without a pot to piss in. If anything, he was having an even rougher time of it than I was. Most of his work was unpublished, and he supported himself by bouncing from one pathetic temporary job to another, aimlessly travelling around the country in search of strange, down-and-out adventures. He had recently landed in New York again and was working in a toy store somewhere in Manhattan, part of the brigade of surplus help who stand behind the counters during the Christmas-shopping season. I picked him up at the train station, and during the half-hour ride back to the house we mostly talked about toys and games, the things he sold in the store. For reasons that still mystify me, this conversation dislodged a small pebble that had been stuck somewhere in my unconscious, an obstruction that had been sitting over a tiny pinprick-hole of memory, and now that I was able to look down that hole again, I found something that had been lost for nearly twenty years. Back when I was ten or twelve, I had invented a game. Using an ordinary deck of fifty-two playing cards, I had sat down on my bed one afternoon and figured out a way to play baseball with them. Now, as I went on talking to my friend in the car, the game came rushing back to me. I remembered everything about it: the basic principles, the rules, the whole set-up down to the last detail.

Under normal circumstances, I probably would have forgotten all about it again. But I was a desperate man, a man with my back against the wall, and I knew that if I didn't think of something fast, the firing squad was about to fill my body with bullets. A windfall was the only way out of my predicament. If I could rustle up a nice large chunk of cash, the nightmare would suddenly stop. I could bribe off the soldiers, walk out of the prison yard, and go home to become a writer again. If translating books and writing magazine articles could no longer do the job, then I owed it to myself and my family to try something else. Well, people bought games, didn't they? What if I worked up my old baseball game into something good, something really good, and managed to sell it? Maybe I'd get lucky and find my bag of gold after all.

It almost sounds like a joke now, but I was in dead earnest. I knew that my chances were next to nil, but once the idea grabbed hold of me, I couldn't shake free of it. Nuttier things had happened, I told myself, and if I wasn't willing to put a little time and effort into having a go at it, then what kind of spineless shit was I?

The game from my childhood had been organized around a few simple operations. The pitcher turned over the cards: each red card from ace to ten was a strike; each black card from ace to ten was a ball. If a face card was turned over, that meant the batter swung. The batter then turned over a card. Anything from ace to nine was an out, with each out corresponding to the position numbers of the defensive players: pitcher—ace (one); catcher—two; first baseman—three; second baseman—four; third baseman—five; shortstop—six; left fielder—seven; center fielder—eight; right fielder—nine. If the batter turned over a five, for example, that meant the out was made by the third baseman. A black five indicated a ground ball; a red five indicated a ball hit in the air (diamond—pop-up; heart—line drive). On balls hit to the outfield (seven, eight, nine), black indicated a shallow fly ball, red a deep fly ball. Turn over a ten, and you had yourself a single. A jack was a double, a queen was a triple, and a king was a home run.

It was crude but reasonably effective, and while the distribution of hits was mathematically off (there should have been more singles than doubles, more doubles than home runs, and more home runs than triples), the games were often close and exciting. More importantly, the final scores looked like the scores of real baseball games—three to two, seven to four, eight to nothing—and not football games or basketball games. The fundamental principles were sound. All I had to do was get rid of the standard deck and design a new set of cards. That would allow me to make the game statistically accurate, add new elements of strategy and decision-making (bunts, stolen bases, sacrifice flies), and lift the whole thing to a higher level of subtlety and sophistication. The work was largely a matter of getting the numbers right and fiddling with the math, but I was well versed in the intricacies of baseball, and it didn't take me long to arrive at the correct formulas. I played out game after game after game, and at the end of a couple of weeks there were no more adjustments to be made. Then came the tedious part. Once I had designed the cards (two decks of ninety-six cards each), I had to sit down with four fine-tipped pens (one red, one green, one black, one blue) and draw the cards by hand. I can't remember how many days it took me to complete this task, but by the time I came to the end, I felt as if I had never done anything else. The design was nothing to brag about, but since I had no experience or talent as a designer, that was to be expected. I was striving for a clear, serviceable presentation, something that could be read at a glance and not confuse anyone, and given that so much information had to be crammed on to every card, I think I accomplished at least that. Beauty and elegance could come later. If anyone showed enough interest to want to manufacture the game, the problem could be turned over to a professional designer. For the time being, after much dithering back and forth, I dubbed my little brainchild Action Baseball.

Once again, my stepfather came to the rescue. He happened to have a friend who worked for one of the largest, most successful American toy companies, and when I showed the game to this man, he was impressed by it, thought it had a real chance of appealing to someone. I was still working on the cards at that point, but he encouraged me to get the game in order as quickly as I could and take it to the New York Toy Fair, which was just five or six weeks down the road. I had never heard of it, but by all accounts it was the most important annual event in the business. Every February companies from around the world gathered at the Toy Center at Twenty-third Street and Fifth Avenue to display their products for the upcoming season, take note of what the competition was up to, and make plans for the future. What the Frankfurt Book Fair is for books and the Cannes Film Festival is for films, the New York Toy Fair is for toys. My stepfather's friend took charge of everything for me. He arranged to have my name put on the list of 'inventors', which qualified me for a badge and an open pass to the fair, and then, as if that weren't enough, set up an appointment for me to meet with the president of his company—at nine o'clock in the morning on the first day of the fair.

I was grateful for the help, but at the same time I felt like someone who had just been booked on a flight to an unknown planet. I had no idea what to expect, no map of the terrain, no guidebook to help me understand the habits and customs of the creatures I would be talking to. The only solution I could think of was to wear a jacket and tie. The tie was the only one I owned, and it hung in my closet for emergency use at weddings and

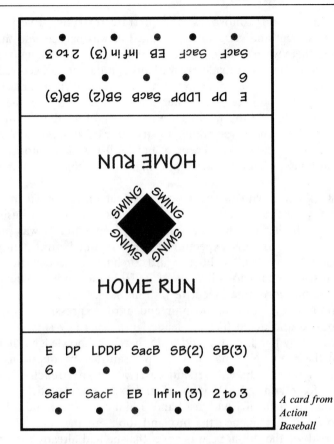

E	DP	LDDP	SacB	SB(2)	SB(3)
6	●	●	●	●	●

SacF	SacF	EB	Inf in (3)	2 to 3
●	●	●	●	●

A card from Action Baseball

funerals. Now business meetings could be added to the list. I must have cut a ridiculous figure as I strode into the Toy Center that morning to collect my badge. I was carrying a briefcase, but the only thing inside it was the game, which was stowed inside a cigar box. That was all I had: the game itself, along with several xeroxed copies of the rules. I was about to go in and talk to the president of a multi-million-dollar business, and I didn't even have a business card.

Even at that early hour, the place was swarming with people. Everywhere you turned, there were endless rows of corporate stands, display booths decked out with dolls and puppets and fire engines and dinosaurs and extraterrestrials. Every kiddie amusement and gadget ever dreamed of was packed into that hall, and there wasn't one of them that didn't whistle or clang or toot or beep or roar. As I made my way through the din, it occurred to me that the briefcase under my arm was the only silent object in the building. Computer games were all the rage that year, the biggest thing to hit the toy world since the invention of the wind-up jack-in-the-box, and I was hoping to strike it rich with an old-fashioned deck of cards. Maybe I would, but until I walked into that noisy fun house, I hadn't realized how likely it was that I wouldn't.

My talk with the company president turned out to be one of the shortest meetings in the annals of American business. It didn't bother me that the man rejected my game (I was prepared for that, was fully expecting bad news), but he did it in such a chilling way, with so little regard for human decency, that it still causes me pain to think about it. He wasn't much older than I was, this corporate executive with his sleek, superbly tailored suit, his blue eyes and blond hair and hard, expressionless face, he looked and acted like the leader of a Nazi spy ring. He barely shook my hand, barely said hello, barely acknowledged that I was in the room. No small talk, no pleasantries, no questions. 'Let's see what you have,' he said curtly, and so I reached into my briefcase and pulled out the cigar box. Contempt flickered in his eyes. It was as if I had just handed him a dog turd and asked him to smell it. I opened the box and took out the cards. By then I could see that all hope was gone, that he had already lost interest, but there was nothing to do but forge ahead and start playing the game. I shuffled the decks, said something about how to read the three levels of information on the cards, and then got down to it. One or two batters into the top half of the first inning, he stood up from his chair and extended his hand to me. Since he hadn't spoken a word, I had no idea why he wanted to shake my hand. I continued to turn over cards, describing the action as it unfolded: ball, strike, swing. 'Thank you,' the Nazi said, finally taking hold of my hand. I still couldn't figure out what was going on. 'Are you saying you don't want to see any more?' I said. 'I haven't even had a chance to show you how it works.' 'Thank you,' he said again. 'You can leave now.' Without another word, he turned and left me with my cards, which were still spread out on the table. It took me a minute or two to put everything back in the cigar box, and it was precisely then, during those sixty or ninety seconds, that I hit bottom, that I reached what I still consider to be the low point of my life.

Somehow or other, I managed to regroup. I went out for breakfast, pulled myself together, and returned to the fair for the rest of the day. One by one, I visited every game company I could find, shook hands, smiled, knocked on doors, demonstrated the wonders of Action Baseball to anyone willing to spare me ten or fifteen minutes. The results were uniformly discouraging. Most of the big companies had stopped working with independent inventors (too many lawsuits), and the small ones either wanted pocket-sized computer games (beep beep) or else refused to look at anything connected with sports (low sales). At least these people were polite. After the sadistic treatment I'd been given that morning, I found some consolation in that.

Some time in the late afternoon, exhausted from hours of fruitless effort, I stumbled on to a company that specialized in card games. They had produced only one game so far, but that one had been wildly successful, and now they were in the market for a second. It was a small, low-budget operation run by two guys from Joliet, Illinois, a back-porch business with none of the corporate trappings and slick promotional methods of the other companies at the fair. That was a promising sign, but best of all, both partners admitted to being avid baseball fans. They weren't doing much at that hour, just sitting around their little booth and chewing the fat, and when I told them about my game, they seemed more than happy to have a look at it. Not just a peek, but a thorough viewing—to sit down and play a full nine-inning contest to the end.

If I had rigged the cards, the results of the game I played with them could not have been more exciting, more true to life. It was nip and tuck the whole way, tension riding on every pitch, and after eight-and-a-half innings of threats, rallies and two-out strike-outs with the bases loaded, the score stood at two to one. The Joliet boys were the home team, and when they came up for their last turn at bat, they needed a run to tie and two to win. The first

two batters did nothing, and quickly they were down to their last
out, with no runners on base. The following batter singled,
however, to keep them alive. Then, to everyone's astonishment,
with the count at two balls and two strikes, the next batter hit a
home run to win the game. I couldn't have asked for more than
that. A two-out, two-run homer in the bottom of the ninth inning
to steal a victory on the last pitch. It was a classic baseball thriller,
and when the man from Joliet turned over the final card, his face
lit up with an expression of pure, undisguisable joy.

They wanted to think about it, they said, to mull it over for a
while before giving me an answer. They would need a deck to study
on their own, of course, and I told them I would send a colour
Xerox copy to Joliet as soon as possible. That was how we left it:
shaking hands and exchanging addresses, promising each other
to be in touch. After all the dismal, demoralizing events of that
day, there was suddenly cause for hope, and I walked out of the
Toy Fair thinking that I might actually get somewhere with my
crazy scheme.

Colour xeroxing was a new process then, and it cost me a small
fortune to have the copies made. I can't remember the exact
amount, but it was more than a hundred dollars, I think, perhaps
even two hundred. I shipped the package off to them and prayed
they would write back soon. Weeks passed, and as I struggled to
concentrate on the other work I had to do, it gradually dawned
on me that I was in for a disappointment. Enthusiasm meant
speed, indecision meant delay, and the longer they delayed, the
worse the odds would be. It took almost two months for them to
answer, and by then I didn't even have to read the letter to know
what was in it. What surprised me was its brevity, its utter lack of
personal warmth. I had spent close to an hour with them, had felt
I'd entertained them and aroused their interest, but their rejection
consisted of just one dry, clumsily written paragraph. Half the
words were misspelt, and nearly every sentence had a grammatical
error in it. It was an embarrassing document, a letter written by
dunces, and once my hurt began to wear off a little, I felt ashamed
of myself for having misjudged them so thoroughly. Put your faith
in fools, and you end up fooling only yourself.

Still, I wasn't quite ready to give up. I had gone too far to allow one setback to throw me off course, and so I put my head down and plunged ahead. Until I had exhausted all the possibilities, I felt duty-bound to continue, to see the whole misbegotten business through to the end. My in-laws put me in touch with a man who worked for Ruder and Finn, a prominent New York public-relations firm. He loved the game, seemed genuinely enthused when I showed it to him, and made an all-out effort to help. That was part of the problem. Everyone liked Action Baseball, enough people at any rate to keep me from abandoning it, and with a kind, friendly, well-connected man like this one pushing on my behalf, it wouldn't have made sense to give up. My new ally's name was George, and he happened to be in charge of the General Foods account, one of Ruder and Finn's most important clients. His plan, which struck me as ingenious, was to get General Foods to put Action Baseball on the Wheaties box as a special coupon offer. ('Hey, kids! Just mail in two Wheaties box tops and a cheque or money order for $3.98, and this incredible game can be yours!')

George proposed it to them, and for a time it looked as if it might happen. Wheaties was considering ideas for a new promotional campaign, and he thought this one might just do the trick. It didn't. They went with the Olympic decathlon champion instead, and for the next umpteen years, every box of Wheaties was adorned with a picture of Bruce Jenner's smiling face. You can't really fault them. It was the Breakfast of Champions, after all, and they had a certain tradition to uphold. I never found out how close George came to getting his idea through, but I must confess (somewhat reluctantly) that I still find it hard to look at a box of Wheaties without feeling a little twinge.

George was almost as disappointed as I was, but now that he'd caught the bug, he wasn't about to quit trying. He knew someone in Indianapolis who was involved with the Babe Ruth League (in what capacity I forget) and thought something good might happen if he put me in contact with this man. The game was duly shipped to the Midwest again, and then followed another inordinately long silence. As the man hastened to explain to me when he finally wrote, he wasn't entirely responsible for the delay:

47

'I am sorry to be so late in acknowledging receipt of your June 22 letter and your game, Action Baseball. They were late reaching me because of a tornado that wiped out our offices. I've been working at home since and did not get my mail until ten days or so ago.'

My bad luck was taking on an almost biblical dimension, and when the man wrote again several weeks later to tell me that he was passing on my game (sadly, with much regret, in the most courtly terms possible), I barely even flinched. 'There is no question that your game is unique, innovative and interesting. There may well be a market for it since it is the only table-top baseball game without a lot of trappings, which makes it faster-moving, but the consensus here is that without big-league players and their statistics, the established competition is insurmountable.'

I called George to give him the news and thank him for his help, but enough was enough, I said, and he shouldn't waste any more time on me.

Things stalled for a couple of months after that, but then another lead materialized, and I picked up my lance and sallied forth again. As long as there was a windmill somewhere in sight, I was prepared to do battle with it. I had not the least shred of hope any more, but I couldn't quite let go of the stupid thing I had started. My stepfather's younger brother knew a man who had invented a game, and since that game had earned him a pile of money, it seemed reasonable for me to contact him and ask for advice. We met in the lobby of the Roosevelt Hotel, not far from Grand Central Station. He was a fast-talking wheeler-dealer of around forty, a wholly antipathetical man with every kind of bluff and angle up his sleeve, but I must admit that his patter had some verve to it.

'Mail order,' he said, 'that's the ticket. Approach a major league star, get him to endorse the game for a share of the profits, and then take out ads in all the baseball magazines. If enough orders come in, use the money to produce the game. If not, send the money back and call it quits.'

'How much would a thing like that cost?' I asked.

'Twenty, twenty-five thousand dollars. Minimum.'

'I couldn't come up with that much,' I said. 'Not even if my life depended on it.'

'Then you can't do it, can you?'

'No, I can't do it. I just want to sell the game to a company. That's all I've ever had in mind—to make some royalties from the copies they sold. I wouldn't be capable of going into business for myself.'

'In other words,' the man said, finally realizing what a numskull he was talking to, 'you've taken a shit and now you want someone to flush the toilet for you.'

That wasn't quite how I would have expressed it myself, but I didn't argue with him. He clearly knew more than I did, and when he went on to recommend that I find a 'game broker' to talk to the companies for me, I didn't doubt that he was pointing me in the right direction. Until then, I hadn't even known of the existence of such people. He gave me the name of someone who was supposed to be particularly good, and I called her the next day. That turned out to be my last move, the final chapter of the whole muddled saga. She talked a mile a minute to me, outlining terms, conditions and percentages, what to do and what not to do, what to expect and what to avoid. It sounded like her standard spiel, a furious condensation of years of hard knocks and cut-throat manoeuvres, and for the first several minutes I couldn't get a word in edgewise. Then, finally, she paused to catch her breath, and that was when she asked me about my game.

'It's called Action Baseball,' I said.

'Did you say *baseball*?' she said.

'Yes, baseball. You turn over cards. It's very realistic, and you can get through a full nine-inning game in about fifteen minutes.'

'Sorry,' she said. 'No sports games.'

'What do you mean?'

'They're losers. They don't sell, and nobody wants them. I wouldn't touch your game with a ten-foot pole.'

That did it for me. With the woman's blunt pronouncement still ringing in my ears, I hung up the phone, put the cards away, and stopped thinking about them for ever. □

SERIOUS AT THE ROYAL FESTIVAL HALL

RFH2 Saturday **21** June	LE GRAND TANGO - A HOMMAGE TO ASTOR PIAZZOLLA GIDON KREMER and his tango group *part of Laurie Anderson's Meltdown*
RFH2 Monday **23** June	IVOR CUTLER *part of Laurie Anderson's Meltdown*
RFH Sunday **13** July	RAY CHARLES + DIANA KRALL
RFH Tuesday **15** July	HERBIE HANCOCK 'The New Standard All-Stars' featuring Michael Brecker, John Scofield, Dave Holland, Jack DeJohnette, Don Alias
RFH Wednesday **16** July	IVAN LINS + DJAVAN
RFH Friday **18** July	PAOLO CONTE
RFH Saturday **19** July	ROBBEN FORD + Ronnie Earl & The Broadcasters
RFH Sunday **27** July	BURNING SPEAR

RFH Royal Festival Hall   RFH2 Queen Elizabeth Hall

0171 960 4201/4242

Ticketmaster 0171 344 4444, HMV & Tower Records

SERIOUS AT THE BARBICAN

GILBERTO GIL + MONICA VASCONCELOS
Saturday **21** June

MIKE STERN + **IAIN BALLAMY**
Wednesday **2** July

JOSHUA REDMAN + **GERI ALLEN**
Saturday **5** July

Barbican Centre 0171 638 8891

Ticketmaster 0171 344 4444, HMV & Tower Records

Herb Alpert

A master trumpet player, whose seminal records with the Tijuana Brass created a new Latin sound, returns with a new harder-edged album exploring jazz rhythm and groove.

WITH JUSTO ALMARIO, HUMBERTO RAMIREZ, WALTER RODRIGUEZ, MICHITO SANCHEZ, ROE ROTONDI JR. OSKAR CARTAYA, KEVIN RICARD, OTMARO RUIZ

Friday **4** July Shepherd's Bush Empire 0181 740 7474

Ticketmaster 0171 344 4444, HMV & Tower Records

New album *Passion Dance* out soon on Almo

If you would like to be kept up to date with all our events join our
FREE MAILING LIST
Please write to: Serious (Mailing list),Windsor House,
83 Kingsway, London WC2B 6SD

DORIS LESSING
THE ROADS OF LONDON

Denbigh Road, W11

High on the side of the tall ship I held up my little boy and said, 'Look, there's London.' Dockland: muddy creeks and channels, greyish rotting wooden walls and beams, cranes, tugs, big and little ships. The child was probably thinking, But ships and cranes and water was Cape Town, and now it's called London. As for me, real London was still ahead, like the beginning of my real life, which would have happened years before if the war hadn't stopped me coming to London. A clean slate, a new page, everything still to come.

I was full of confidence and optimism, though my assets were minimal: rather less than £150; the manuscript of my first novel, *The Grass is Singing*, already bought by a Johannesburg publisher who had not concealed the fact he would take a long time publishing it, because it was so subversive; and a few short stories. I had a couple of trunkfuls of books, for I would not be parted from them, some clothes, some negligible jewellery. I had refused the pitiful sums of money my mother had offered, because she had so little herself, and besides, the whole sum and essence of this journey was that it was away from her, from the family and from that dreadful provincial country Southern Rhodesia, where, if there was a serious conversation, then it was—always—about the Colour Bar and the inadequacies of the blacks. I was free. I could at last be wholly myself. I felt myself to be self-created, self-sufficient. Is this an adolescent I am describing? No, I was nearly thirty. I had two marriages behind me, but I did not feel I had been really married.

I was also exhausted, because the child, two-and-a-half, had for the month of the voyage woken at five, with shouts of delight for the new day, and had slept reluctantly at ten every night. In between he had never been still, unless I was telling him tales and singing him nursery rhymes, which I had been doing for four or five hours every day. He had had a wonderful time.

I was also having those thoughts—perhaps better say feelings—that disturb every arrival from Southern Africa who has not before seen white men unloading a ship, doing heavy manual labour, for this had been what black people did. A lot of white people, seeing whites work like blacks, had felt uneasy and threatened; for me, it was not so simple. Here they were, the workers, the working class, and at that time I believed that the logic of history would make it inevitable they should inherit the earth. They—those tough, muscled labouring men down there and, of course, people like me—were the vanguard of the working class. I am not writing this down to ridicule it. That would be dishonest. Millions, if not billions, of people were thinking like that, using this language.

A little book called *In Pursuit of the English*, written when I was still close to that time, will add depth and detail to those first months in London. At once, problems—literary problems. What I say in it is true enough. A couple of characters were changed for libel reasons and would have to be now. But there is no doubt that while 'true', the book is not as true as what I would write now. It is a question of tone, and that is no simple matter. That little book is more like a novel; it has the shape and the pace of one. It is too well shaped for life. In one thing at least it is accurate: when I was newly in London I was returned to a child's way of seeing and feeling, every person, building, bus, street, striking my senses with the shocking immediacy of a child's life, everything oversized, very bright, very dark, smelly, noisy. I do not experience London like that now. That was a city of Dickensian exaggeration. I am not saying I saw London through a veil of Dickens, but rather that I was sharing the grotesque vision of Dickens, on the verge of the surreal.

That London of the late 1940s, the early 1950s, has vanished, and now it is hard to believe it existed. It was unpainted, buildings were stained and cracked and dull and grey; it was war-damaged, some areas all ruins, and under them holes full of dirty water, once cellars, and it was subject to sudden dark fogs—that was before the Clean Air Act. No one who has only known today's London of self-respecting clean buildings, crowded cafés and restaurants, good food and coffee, streets full until after midnight with mostly young people having a good time, can believe what London was like then. No cafés. No good restaurants. Clothes were still 'austerity' from the war, dismal and ugly. Everyone was indoors by ten, and the streets were empty. The Dining Rooms, subsidized during the war, were often the only places to eat in a whole area of streets. They served good meat, terrible vegetables, nursery puddings. Lyons restaurants were the high point of eating for ordinary people—I remember fish and chips and poached eggs on toast. There were fine restaurants for the well-off, and they tended to hide themselves away out of embarrassment, because in them, during the war, the rigours of rationing had been so ameliorated. You could not get a decent cup of coffee anywhere in the British Isles. The sole civilized amenity was the pubs, but they closed at eleven, and you have to have the right temperament for pubs. Or, I should say, had to have, for they have changed so much, no longer give the impression to an outsider of being like clubs, each with its members, or 'regulars', where outsiders go on sufferance. Rationing was still on. The war still lingered, not only in the bombed places but in people's minds and behaviour. Any conversation tended to drift towards the war, like an animal licking a sore place. There was a wariness, a weariness.

On New Year's Eve 1950, I was telephoned by an American from the publishing scene to ask if I would share the revels with him. I met him in my best dress at six o'clock in Leicester Square. We expected cheerful crowds, but there was no one on the streets. For an hour or so we were in a pub but felt out of place. Then we looked for a restaurant. There were the expensive restaurants, which we could not afford, but nothing of what we now take for granted—the Chinese, Indian, Italian restaurants, and dozens of other nationalities. The big hotels were all booked up. We walked up and down and back and forth through Soho and around Piccadilly. Everything was dark and blank. Then he said, To hell with it, let's live it up. A taxi driver took us to a club in Mayfair, and there we watched the successors of the Bright Young Things getting drunk and throwing bread at each other.

But by the end of the decade, there were coffee bars and good ice cream, courtesy of the Italians, and good cheap Indian restaurants. Clothes were bright and cheap and irreverent. London was painted again and was cheerful. Most of the bomb damage was gone. Above all, there was a new generation not made tired by war. They did not talk about the war, or think about it.

The first place where I lived was in Bayswater, which was then rather seedy and hard to associate with the grandeur of its earlier days. Prostitutes lined the streets every evening. I was supposed to be sharing a flat with a South African woman and her child: I wrote about this somewhat unsatisfactory experience in *In Pursuit of the English*. The flat we were in was large and well furnished. Two rooms were let to prostitutes. When I discovered this—I did not realize at once who these smartly dressed girls were who tripped up and down the stairs with men—and tackled the South African woman, because I did not think this was good for the two small children, she burst into tears and said I was unkind.

I spent six weeks looking for a place that would take a small child. There was a heatwave, and I couldn't understand why people complained about the English weather. My feet gave in on the hot pavements, and my morale almost did, but then a household of Italians welcomed the child and me, and my main problem was solved. This was Denbigh Road. My son, Peter, had been accepted by a council nursery. Circumstances had taught him from his very first days to be sociable, and he loved going there. When he came back from the nursery he disappeared at once into the basement, where there was a little girl his age. The house, dispiriting to me, because it was so grim and dirty and war-damaged, was a happy place for him.

We were at the beginning—but literally—in a garret, which was too small for me even to unpack a typewriter. I sent some short stories to the agent Curtis Brown, chosen at random from the *Writers' and Artists' Yearbook*, and Juliet O'Hea wrote back what I later knew was a form letter: yes, but did I have a novel or was I thinking of writing one? I said there was a novel, but it had been bought by a Johannesburg publisher. She asked to see the contract, was shocked and angry when she saw it—they were going to take fifty per cent of everything I earned, as a reward for risking themselves over this dangerous book. She sent them a telegram saying that if they didn't at once release me from the contract, she would expose them as crooks. She then sold the book over the weekend to Michael Joseph.

Ihad very little money left. The £150 advance from Michael
Joseph was at once swallowed up by rent and fees for the
nursery school. I took a secretary's job for a few weeks, where I
did practically no work at all, for it was a new engineering firm,
with young, inexperienced partners. I had taken the child out of
the council nursery and put him in a rather expensive private
nursery. How was I going to pay for this? But my attitude always
was: decide to do something and then find out the way to pay for
it. Soon I knew I was being stupid. I was supposed to be a writer:
publishers enquired tenderly about what I was writing. But I had
no energy for writing. I woke at five, with the child, as always—he
went on waking at five for years, and I with him. I read to him,
told him stories, gave him breakfast, took him by bus down to the
nursery school, went to work. There I sat about, doing nothing
much, or perhaps covertly writing a short story. At lunchtime I
shopped. At five I fetched the child from the nursery, went back
by bus, and then the usual rumbustious rowdy evening for him,
downstairs, while I cleaned the place up. He did not sleep until ten
or so. But then I was too tired to work.

I gave up the job. Meanwhile the publishers rang—twice to
say they were reprinting, and that was before publication. I said,
'Oh good.' I thought this happened to every writer. My ignorance
was absolute. They thought I was taking my success for granted.

Michael Joseph invited me to the Caprice for lunch, then the
smartest show-business restaurant. I had moved downstairs from
my garret and was in a large room that had been once—and
would be again—beautiful but was now dirty and draughty,
heated by an inadequate fireplace. The whole house was cracked
and leaking because of the bombing. There was a tiny room,
where Peter slept. The Caprice was adazzle with pink tablecloths,
silver, glass and well-dressed people. Michael Joseph was a
handsome man, worldly, at home there, and he talked of Larry
and Viv, and said it was a pity they weren't lunching that day.
Michael Joseph, for some reason unfit for fighting, had started the
firm during the war, against the advice of everybody, for he did
not have much capital. The firm was at once successful, chiefly
because he had been an agent with Curtis Brown, and Juliet
O'Hea, his good friend, saw that he got sent new books. He

enjoyed his success, ran a racehorse or two, frequented London's smart places. He kept greeting the people at other tables: 'Let me introduce you to our new writer—she's from Africa.'

The purpose of this lunch was not only because writers were supposed to feel flattered but because he was concerned that this author should not expect him to advertise. He told me exemplary tales, such as that a certain little book, *The Snow Goose*, by Paul Gallico, published during the war, was reprinted several times before publication on word of mouth alone: 'Advertising has no effect at all on the fate of a book.' All publishers talk like this.

In certain military academies is set this exercise: the examinee is to imagine that he is a general in command of a battlefront. In one area his troops are only holding their own, in another are being routed, in a third are driving back the enemy. With limited resources, where is he to send support? The correct answer is: to the successful sector; the rest must be left to their fate. It seems few people know the right answer; they mislead themselves with compassionate thoughts for the less successful soldiers. This is how publishers think. An already successful or known author gets advertisements, but struggling or unknown ones are expected to sink or swim. When people see advertisements for a novel on the underground, they are seeing reserves being sent to a successful sector of the battlefront. They are seeing a bestseller being created from a novel that is already a success.

Inspired by the atmosphere of the Caprice, I told Michael Joseph that if there was one thing I adored above all else, it was chocolate éclairs, and no sooner had I got back to my slum than a long black car purred to a stop outside it, and a pretty pink box was delivered by the chauffeur. It contained a dozen chocolate éclairs. These were added to the already bounteous family supper downstairs.

Nothing I experienced in that household matched what I had expected to find, which was rationing, a dour self-sufficiency, even semi-starvation. I had sent food parcels to Britain. The woman of the house, Italian, was one of the world's great cooks. I don't think she had ever seen a recipe book. She took six ration books to a shop in Westbourne Grove, then a slummy road. But she always got three or four times the rationed amounts of butter, eggs, bacon, cooking fat, cheese. How did she manage it? She was scornful when I asked. It's time you knew your way around, she said. There were a couple of bent policemen, always dropping in and out, who were given butter and eggs from her spoils, in return for turning a blind eye. Did I share in this lawlessness? Yes, I did: our two ration books were given to her to manage. To make little shows of morality in that atmosphere would not only have seemed absurd but would have been incomprehensible to these amiable crooks. Besides, the newspapers were already clamouring for the end of rationing. There was no longer any need for it, they said. Never have I eaten so well. The rent did not include food, but like most fine cooks, our landlady could not bear not to feed anyone around who would sit down at her table. I ate downstairs two or three times a week, Peter most evenings. She asked for money for shopping when she ran out. Hers was an economy that absorbed not only me but other people in the house in complicated borrowings, lendings, cigarettes, a dress or shoes she fancied.

When I told middle-class acquaintances about the bent policemen and the butter and eggs and cheese, they were cold and they were angry. 'Our policemen are not corrupt,' they said. They saw my sojourn on that foreign shore—the working class—as a whimsical foray for the sake of my art, for Experience. They waited for little anecdotes about the comic working classes, in the spirit of the snobbish *Punch* cartoons about servants.

From then until decades later, when it was admitted by Authority that all was not well with our policemen, I was treated by nearly everyone with the hostile impatience I was already earning when I said that South Africa was a hell-hole for the blacks and the Coloureds—for this was still not acknowledged, in spite of Alan Paton's *Cry, the Beloved Country*, which had just come out, a little before *The Grass is Singing*—and even more when I insisted that Southern Rhodesia was as bad and, some blacks thought, even worse than South Africa. Only reds and malcontents said this kind of thing.

In the household in Denbigh Road, Southern Africa was not of interest. Nothing was, outside this little area of streets. They talked of going up to the West End, a mile or so away, as a serious excursion.

The exuberance, the physical well-being of that household was certainly not general then. They were a tired people, the British. Stoical. The national low vitality, that aftermath of war, as if the horrors or endurances of war are eating away silently, out of sight, swallowing energy like a black hole, was balanced by something very different. That is what strikes me most about that time, the contrast. On the one hand, the low spirits, a patient sticking it out, but on the other, an optimism for the future so far from how we are thinking now it seems almost like the symptom of a general foolishness. A New Age was dawning, no less. Socialism was the key. The troops returning from all over the world had been promised everything, the Atlantic Charter (seen sardonically at the time) was merely the summing-up of those Utopian hopes, and now the people had returned a Labour government to make sure they would get it. The National Health Service was their proudest achievement. In the Thirties, before the war, an illness or an accident could drag a whole family down to disaster. The poverty had been terrible and had not been forgotten. All that was finished. No longer was there a need to dread illness and the dole and old age. And this was just a beginning: things were going to get steadily better. Everyone seemed to share this mood. You kept meeting doctors who were setting up practices that would embody this new socialist medicine, who saw themselves as builders of a new era. They could be communists, they could be Labour, they could be Liberals. They were all idealists.

And now . . . what was I going to write next? What the publishers wanted was a novel. What I was writing was short stories. All of them were set in The District—Banket, Lomagundi—and they were about the white community and how its members saw themselves, preserved themselves, saw the blacks around them. I would call it *This Was the Old Chief's Country*. Juliet O'Hea said if that is what I wanted to do, then of course, but no publisher would be delighted at the news of short stories, which did not sell. In fact, I proved them wrong, for they did sell, and very well—for short stories—and have gone on selling ever since. But it was a novel I should be thinking about. And so I did think hard and long about the book that would be *Martha Quest*.

I started to write *Martha Quest* while still in Denbigh Road, and it was going along at a good rate, but I had to interrupt myself, I had to get out of that house, that street—which for a long time now has been a fashionable area. Sometimes I drive or walk through it and see those discreetly desirable residences, and I think, I wonder what you people would say if you could see how these houses were and how carelessly they were 'done up' by War Damage.

The trouble was the little boy, Peter, was happy there, and I knew I would not easily find anything as good. For him, that is.

By chance I went to an evening party, in the flat of the brother of a farmer in Southern Rhodesia, who was the essence of white conformity. But this brother was left-wing and pro-Soviet, as was then common. He had an elderly girlfriend, who had once been beautiful, as the photographs that stood about everywhere averred, and whom he called Baby. Baby, with her great dark eyes in her painted pretty old face, her little ruffles and bows, dominated the scene, but there was another focus of attention, a vibrant, dark-eyed, dark-haired stocky young woman, who at first I thought was French. She wore a tight black skirt, a white shirt, and a cheeky black beret. We talked; she heard how I was living; she at once responded with practical sympathy. She had herself been a young woman with a small child in one bed-sit room in New York. She had been rescued by a woman friend, with the offer of a flat in her house. 'You can't live like this,' she had said. And now Joan Rodker said to me that she was getting rid of an unsatisfactory tenant, and she had been thinking for some time how to help some young woman with a child. There was a small flat at the top of her house, and I could live there, provided she liked Peter. So on the next Sunday I took Peter to see her, and they liked each other at once. So you could say that it was Peter who solved my housing problem for me.

And so I moved into Church Street, Kensington, an attractive little flat at the top of the house, where I lived for four years. It was summer 1950. But before I left Denbigh Road I saw the end of an era, the death of a culture: television arrived. Before, when the men came back from work, the tea was already on the table, a fire was roaring, the radio emitted words or music softly in a corner, they washed and sat down at their places, with the woman, the child, and whoever else in the house could be inveigled downstairs. Food began emerging from the oven, dish after dish, tea was brewed, beer appeared, off went the jerseys or jackets, the men sat in their shirtsleeves, glistening with well-being. They all talked, they sang, they told what had happened in their day, they talked dirty—a ritual; they quarrelled, they shouted, they kissed and made up and went to bed at twelve or one, after six or so hours of energetic conviviality. I suppose that this level of emotional intensity was not usual in the households of Britain: I was witnessing an extreme. And then, from one day to the next—but literally from one evening to the next—came the end of good times, for television had arrived and sat like a toad in the corner of the kitchen. Soon the big kitchen table had been pushed along the wall, chairs were installed in a semicircle and, on the chair arms, the swivelling supper trays. It was the end of an exuberant verbal culture.

Church Street, W8

I had made a life for me and for Peter. That was an achievement, and I was proud of myself. The most important part was Peter, who was enjoying his life, particularly the nursery school in Kensington, and then the family atmosphere with Joan and Ernest. Never has there been a child so ready to make friends. Our days still began at five. Again I was reading to him and telling him stories for a couple of hours after he woke, because Joan's bedroom was immediately below, and the floors were thin, and she did not wake till later. Or he listened to the radio. We have forgotten the role radio played before television. Peter loved the radio. He listened to everything. He listened to two radio plays based on novels by Ivy Compton-Burnett, each an hour long, standing by the machine, absolutely riveted. What was he hearing? Understanding? I have no idea. It is my belief that children are full of understanding and know as much as and more than adults, until they are about seven, when they suddenly become stupid, like adults. At three or four, Peter understood everything, and at eight or nine read only comics. And I've seen this again and again with small children. A child of three sits entranced through the film *2001: A Space Odyssey*, but four years later can tolerate only Rupert Bear.

I was writing *Martha Quest*, a conventional novel, though the demand then was for experimental novels. I played in my mind with a hundred ways of doing *Martha Quest*, pulling shapes about, playing with time, but at the end of all this, the novel was straightforward. I was dealing with my painful adolescence, my mother, all that anguish, the struggle for survival.

And now there arrived a letter from my mother, saying she was coming to London, she was going to live with me and help me with Peter, and—here was the inevitable, surreal, heart-breaking ingredient—she had taught herself typing and would be my secretary.

I collapsed. I simply went to bed and pulled the covers over my head. When I had taken Peter to nursery school, I crept away into the dark of my bed and stayed there until I had to bring him home.

And now—again—there is the question of time, tricksy time, and until I came to write this and was forced to do my work with calendars and obdurate dates, I had thought, vaguely, that I was in Denbigh Road for . . . well, it was probably three years or so. But that was because, having been resumed to child-seeing, everything new and immediate, I had been resumed—partly—to child-time. No matter how I wriggled and protested, No, it can't have been only a year, it was a year before I went to Joan's, and I had been there only six months or so when the letter came from my mother.

Yet those months seem now like years. Time is different at different times in one's life. A year in your thirties is much shorter than a child's year—which is almost endless—but long compared with a year in your forties; whereas a year in your seventies is a mere blink.

Of course she was bound to come after me. How could I have been so naive as to think she wouldn't, as soon as she could? She had been in exile in Southern Rhodesia, dreaming of London, and now . . . She and her daughter did not 'get on', or, to put it

63

truthfully, had always fought. Oh, never mind, the girl was wrongheaded; she would learn to listen to her mother. She was a communist? She always had disreputable friends? That was all right; her mother would introduce her to really nice people. She had written *The Grass is Singing*, which had caused her mother anguish and shame, because it was so hated by the whites? And those extremely unfair short stories about The District? Well, she—the girl's mother—would explain to everyone that no one outside the country could really understand the whites' problems and . . . But the author had been brought up in the country? Her views were wrong, and in time she would come to see that . . . She proposed to live with a daughter who had broken up her first marriage, leaving two children, had married a German refugee at the height of the war, who was a kaffir-lover and scornful of religion?

Well, how did she see it? Now I believe she did not think about it much. She could not afford to. She longed to live in London again, but it was the London she had left in 1919. She had no friends left, except for Daisy Lane, with whom she had been exchanging letters, but Daisy Lane was now an old lady, living in Richmond with her sister, an ex-missionary from Japan. There was her brother's family, and she was coming home in time for the daughter's wedding. Her brother's sister-in-law had already said, 'I hope Jane doesn't imagine she is going to take first place at the wedding.' (Jane: Plain Jane, the loving family nickname, making sure that Maude didn't imagine she possessed any attractions.) And had written to my mother saying she must take a back seat.

Over twenty-five years: 1924 to 1950. That was then the term of my mother's exile in Africa. Now I have reached the age to understand that twenty-five years—or thirty—can seem nothing much, I know that for her time had contracted and that unfortunate experience, Africa, had become an irrelevance. But for me, just over thirty, it was the length of my conscious life, and my mother lived in, belonged to, Africa. Her yearnings after London pea-soupers and jolly tennis parties were mere whimsies.

How could she come after me like this? Yet of course she had been bound to. How could she imagine that . . . But she did. Soon she would toil up those impossible narrow stairs, smiling bravely, walk into my room, move the furniture about, look through my clothes and pronounce their unsuitability, look at the little safe on the wall—no fridge—and say the child was not getting enough to eat.

These days, everyone goes to a therapist, or is a therapist, but then no one did. Not in England, only in America, and even there the phenomenon was in its infancy. And particularly communists did not go 'into analysis', for it was 'reactionary' by definition, or rather without the need for definition. I was so desperate I went. I went two or three times a week, for about three years. I think it saved me. The process was full of the wildest anomalies or ironies—the communist word 'contradictions' seems too mild. First, Mrs Sussman was a Roman Catholic, and Jungian, and while I liked Jung, as all artists do, I had no reason to love Roman Catholics. She was Jewish, and her husband, a dear old man, like a Rembrandt portrait, was a Jewish scholar. But she had converted to Roman Catholicism. This fascinated me, the improbability of it, but she said my wanting to discuss it was merely a sign of my evading real issues. Enough, she said, that Roman Catholicism had deeper and higher levels of understanding, infinitely removed from the crudities of the convent. (And Judaism did not have such higher reaches or peaks? 'We were talking about your father, I think, my dear. Shall we go on?') Mrs Sussman specialized in unblocking artists who were blocked, could not write or paint or compose. This is what she saw as her mission in life. But I did not suffer from a 'block'. She wanted to discuss my work. I did not want to. I did not see the need for it. So she was perpetually frustrated, bringing up the subject, while I deflected her. Mrs Sussman was a cultivated, civilized, wise old woman, who gave me what I needed, which was support. Mostly support against my mother. When the pressures came on, all of them intolerable, because my mother was so pathetic, so lonely, so full of emotional blackmail—quite unconscious, for it was her situation that undermined me—Mrs Sussman simply said, 'If you don't stand firm now, it will be the end of you. And the end of Peter too.'

My mother was . . . but I have forgotten which archetype my mother was. She was one, I know. Mrs Sussman would often bring some exchange to a close: she, he, is such and such an archetype . . . or is one at this time. I, for example, at various times was Electra, Antigone, Medea. The trouble was, while I was instinctively happy with the idea of archetypes, those majestic eternal figures, rising from literature and myth like stone shapes created by nature out of rock and mountain, I was hating the labels. Unhappy with communism, I was unhappiest with its language, with the labelling of everything, and the vindictive or automatic stereotypes, and here were more of them, whether described romantically as 'archetypes' or not. I did not see why she minded my criticisms, for she liked the dreams I 'brought' her. Psychotherapists are like doctors and nurses who treat patients like children: 'Just a little spoonful for me.' 'Put out your tongue for me.' When we have a dream, it is 'for' the therapist. Often it is: I swear I dreamed dreams to please her, after we had been going along for a while. But at my very first session she had asked for dreams, preferably serial dreams, and she was pleased with my ancient lizard dream and the dreams I was having about my father, who, too shallowly buried in a forest, would emerge from his grave, or attract wolves who came down from the hills to dig him up. 'These are typically Jungian dreams,' she would say gently, flushed with pleasure. 'Sometimes it can take years to get someone to dream a dream on that level.' Whereas Jungian dreams had been my night landscape for as long as I could remember, I had not had 'Freudian' dreams. She said she used Freud when it was appropriate, and that was, I gathered, when the patient was still at a very low level of individuation. She made it altogether clear that she thought I was.

'Jungian dreams'—wonderful, those layers of ancient common experience, but what was the use of that if I had to go to bed with the covers over my head at the news my mother was about to arrive? Here I was. Here I am, Mrs Sussman. Do what you will with me, but for God's sake cure me.

I needed support for other reasons.

One of them was my lover. My friend Moidi Jokl had suggested that I should go with her one evening to a party, and there I met a man I was destined—so I felt then—to live with, and to have and to hold and be happy with.

Yes, he had a name. But as always, there is the question of children and grandchildren. Since *Under My Skin* came out, I have met not a few grandchildren, children, of my old mates from those far-off times and learned that the views of contemporaries about each other need not share much with the views of their children. Whole areas of a parent's, let alone a grandparent's, life can be unknown to them. And why not? Children do not own their parents' lives, though they—and I too—jealously pore over them as if they hold the key to their own.

I say to a charming young man who has come to lunch to discuss his father, 'When James was working on the mines on the Rand—'

'Oh, I'm sure he never did that,' comes the confident reply.

To another: 'You didn't know your father was a great lover of women?' A faintly derisive smile, meaning: What, that old stick? So then of course you shut up; after all, it has nothing to do with him.

I will call this man Jack. He was a Czech. He had worked as a doctor with our armies throughout the war. He was—what else?—a communist.

He fell in love with me, jealously, hungrily, even angrily— with that particular degree of anger that means a man is in conflict. I did not at once fall in love with him. At the start, what I loved was his loving me so much: a nice change after my second husband, Gottfried. The way I saw this—felt this—was that now I was ready for the right man: my 'mistakes' were over, and I was settled in London, where I intended to stay. All my experiences had programmed me for domesticity. I might now tell myself—and quite rightly—that I had never been 'really' married to Frank Wisdom, but for four years we had a conventional marriage. Gottfried and I had hardly been well matched, but we had lived conventionally enough. The law and society saw me as a woman who had had two marriages and two divorces. I felt that these marriages did not count. I had been too young, too immature. The fact that the bouncy, affectionate, almost casual relationship I had had with Frank was hardly unusual— particularly in those war years, when people married far too easily—did not mean I did not aspire to better. With Gottfried it

67

had been a political marriage. I would not have married Gottfried if the internment camp was not still a threat. Then, people were always marrying to give someone a name, a passport, a place; in London there were organizations for precisely this—to rescue threatened people from Europe. But now, in these luckier times, people have forgotten that such marriages were hardly uncommon. No, my real emotional life was all before me. And I had all the talents needed for intimacy. I was born to live companionably—and passionately—with the right man, and here he was.

Jack had been one of thirteen children, the youngest, of a very poor family in Czechoslovakia. He had had to walk miles to school and back—just like Africans now in many parts of Africa. They scarcely had enough to eat or to cover themselves with. This was a common enough story, then, in Europe and in some parts of Britain too: people don't want to remember the frightful poverty in Britain in the Twenties and Thirties. Jack had become a communist in his early teens, like all his schoolfellows. He was a real communist, for whom the Party was a home, a family, the future, his deepest and sanest self. He wasn't at all like me who had had choices. When I met him, his closest friends in Czechoslovakia, the friends of his youth, the top leadership of the Czech Communist Party, had just been made to stand in the eyes of the world as traitors to communism, and then eleven of them were hanged, Stalin the invisible stage manager. For Jack it had been as if the foundations of the world had collapsed. It was impossible for these old friends to have been traitors, and he did not believe it. On the other hand, it was impossible for the Party to have made a mistake. He had nightmares, he wept in his sleep. Like Gottfried Lessing. Again I shared a bed with a man who woke from nightmares.

That was the second cataclysmic event of his life. His entire family—mother, father, and all his siblings, except one sister who had escaped to America—had died in the gas chambers.

This story is a terrible one. It was terrible then, but taken in the context of that time, not worse than many others. In 1950 in London, everybody I met had come out of the army from battlefields in Burma, France, Italy, Yugoslavia, had been present when the concentration camps were opened, had fought in the Spanish war or was a refugee and had survived horrors. With my background, the trenches and the nastiness of the First World War dinned into me day and night through my childhood, Jack's story was felt by me as a continuation: Well, what can you expect? We understood each other well. We had everything in common. Now I assess the situation in a way I would then have found 'cold'. I look at a couple and I think, Are they suited emotionally . . . physically . . . mentally? Jack and I were suited in all three ways, but perhaps most emotionally, sharing a natural disposition towards the grimmest understanding of life and events that in its less severe manifestations is called irony. It was our situations, not our natures, that were incompatible. I was ready to settle down for ever with this man. He had just come back from the war, to find his wife, whom he had married long years before, a stranger, and children whom he hardly knew.

It is a commonplace among psychiatrists that a young woman who has been close to death, has cut her wrists too often, or has been threatened by parents, must buy clothes, be obsessed with clothes and with the ordering of her appearance, puzzling observers with what seems like a senseless profligacy. It is life she is keeping in order.

And a man who has been running a step ahead of death for years—if Jack had stayed in Czechoslovakia it is likely he would have been hanged as a traitor, together with his good friends, if he hadn't already perished in the gas chambers—such a man will be forced by a hundred powerful needs to sleep with women, have women, assert life, make life, move on.

In no way can I—or could I then—accuse Jack of letting me down, for he never promised anything. On the contrary, short of actually saying, 'I am sleeping with other women; I have no intention of marrying you,' he said it all. Often joking. But I wasn't listening. What I felt was: When we get on so wonderfully in every possible way, then it isn't sensible for him to go away from me. I wasn't able to think at all; the emotional realities were too powerful. I think this is quite common with women. 'Really, this man is talking nonsense, he doesn't know what is right for him. And besides, he says himself his marriage is no marriage at all. And obviously it can't be, when he is here most nights.' How easy to be intelligent now, how impossible then.

Impossible to describe a writer's life, for the real part of it cannot be written down. How did my day go in those early days in London, in Church Street? I woke at five, when the child did. He came into my bed, and I told or read stories or rhymes. We got dressed, he ate, and then I took him to the school up the street. But soon I put him on the bus, and he took himself the two stops to the school. I suppose now one couldn't do this. I shopped a little, and then my real day began. The feverish need to get this or that done—what I call the housewife's disease: 'I must buy this, ring so-and-so, don't forget this, make a note of that'—had to be subdued to the flat, dull state one needs to write in. Sometimes I achieved it by sleeping for a few minutes, praying that the telephone would be silent. Sleep has always been my friend, my restorer, my quick fix, but it was in those days that I learned the value of a few minutes' submersion in . . . where? And you emerge untangled, quiet, dark, ready for work.

Often when Peter went to the Eichners' in the country for a few days or the weekend, or my mother had taken him off somewhere, I simply went to bed, sliding into that restorative underwater state where you lie limp, rising towards the surface, just reaching it, sinking, rising . . . You are not really conscious when you are reaching wakefulness, and the sleep itself is lightened by the half-knowledge you are asleep. An hour . . . a day even, if I had become too frenetic. As I grew older, and became cleverer at managing my emotional economy, I began to wonder if the condition of being awake accumulates some kind of substance, which jangles and vibrates, making you tense and sharp, and that this is exaggerated a hundred times if you are writing: but even a few minutes' sleep, the merest dip into that other dimension, dissolves it, leaving you calm again, newborn.

And now, on the little table that has been cleared of breakfast things, replaced by scattered sheets of paper, is the typewriter, waiting for me. Work begins. I do not sit down but wander about the room. I think on my feet, while I wash up a cup, tidy a drawer, drink a cup of tea, but my mind is not on these activities. I find myself in the chair by the machine. I write a sentence . . . will it stand? But never mind, look at it later, just get on with it, get the flow started. And so it goes on. I walk and I prowl, my hands busy with this and that. You'd think I was a paragon of concern for housekeeping if you judged by what you saw. I drop off into sleep for a few minutes, because I have wrought myself into a state of uncomfortable electric tension. I walk, I write. If the telephone rings I try to answer it without breaking the concentration. And so it goes on, all day, until it is time to fetch the child from school or until he arrives at the door.

This business of the physical as a road into concentration: you see painters doing it. They wander about the studio, apparently at random. They clean a brush. They throw away another. They prepare a canvas, but you can see their minds are elsewhere. They stare out of the window. They make a cup of coffee. They stand for a long time in front of the canvas, the brush on the alert in their hands. At last, it begins: the work.

There are no attempts to write when the child is there, for that only results in irritation on both sides. He is read to, we play board games. He listens to the radio, grown-up plays as well as the children's programmes. Supper. If Joan or Ernest are there he goes down to see them. He is put to bed at eight, but he has never been a sleeper, and he will lie awake until nine or so—later. Meanwhile Jack arrives. We eat. We talk. Jack works very hard at the Maudsley Hospital. This is the leading psychiatric hospital in Britain, and it is a time of ferment and discovery. Many psychiatric beliefs and practices we now take for granted were being established then. Jack was the kind of doctor probably now obsolete. He illustrated the Maudsley theories and practices, or incidents with patients, with comparisons from music—for he knew a good deal about music—or from composers' lives, or incidents from literature. A poor man from London's East End would be matched with a character from Dostoevsky, a mad girl with a story from opera. He suffered over the sufferings of his patients. He was often dubious about the experiments that went on. He described, for instance, experiments in hypnosis. If you take someone—anyone—hypnotize them and ask them to say what happened let's say on the second of May in some far-off year, when this person was ten years old, or twenty, they will come up with a complete account of that day: 'I woke in a bad mood, I quarrelled with my husband, I went to the shops, I cooked supper . . . ' and so on. It is all stored in the mind somewhere. What we call memory is a tiny part of what is in our brains, and it is easy to think of it as a kind of overspill from the full, real record. 'What right have we to intrude into another person's mind like this?' He told me how he stood in front of him a line of people chosen at random and went along the line, snapping his fingers, and—'They're out! Just like that! You can do what you like with them. No human being should be treated like that.' He was always saying that human beings should not be treated like this, or like that. He may have been a communist, had been a Stalinist, was still, he said, a Marxist, but he was an old-fashioned humanist, and that was true of all communists with the literary tradition in their blood.

And then we went to bed. The dark, and love.

In the morning he was often off as the child woke. 'I have to pick up a clean shirt from home,' was the formula.

'You could always keep your clean shirts here.'

'Now come on—why should you have the bother of my shirts?'

This exchange, archetypical between man and mistress, went on, in one form or another, for the four years we were together.

So that's the outline of a day. But nowhere in it is there the truth of the process of writing. I fall back on that useful word 'wool-gathering'. And this goes on when you are shopping, cooking, anything. You are reading but find the book has lowered itself: you are wool-gathering. The creative dark. Incommunicable. And what about the pages discarded and thrown away, the stories that were misbegotten—into the waste-paper basket, the ideas that lived in your mind for a day or two, or a week, but haven't any life, so out with them. What life, what is it, why is one page alive and another not, what is this aliveness, which is born so very deep, out of sight, fed by love? But describing a day like this: I got up, the child went to school, I wrote, he came back, and the next day was the same—that is hardly the stuff that keeps the reader turning pages.

Like all authors, I survived from cheque to cheque. Joan did not mind my weekly rent being paid two weeks or three weeks late. Once, the debt ran on until it was five weeks overdue, and this made me sick with worry, because she did not have much money either. These little sharp memories correct generalizations, like: 'Having no money did not worry me.' (I was actually saying this for a time.) There were times when I was worried, all right. I was walking down Church Street, having dropped the child at school, and I was crying because I couldn't buy food. A man walked rapidly up the street towards me, stopped, and said, Why are you crying? I said, I haven't any money. He said, Well, cheer up; you will have by this time next week, won't you? This being true enough, since money always did turn up from somewhere, I did cheer up. I sold my mother's jewellery. Giving me her heavy gold chain, her gold brooch, her gold bracelets, some Victorian trinkets, was a ritual: mothers hand on their good jewellery to their daughters. I did not want it, asked her to keep it, but she insisted. When I took it to the jeweller's I was positively asking to be cheated, to be done down, so low was my morale. The jewellery was not fashionable. I remember even pointing this out, apologetically. I was paid less than thirty shillings for what ten years later, when Victoriana became fashionable, would be worth hundreds of pounds. Similarly, I had a Victorian sewing table, from my aunt Daisy. It was very pretty, full of little drawers, fretwork compartments, padded pin-and-needle cushions—a gem of a piece. There was an antique shop downstairs. I begged them to buy it. They refused, said there was no market for it. Soon it was worth a lot of money.

The vicissitudes of a writer's life mean complicated tax returns. One year I had no money to pay tax. The year before I had earned well. The income tax official came, was sympathetic, but it was no good: I had to pay it. How I don't remember. Probably I asked for books to review. I don't think there were allowances then for women in my position—a child, and no support from the father. Even if there had been, I would have scorned to take them; a question of pride.

If you are thinking, But you had a lover; why didn't he help? I always paid my way with Jack. It was a question of principle. Besides, he had a wife and family to support. Yet, if this was poverty, I can't remember really going without anything much, pining for something I couldn't afford.

And we ate well. Joan and I both cooked wonderful meals and invited each other. I made good use of that standby for people during hard times, the soup-stew which was continually added to and became better as the days passed.

Sometimes I must have despaired, though, because I applied for a secretary's job in Mayfair. Seven pounds a week. I said to the employer that it wasn't a living wage, and he said apologetically: 'I am afraid we expect them to live at home.'

I sent short stories to the *New Yorker*, sold them two, neither of them my best. Nadine Gordimer had had a short story accepted, told them to look out for me (we had not then met). I sent back a batch they had just returned, and they took one.

From the time I met him, I was under pressure from Jack to get myself my own place. 'You are a big girl now.' He said Joan bossed me about, but I knew his attitude to Joan was to do with some 'unresolved conflict' of his own. The ways in which I had or had not turned Joan into my mother were of course discussed with Mrs Sussman. I thought Jack missed the point, which was that it was good for Peter to be in Joan's house, for he loved her, and she him, and Ernest was as good as an older brother. Surely Jack could see this. He was a psychiatrist, wasn't he? This was truly naïve, but in those early days psychoanalysts and psychiatrists were considered infallible or at least given credit for insights in ways that would be impossible now: we know they are mere human beings, like the rest of us.

Now, there is no woman in the world whose lover urges her into leaving all others to find a place of her own who does not feel what he says, even if her mind is saying something else, as a promise. I was seeing less of Jack than I had. I thought I would see more of him when I achieved my own place.

I was missing the essential thing. It was not only me but other woman friends of his who were being told they must get their own homes. This was a man who had been very poor all his childhood, in a country and culture where security was a chimera. For a poor person, the first step into security is a roof over one's head. Decades later, when I was involved with some very poor old women, I heard all the time: 'a roof over my head'; 'I got a roof over my head'; 'You must keep the roof over your head'. Jack's advice to everyone was to find a house or flat in an unfashionable area, get a mortgage, and be sure there is enough space to let a room or two, which will cover expenses. This is the recipe for survival in hard times. But I had never thought like that, had moved so many times in my life I could no longer remember when or where, felt nervous at the thought of staying in one place. I had been at Joan's for four years—1950–1954.

It was not that I had not tried. I had been urged to buy a vast house in Blenheim Crescent, in bad repair, going for £2,500, ludicrously cheap even then. I asked the bank manager for a loan, but he said that house prices were so unreasonably high they were bound to fall, and he would not advise his wife or his daughter to make such a terrible mistake. Experts. (For a time I kept a file, 'Experts', but I lost it in one of the moves.) If he had given me this loan, my years-long, decades-long worries over getting and keeping a roof over my head would have ended right at the beginning of my time in London.

Suddenly there was a telephone call from Pamela Hansford Johnson at Michael Joseph, who asked me why I had not put in for the Somerset Maugham Award. It was then £400, with the proviso that it had to be spent travelling for at least three months. This was because Somerset Maugham felt that English writers were provincial, knew only England, and should travel. It was before the tourist explosion. I said that since I had been brought up outside the country, I thought I didn't qualify. Never mind that, said she. She was always kind to younger writers. (In my experience, older writers are kind to the young ones.) And so I won the Somerset Maugham Award, but I had to promise to spend the £400 out of Britain. This was like being handed an apple when you are starving and told to eat it next month. I needed that £400 badly. This proviso of Maugham's taught me that if you are going to give something, then don't make conditions. Previous recipients, also desperate for a roof over their heads, or to eat, had cheated. One had fulfilled the letter of the law by putting the money in a bank and travelling round Italy for three months with his guitar, singing for his supper and sleeping rough. Or with kindly girls.

There was a flat going in Warwick Road, controlled rent, for

£250. It was large enough to let rooms. I gave this sum as a deposit to an Australian mother and daughter going back home. I was getting all their furniture, 'such as it is', included. I would go to Paris for a month. Peter would go to the Eichners' for a month, my mother and Joan would cope for a month. Then in his holidays, I would take him to the Mediterranean for a month.

Jack was with me when the telephone call came that I had won the Somerset Maugham prize. I was afraid to tell him— rightly, as it turned out—for he at once exclaimed, 'And that's it, that's the end.' It came from his depths, from his deep dark male depths. I was so shocked. I was so frightened. I expostulated. I begged. I appealed for justice, but that was the end, and I knew it.

'You don't love me; you only care about your writing.'

I am sure there is not one woman writer, ever, at any time in the world's history, who has not heard these words from her man.

It was unjust. Far from being like George Sand, who rose from the bed of love to write all night by candlelight, while her lover lay alone, I never put writing before love, or before Jack; was infinitely amenable to any suggestions from him, giving up any writing plans for him; and in short was like Jane Austen, writing . . . well, if not under the cover of a blotter, then only when he was not around or expected. But we do touch here on something deeper. A woman writer, putting love before literature, when love lets her down will then make literature out of love. 'Well, whose fault is it!'

I put myself in a cheap hotel on the Left Bank and set myself to spend as little money as possible. Twenty-five—that's the age for Paris; young, fancy-free, unworried. I was in my mid-thirties. I spent my days writing, but I was not living the life of a writer in Paris. I sat in cafés trying to understand the talk around me, got into clumsy conversations with strangers but made no attempt to make friends. I was low and sad, and worried, waiting for Jack to arrive, when he would see that I was not having mad passionate love affairs with all and sundry. It is no good saying now I wish I had—what a waste of Paris! Jack came for a weekend. There could scarcely have been a more misused visit to Paris than that one, but it cost very little, which was the point. Then Peter arrived, by plane, and we went down to St-Maxime for the other month. I found an extremely cheap room at the bottom of a house, large and cool, with nothing in it but a couple of mattresses on the floor, two hard chairs, and an electric plate. Small black ants were everywhere. I have never been more bored in my life, but the child, of course, loved every second, because we were out on the beach from six or seven till the sun went down. We ate picnics in our room. There were other children, but they were French and not interested in an English boy. The much reprinted and anthologized story 'Through the Tunnel' comes from that holiday, so you could say it paid for itself. Also a little sour story called 'Pleasure', about enjoying oneself.

Back in London, it was time to move. Mrs Sussman was supporting me. She always did. I do know how lucky I was to find her, having since seen in action therapists who do more harm than good. She told me, when I said I was worried about Jack, whom I was seeing so much less of, just as I was preparing to share a home with him, 'But you are married to him.' I will skip reflections on what being really married means. But probably he was married to more than one of us, apart from his wife. Like me, he had a talent for intimacy. The Shona people say that it may take years for a man and a woman to be really married. By definition, that must mean: within a framework of polygamy.

Going to Mrs Sussman twice or thrice a week, which I did for about three years, saved me. I knew that then; it has not taken the passing of time to tell me. She was a friend. Perhaps if I had had a good older friend, I would not have needed Mrs Sussman. I didn't care about the ideologies—Freud, Jung and so forth. When she started 'interpreting' according to whichever creed it was, I waited for her to finish. For one thing, I had always been at home in these realms.

Joan reached me where it hurt when she said moving would be bad for Peter. I knew that, but the flat was too small. By then he was a vigorous boy of eight. He needed more room. But what he needed most was a father, and Ernest was at least a big brother.

Before leaving Joan's I wrote to Somerset Maugham, thanking him for the £400. I got a grudging letter back, saying that, first, he had nothing to do with the choosing of prizewinners and, two, he had never read anything I had written and, three, no one before me had ever written to thank him. So much for good manners. 'You must always write bread-and-butter letters saying thank you.' Or, 'Doddis is a *good* little baba.' (*Under My Skin*). This letter from Maugham hurt. It was meant to. But I owed him a roof over my head.

Warwick Road, SW5

The flat was in Warwick Road, a singularly ugly street, where lorries thundered all day and most of the night. It consisted of a large kitchen, a very large living room, and upstairs two decent bedrooms and two small ones. A 'maisonette'. This was the first place I could call mine, of all the many rooms, flats, houses I had lived in. It was all brown wood and cream paint, twenty years later to be the last word in chic, but then the very essence of dowdy provincialism. I could not have lived with it. I painted it white, all of it, and that took two-and-a-half months. I balanced on ladders, and window sills, on contraptions of ladders and chairs and planks, even over stairwells: I now shudder to think of what I did. A painter dropping in from downstairs, hearing that this female was usurping his place in the economy, looked at the paint rollers, just invented, and said no decent workman would use such rubbish. 'No one can do a good job with rollers.' Experts.

The furniture that came with the flat was quite awful. I painted some of it. I put up cheap but pretty curtains. I dyed the ancient carpet green. A friend told me the other day that when she came into the flat and saw I had a black cover on the bed she was shocked. But it was red, surely? I remember dyeing a 'brocade' bedcover dark red. At first I took one of the tiny rooms as a bedroom, but then when Jack ditched me, I moved downstairs, and the big living room was where I slept, worked, lived.

When I went into this flat or 'maisonette', which was really like a little house, was my approach much different from someone conquering a bit of wilderness? This flat was mine. I was not renting a corner in someone else's home. We put our mark on new houses, flats, with curtains, colours, furniture, but I did not have the money for all that. What I hung at the windows was not what I would have chosen. It was the dazzling skin of white over every inch of the walls that was my mark. I had thought my kitchen was mine—blue linoleum floor, white woodwork, a red wallpaper—but Jack stood in it, smiling, and said, 'What a colour box! You share more than you know with my wife. She's got the same wallpaper in her kitchen.' In those days there wasn't so much choice as now, not hundreds of possible kitchen wallpapers, so this was not really so surprising. But deflating, yes.

I could not have afforded this flat without letting a room, at least when I began. The rent was very low, but no one could let such rooms these days, even in the provinces. There were merely adequate beds, dressing tables and wardrobes; painted board floors, everything bright and cheap. The bathroom and lavatory were shared. Peter had one of the big rooms. There was a succession of tenants: I had entered that world of the lost, the lonely, the misfits, the waifs and strays that drift from one let room to another in big cities. It was a nasty experience. It didn't help that I was a youngish woman, by myself. My highest social point as a landlady was when a couple of minor diplomats from the French Embassy took a big room and a small one. They were charming, affectionate in the caressing French man-to-woman way, and that was certainly good for my morale. They brought me flowers, offered to do all kinds of little jobs I found difficult, like moving heavy furniture. They were good to Peter. They were fascists—I mean, real ones. This was when the French were fighting the rearguard action in Vietnam, and they called the Vietnamese little brown scared bunnies. The two handsome young men staged a rabbit hunt through the four rooms upstairs, frightening Peter because they were violent and vicious, though they were making a joke of it. They were anti-Semitic, in a conventional way. They complained about the black people in the streets: 'They should go back where they came from.' So depressing was this experience of letting rooms that after a few months I decided I would chance it and live on what came in, hoping it would be enough. It was, more or less.

Peter was not happy. He had done well at his first school, had enjoyed it, or seemed to, and when it came to choosing the

next school, I thought, Well, why not stay with what has worked
well up till now? Most of the children from the junior school
moved up to its senior school, which was next door, near Notting
Hill Gate. Peter at once became sullen and miserable and was at
the bottom of the class. Then he said the headmaster had beaten
him. No one had ever so much as smacked him before. I went to
see the headmaster, who was an unpleasant little bully. He said,
Spare the rod, spoil the child, and called Peter 'Lessing the
Blessing'. I knew that Peter was earning—far from the last time in
his life—punishments for being my son. The children of the
successful can have a hard time of it. He made drawling envious
remarks about my books. The worst thing about this man was his
cold, sarcastic, cutting voice, the voice which, when I was a child,
shrivelled me up. There followed two unsuccessful schools. I
thought that this most gregarious child was suffering from being
so much of the time alone with me; he still did not sleep until nine
or ten, still woke at five or six. He went to a school as a weekly
boarder, coming home at weekends, but he hated it. He hated
Warwick Road, as much as I did. During the time I had lodgers
he was resentful and suspicious of them. He was used to a
household with a lively family atmosphere—Joan's—and now he
had to be quiet for fear of disturbing these strangers who were in
his home. I made a mistake and refused to buy a television,
though he begged for one. Bad enough, I thought, the 'comics'
which he read for hours every day. So he used to go after school
to friends' houses to watch their television. We became engaged in
a battle of wills on this and it seems on every other issue. I knew
that what he needed was a father. When Gottfried dropped him,
just like that, and he was so unhappy, I made a point of creating a
picture of Gottfried as a brave, heroic figure fighting for the poor
and dispossessed. This was hardly the truth, but I believed it
would be bad for the child to know too much about the failures of
communism. I made up stories about how he—Peter—and
Gottfried tackled all kinds of difficult and dangerous situations,
from solving housing problems in slum areas to fighting landlords
(this was the time of the landlord Rachman whose name is still
synonymous with the wicked exploitation of tenants) or routing
whole divisions of Nazi soldiers. Later, in his teens, when Peter

went to visit Gottfried, he found that his father was vilifying me in every way he could and that he had been doing so for years.

There was a child in the flat downstairs for a while, a boy Peter's age. The parents hoped the children would be friends, as parents so often do, but they did not like each other. One day this happened: I had started Peter off on a stamp album; we bought stamps, sent for stamps, he swapped stamps. The little boy downstairs took the album and stole half the stamps. Peter was miserable, in that frantic resentful way of children who feel themselves trapped by circumstances. I asked the mother to get the stamps back for Peter, but all she said was: 'Poor little boy'—meaning her son. Peter was hurt by the injustice of it, and I felt an only too familiar cold discouragement—that so often things went wrong for him and I could not put them right.

I will leave this theme here. Women who have brought up a son without a father will know how difficult it is, and those without the experience will have no idea of it. One may easily describe a single dramatic event—like a traveller arriving at the door with a present for Peter from his father, a plastic whale, for instance, but there was no word from his father, no letter, nothing. One may describe the pain of that for the child, his bewilderment and the mother's anger, but not the day-in, day-out slog of it all, trying to be what is impossible, a father as well as a mother.

When Jack finally left me, we were in Paris. He was going to some hospital abroad somewhere. I knew he had arranged it to break with me. We both knew this was the end but were saying things like: 'Well, it's only six months.' He was off to the airport, but he went with me to the ticket office at the station, where I would buy my ticket back to London. We embraced. He left. I stood immobilized, tears flooding. The young man at the window made sympathetic noises. No queue. Seeing I had a packet of Gîtanes in my hand, he nipped out from his little office, put a cigarette in my mouth, lit it, clicked his tongue, Tsk-tsk, patted me, said *'Pauvre petite'* several times, and nipped back to serve a customer. When I finally was able to ask for a ticket, he said love was a very serious matter, but cheer up, I'd find another lover soon.

It was very bad. The 'affair', which had lasted four years, was in fact a marriage, more of one than either of my two legal marriages. I had been uncooked, raw, not involved with more than a small part of myself. But with this man, it had been all or nothing. How absurd that was: he had never ever said he would marry me, made any promises. And yet I had been committed to him. This was the most serious love in my life. So little did he understand how it was for me that he turned up later, three times in all, the last being in the Seventies, to say that since we had done so well, we should start again. And with a look at the bed. That was where we understood each other . . . But surely in a good many other ways too? In *Under My Skin* I describe leaving two small children, and I earned criticism for not going into what I felt about it. It seemed to me obvious that I was bound to be unhappy, and any intelligent reader would understand that without ritual beatings of the breast. Now I feel the same. There is no one who hasn't suffered over love at some time, and so it should be enough to say that being thrown over by this man was bad for me. It was the worst. I was unhappy for a long time. Men fell in love with me, but it was no good, I could not care for them. And then I did something foolish, after misguided reflection. My two marriages I did not think of as having been chosen by me: the first was because of the approach of war, always as good as a marriage broker, the second was a political marriage. My great love, with Jack, had ended badly. Why did I not do as people have been doing for centuries—choose a man for compatibility, similarity of tastes and ideas (at that time these had to include politics)? Among the men interested in me was one who could not have fitted the bill better, as well as being amiable with Peter, who liked him. We embarked on an affair. This was a bad experience for him. He was in love with me, but seriously, and I had to bring the thing to an end. I felt suffocated by him. There was no rational reason, and I have never understood it. We'd meet, with pleasure, talk, walk, go for a meal, I found him delightful—and then it would begin, an irritable need to escape, get away; and in bed it was the same, though on the face of it there was nothing wrong. I couldn't breathe. It had never happened to me before, and it hasn't happened since. I was shocked at myself for letting him in for such pain, because he was badly hurt by it.

Y ou have to be grown up, really grown up, not merely in years, to understand your parents. I was middle-aged when it occurred to me that I had never known my father, as he really was, as he would have been, without that terrible war. Young, he was optimistic and robust, played football, played cricket and billiards for his county, walked and—what he enjoyed most—danced at all the dances for miles around, thought nothing of walking ten miles to a dance, dancing all night, walking back again. The war had killed that young man and left a sombre, irascible man, soon to become a semi-invalid, and then a very ill man. If I had ever met that young Alfred Tayler, would I have recognized him? And, similarly, my mother. Yes, I knew that the war had done her in too, not least because it killed the great love of her life, so that in the end she married one of its victims—and spent the rest of her life nursing him. But it took me a long time to see something else. This was the girl who had defied her father to become a nurse, standing up to years of his refusal even to speak to her. This was the woman who impressed everyone she met by her vigour, her competence, her independence, her humour. I cannot imagine that had I met the young Emily Maude McVeagh I would have had much to say to her, but I would have had to admire her.

I think what happened was this: when she arrived on the Rhodesian farm, which was still virgin bush, with not so much as a field cleared on it, not a house or farm building—nothing; when she knew that this would be her future, a lonely one, because of her neighbours, with whom she had nothing in common; when she knew that the forward drive of her life, which had been towards some form of conventional middle-class living, was blocked; when she knew her husband was an invalid and would not be able to keep his grasp on life; when she knew that nothing she had hoped for could ever happen—then she had a breakdown and took to her bed. But words like 'breakdown' and 'depression' were not used then as they are now: people could be suffering from neurasthenia, or low spirits. She said she had a bad heart and probably believed it, as she lay in bed with her heart pounding from anxiety, looking out over the African bush, where she would never ever feel at home. She lay there for months, saying to her little children, 'Poor mummy, poor sick mummy,' begging for their love and sympathy, and that was so unlike her it should have given me reason to think. And then she got out of bed, because she had to. But *who* got out of that bed? Not the young Emily Maude (she had become Maude by then, the Emily had gone—she had dropped her mother's name). A woman who kept telling her children she had sacrificed her life for them, that they were ungrateful and unfeeling and . . . all the litany of reproaches that are the stock-in-trade of the female martyr. A creature I am sure she would have hated and despised when being herself and still young—and undamaged by war.

She went back to Southern Rhodesia, after four disappointing years in England, told her son and his wife that she would devote her life to them, and her daughter-in-law said to her son, Either her or me. And she began on a round of visits to friends. In the letters she wrote, she said, I hope I shall make myself useful; I don't want to be a burden. □

J. M. COETZEE
MAKE HIM SING

He shares nothing with his mother. His life at school is kept a tight secret from her. She shall know nothing, he resolves, but what appears on his quarterly report, which shall be impeccable. He will always come first in class. His conduct will always be Very Good, his progress Excellent. As long as the report is faultless, she will have no right to ask questions. That is the contract he establishes in his mind.

What happens at school is that boys are flogged. It happens every day. Boys are ordered to bend over and touch their toes and are flogged with a cane.

He has a classmate in Standard Three named Roy Roe whom the teacher particularly loves to beat. The Standard Three teacher is an excitable woman with hennaed hair named Miss Oosthuizen. From somewhere or other his parents know of her as Manie Oosthuizen: she takes part in theatricals and has never married. Clearly she has a life outside the school, but he cannot imagine it. He cannot imagine any teacher having a life outside school.

Miss Oosthuizen flies into rages, calls Roy Roe out from his desk, orders him to bend, and flogs him across the buttocks. The blows come fast one upon another, with barely time for the cane to swing back. By the time Miss Oosthuizen has finished with him, Roy Roe is flushed in the face. But he does not cry; in fact, he may be flushed only because he was bending. Miss Oosthuizen, on the other hand, heaves at the breast and seems on the brink of tears—of tears and of other outpourings too.

After these spells of ungoverned passion the whole class is hushed, and remains hushed until the bell rings.

Miss Oosthuizen never succeeds in making Roy Roe cry; perhaps that is why she flies into such rages at him and beats him so hard, harder than anyone else. Roy Roe is the oldest boy in the class, nearly two years older than himself (he is the youngest); he has a sense that between Roy Roe and Miss Oosthuizen there is something going on that he is not privy to.

Roy Roe is tall and handsome in a devil-may-care way. Though Roy Roe is not clever and is perhaps even in danger of failing the standard, he is attracted toward him. Roy Roe is part of a world he has not yet found a way of entering: a world of sex and beating.

As for himself, he has no desire to be beaten by Miss Oosthuizen or anyone else. The very idea of being beaten makes him squirm with shame. There is nothing he will not do to save himself from it. In this respect he is unnatural and knows it. He comes from an unnatural and shameful family in which not only are children not beaten, but older people are addressed by their first names, and no one goes to church, and shoes are worn every day.

Every teacher at his school, man or woman, has a cane and is at liberty to use it. Each of these canes has a personality, a character, which is known to the boys and talked about endlessly. In a spirit of knowing connoisseurship the boys weigh up the characters of the canes and the quality of pain they give, compare the arm and wrist techniques of the teachers who wield them. No one mentions the shame of being called out and made to bend and being beaten on one's backside.

Without experience of his own, he cannot take part in these conversations. Nevertheless, he knows that pain is not the most important consideration. If the other boys can bear the pain, then so can he, whose will-power is so much greater. What he will not be able to endure will be the shame. So bad will be the shame, he fears, so daunting, that he will hold tight to his desk and refuse to come when he is called out. And that will be a greater shame: it will set him apart and set the other boys against him too. If it ever happens that he is called out to be beaten, there will be so humiliating a scene that he will never again be able to go back to school; in the end there will be no way out but to kill himself.

So that is what is at stake. That is why he never makes a sound in class. That is why he is always so neat, why his homework is always done, why he always knows the answer. He dare not slip. If he slips, he risks being beaten; and whether he is beaten or whether he struggles against being beaten, it is all the same: he will die.

The strange thing is, it will only take one beating to break the spell of terror that has him in its grip. He is well aware of this: if, somehow, he can be rushed through the beating before he has had time to turn to stone and resist, if the violation of his body can be achieved quickly by force, he will be able to come out on the other side a normal boy, able to join easily in the discussion of the teachers and their canes and the various grades and flavours of pain they inflict. But by himself he cannot leap that barrier.

He puts the blame on his mother for not beating him. At the same time that he is glad he wears shoes and takes out books from the public library and stays away from school when he has a cold—all the things that set him apart—he is angry with his mother for not having normal children and making them live a normal life. His father, if his father were to take control, would turn them into a normal family. His father is normal in every way. He is grateful to his mother for protecting him from his father's normality, that is to say, from his father's occasional blue-eyed rages and threats to beat him. At the same time he is angry with his mother for turning him into something unnatural, something that needs to be protected if it is to continue to live.

Among the canes it is not Miss Oosthuizen's that leaves the deepest impression on him. The most fearsome cane is that of Mr Britz the woodwork teacher. Mr Britz's cane is not long and springy in the style most of the teachers prefer. Instead it is short and thick and stubby, more a stick or a baton than a switch. It is rumoured that Mr Britz uses it only on the older boys, that it would be too much for a younger boy. It is rumoured that with his cane Mr Britz has made even Matric boys blubber and plead for mercy and urinate in their pants and disgrace themselves.

Mr Britz is a little man with close-cropped hair that stands upright and a moustache. One of his thumbs is missing: the stub is neatly covered over with a purple scar. Mr Britz hardly says anything. He is always in a distant, irritable mood, as though teaching woodwork to small boys is a task beneath him that he performs unwillingly. Through most of the lesson he stands at the window staring out over the quadrangle while the boys tentatively measure and saw and plane. Sometimes he has the stubby cane with him, idly tapping his trouser leg while he ruminates. When he comes on his inspection round he disdainfully points to what is wrong, then with a shrug of the shoulders passes on.

It is permitted for boys to joke with teachers about their canes. In fact this is one area in which a certain teasing of the teachers is permitted. 'Make him sing, sir!' say the boys, and Mr

Gouws will flash his wrist and his long cane (the longest cane in the school, though Mr Gouws is only the Standard Five teacher) will whistle through the air.

No one jokes with Mr Britz. There is awe of Mr Britz, of what he can do with his cane to boys who are almost men.

When his father and his father's brothers get together on the farm at Christmas, talk always turns to their schooldays. They reminisce about their schoolmasters and their schoolmasters' canes; they recall cold winter mornings when the cane would raise blue weals on their buttocks, and the sting would linger for days in the memory of the flesh. In their words there is a note of nostalgia and pleasurable fear. He listens avidly but makes himself as inconspicuous as possible. He does not want them to turn to him, in some pause in the conversation, and ask about the place of the cane in his own life. He has never been beaten and is deeply ashamed of it. He cannot talk about canes in the easy, knowing way of these men.

He has a sense that he is damaged. He has a sense that something is slowly tearing inside him all the time: a wall, a membrane. He tries to hold himself as tight as possible to keep the tearing within bounds. To keep it within bounds, not to stop it; nothing will stop it.

Once a week he and his class troop across the school grounds to the gymnasium for PT, physical training. In the changing room they put on white singlets and shorts. Then, under the direction of Mr Barnard, also attired in white, they spend half an hour leapfrogging the pommel horse or tossing the medicine ball or jumping and clapping their hands above their heads.

They do all of this with bare feet. For days ahead he dreads baring his feet for PT, his feet that are always covered. Yet when his shoes and socks are off, it is suddenly not difficult at all. He has simply to remove himself from his shame, to go through with the undressing in a brisk, hurried way, and his feet become just feet like everyone else's. Somewhere in the vicinity the shame still hangs, waiting to return to him, but it is a private shame, which the other boys need never be aware of.

His feet are soft and white; otherwise they look like everyone else's, even those of boys who have no shoes and come to school barefoot. He does not enjoy PT and the stripping for PT but he tells himself he can endure it, as he endures other things.

Then one day there is a change in the routine. They are sent from the gymnasium to the tennis courts to learn paddle tennis. The courts are some distance away; along the pathway he has to tread carefully, picking his steps among the pebbles. Under the summer sun the tarmac of the court itself is so hot that he has to hop from foot to foot to keep from burning. It is a relief to get back to the changing room and put on his shoes again; but by afternoon he can barely walk, and when his mother removes his shoes at home she finds the soles of his feet blistered and bleeding.

He spends three days at home recovering. On the fourth day he returns with a note from his mother, a note whose indignant wording he is aware of and approves. Like a wounded warrior resuming his place in the ranks, he limps down the aisle to his desk.

'Why were you away from school?' whisper his classmates.

'I couldn't walk; I had blisters on my feet from the tennis,' he whispers back.

He expects astonishment and sympathy; instead he gets mirth. Even those of his classmates who wear shoes do not take his story seriously. Somehow they too have acquired hardened feet, feet that do not blister. He alone has soft feet, and soft feet, it is emerging, are no claim to distinction. All of a sudden he is isolated—he and, behind him, his mother. ☐

NELL STROUD
THE JOSSER

I am the ringmaster in a circus in England. Over the next few months I will buy a horse for the show. When I am in the ring next season, on my own horse, in costumes I have made, that will be my dream come true.

People hide in the circus. I went to the circus to run away, and found myself in this demoralized, hard-fighting and uncompromising world, full of people who fight for what they believe in and what they know, and make their lives a sacrifice for their art. We suffer to carry on, they say. It is dangerous work, and difficult, and painful and beautiful: horses, stars, camels, lorries. It is an art form that we will soon, if we are not careful, lose.

I am among circus people, but not of them. I am a josser—in the circus from the outside world. I ran to the circus, and then, after a while, I found that I had run back into myself, and that I felt more myself in the circus than anywhere else in the world.

I was born in Oxford in 1973 and lived there for ten years. The memories of this time are fractured. I remember a party in the street for the Queen's Jubilee: my father, Rick, dressed up as a ringmaster, my sister Emma on her horse, carnival lions in a home-made parade. I was always in the garden. We were clearing out the shed one day, and a rat ran across the lawn, and there was a hot-air balloon overhead. The people in the balloon were laughing. My mum waved. I had a toy monkey—I was obsessed with monkeys—and we were all sitting on the grass with a historian from New College who was making a speech with the monkey. To be or not to be that is the question whether 'tis nobler in the mind to suffer the slings and arrows of outrageous fortune or to take arms against a sea of troubles and by opposing end them. Everyone was laughing and the sun was shining and the grass was warm. My mum was the lion beside me, do you love me more than a thousand monkeys? Of course I do, and she hugs me, the strength and heart of a lion.

When I was ten we moved to the country, to a village called Minety. The three older children, Tom, Emma and Sophy, had grown up and left home. My younger sister, Clover, was my most constant friend. We would play gypsies under the bay tree in Oxford, and then in the country we would see them for real. They used to camp on a bit of land called the Dance, near Minety. We sentimentalized them, would have done anything to be them, parked up in the long grass and the cow parsley. The dogs and the babies and the horses, smoke in the blossom on a summer evening. We longed for this life that we knew nothing about, and a childish inclination can carry you further than you think.

In the year between school and university I joined a circus in America. The iconography burnt itself into my mind at once. There was an electric storm on the first night, and in the yellow flashes the performers appeared, in costumes brighter and more beautiful than any I had seen before.

Back in Oxford, at the university now, I lived in a house with various friends, a large and ever-changing population. We ran a nightclub from the front room, and for a while the house was full of painted mannequins and Day-Glo backdrops, with the sound of hard techno most of the day and night. But the circus was always in my mind. I knew what I wanted to do when I left.

Sometimes, sitting in the box office, I think about Mum and what happened to her, how she suddenly went away and returned a different person. I remember her voice and her laugh and the way she hugged me. The things she would say, the intrigue of her thoughts and the world around her, all gone. What we were to her and her vision of life, all gone too. She would say, don't just think of your great-aunts as being old people, they were young and adventurous like you once, young girls, and I see now what she meant. I wish that she was still here. I cry for her counsel. I think of the fact that she has gone and sometimes I actually say No out loud, as if that will make any difference. Why won't she walk into the room now? Her quick strong walk and big smile, pleased to see you, never let the sun go down on your anger, girls.

She is about thirty and she is standing beside a car, a Citroën. All the doors are wide open, and the bonnet is open too. She has her back to the car, and her hand on her hip, and her feet are neatly together, stripy tights and a denim skirt and sensible shoes, a jersey with a belt and the sleeves rolled up. Her other hand is resting on the edge of the pram and she is looking down at her dog, who is looping about; she is looking down and saying something and smiling. She is surrounded by baskets and bags all sitting in the gravel, loose clothes, and the pram is full of stuff too, saddles, riding hats, blankets, fragments and suggestions of more luggage. I can't think how she is going to get it all into the car, the pram and the dog and everything, and the car looks weighed down already. It is typical, though, she looks so relaxed, talking to the dog, her feet together so neatly. A world goes past and we never even realize it.

It is the back end of the circus season; winter is on its way without a doubt, and with the winter the winds and all the fear of losing the big top. The night before we had to take it down in a gale. The vinyl had cracked and rolled and everyone came out from the caravans to help, the girls and the children and the wives, hanging on to ropes and shouting in the stumbling darkness. Once the poles are out the only things that hold the tent are the guys and the stakes, and the wind gets right underneath the canvas and hauls it upwards, so we ran round undoing the ropes in succession, dragging the tent, folding it, piling it on to the lorry. Jason was standing on the lorry as the tent came down on the flat bed.

Jason is a good boy. He grins at you in the darkness when there is mud on his face and rain in his hair, and the only lights are the lights from the road and the rushing cars and everyone has lost their torches and you are at the outside edge of what you can take; too tired now, too long the hours, too slow the lorries, too violent the wind. I like to run with the boys, get good at it all, get stronger. Jason has slight bow legs and his hands are all wrong for his age. He is a young boy, but his hands are broken open and rough like wood.

The wind was blowing and forcing the tent to hang over to one side, making it impossible to load. We pushed it back, clinging to the sides of the lorry and trying to lean on this vast flapping angry thing that billowed around us. There was a new boy, and he tried to climb up to help, but he didn't know where the footholds were and could not see in the darkness. I was at one end, trying to keep the corners in, and somebody pushed the boy up from underneath, and he lurched forward and disappeared into a fold. The wind gusted, and just as we thought we had it, the tent jerked to one side and Jason flew off the edge of the lorry, on to the ground, twisting and curling as he hit the grass. He lay completely still and then jumped up and walked forwards, his body tipped and wincing at the weight, and he stopped and put his hands on his knees and then straightened again, and someone shouted to him, and he yelled back that he was coming, hang on.

That was all last night. We have put the poles back up today, but not the tent, it is too windy, we have a spare day tomorrow, we can do it then, just sleep tonight and hear the wind and not worry. The man who owns the circus is called Ernest and he is tired. He says that he never sleeps when the wind blows; his whole life would be carried away if the tent went.

What else could I do but the circus, he asked me once. You can see what he means. The circus is the only medium I can think of where life and art are undivided, so the essence of circus life cannot be replicated anywhere else. Once you have been in the circus, then you feel out of it in any other world. But I feel guilty; this is my choice, still. I could walk away from a destroyed tent to other lives. I am inauthentic, a passenger. And I make assumptions, at the back of my head, without realizing. That the others must have different lives too, houses, a normal existence somewhere else. But they don't. There is nothing else for them to fall back on, to go home to. This is it—the wind and the flapping tent and the lorries in the night and the camels slowly passing outside the caravan during tea.

The sun has set in a sky that is coloured by the storm, and the faces are coloured by the sky. The tent is not up, but the caravans are arranged around the ground, and the animals are grazing within this space. The field we are parked in has little hillocks and a gate on to the road. This road leads on to a roundabout and a motorway. You can see it from the field. It runs along the horizon. The trucks look huge, nothing behind them, just the sky. I feel very tired from the long night of driving and the night before, the racing around in the dark and falling in the mud and the work today. I am with Ernest and Jason and Claire beside the tent trailer, whiling the time away a bit, watching the last light and practising handstands. I want to learn to press a handstand, but I am heavy and my wrists feel weak. Ernest's father comes over. He is about eighty and he stands on one hand with his body straight out parallel to the ground and everyone claps. The bull pulls his stake out of the ground and canters about, tossing his head and glancing at us with the whites of his eyes. The boys go after him and they catch him by the horns and knock the stake back in. Jason's dog barks and the boys are laughing, they look like cowboys. The light is bright yellow on the horizon and all their faces are yellow too.

There is more wind forecast, and darkness ahead. It is about five o'clock. I have to sit in the box office for a few hours, waiting for people to buy tickets. It is a converted trailer with a dented steel step set by the door that Elena has just painted white. She says that she loves painting. Her English is broken and articulate and hard. She is Romanian and rolls her Rs, and her face is wide, cat eyes and scarred skin from chickenpox. When she smiles her lips go thin, and her eyes slant; she has arms like a monkey and a short back. She stands on her head on the trapeze; her neck is thick with muscle, and one day she will be in a wheelchair. And then will you push me around, eh, Speary? she says to her husband accusingly, and he says that he married her, babe, in sickness and in health, and she laughs bitterly because she doesn't believe him.

Elena's life seems difficult to me. She lives in a lorry and is always packing things into suitcases and then unpacking them. She is very clever with her costumes; for riding the elephants she makes feather headdresses encrusted with stones stuck on thick wires, and she patiently mends rips in thin tights, weaving in threads of material pulled from the waistband. But she is tired and lazy too, gives up in winter, lives in her bed, watching telly and eating bacon sandwiches. I am sure she doesn't know the extent of her brilliance. She puts the paintbrush into a jar of water and the lid on the paint. Speary calls, and she goes home to the lorry for supper.

I sit in the swivel chair in the box office. The wind is starting again, and I can still see the lorries on the horizon. One of them looks as if it has broken down, and then I see a man climbing the ladder on the side of it. He is dressed in silver and he looks tiny, and the lorry huge. The light is going now and it is dark in the office, too dark to read, and I am sure that no one will stop by. Jason is still laying the electricity cable, ratcheting around in the dark, and until he has finished there will be no light. Speary's generator starts to whirr from across the ground and the animals are in now for the night.

Ernest knocks on the door and looks through the glass window. I open the door, and he steps in. The step is wet, and there is white paint on his soles, and he laughs and says that Elena loves painting, doesn't she. He asks me if I am all right, and he says that the electricity is on now, so I pull the light cord, and the bulb shines. Not much power here, he says, and the bulb is glowing dark yellow, and his face is in deep shadow now all the light in the sky is gone. It is pitch black outside.

I work much harder than the other girls. It is men's work, putting the tent up and taking it down, heavy and very dangerous. The girls know better than me; they wait in their caravans behind the curtains, the noises from outside signalling the progress of this massive operation. The shouts as the rolls of tent are lifted on to the lorry, the squeals of the winches as the kingpoles come down, and then the far-carrying chimes as the stakes are knocked out. A high wind, and they will be compelled to turn out, to help until the tent is packed, beyond danger of ripping. The tent is the hardest taskmaster of all, a mobile building site, a theatre of art and work. This evening, sitting in the box office, I am shattered, not much sleep for two days, the curve of the swinging sledgehammer pulling your shoulders. As the little room lights up, I can see my face reflected in the window. Ernest asks me again if I am all right and he asks if I want to go to the pub.

I don't know, I say.

Are you being difficult? he says. Do you want to go to the pub later? We won't open the box office for long, in this wind what's the point?

The rain has started. You can hear it on the roof.

Ernest goes away, and I can still see my reflection and I don't recognize myself: I look thinner than I think I am, with wild hair and filthy clothes and green eyeliner still left over from the show two days ago. I am tired, too tired even to read. I just sit and stare at my reflection and then out through it to darkness. If I wasn't so tired I would be bored now, but the tiredness takes you away from the monotony. This is a circus night, and I remember my first week with this circus.

The old ringmaster was leaving, and we sat outside having dinner. The ringmaster was called John Paul and he was Irish and spoke with the ease of Irishmen. We were by the sea and we ate crabs and lobster and oysters, platefuls of them, a last warm night in August. There were bulbs on cables hanging from the caravan and a white tablecloth, and we drank whiskey. My dad, Rick, was there. I was very happy; I felt that I had come home. The people were strangers, and yet it was as if they were waiting here for me, as if I knew them already. The sea was in the distance, and I swam in it the next day, with John Paul, drifted in the waves and looked at the sky, the sand dunes and, yes, I felt that I had come home.

There is a knock again, and it is Claire, Jason's girlfriend. She is a tall, big-boned girl, with long black hair and she throws knives and whirls a forty-foot lasso. She is a gossip, old Claire, an information sieve—you can't really tell her anything; but she is tough and funny. She looks like a Red Indian princess, I think, with her black hair and her dogs. Her caravan is beautiful: glossy, clean and spacious with a cut-glass door and a honey-coloured wooden floor. In the back of the lorry Jason has built a bath, with wooden walls and a built-in radio. Costumes, tumble-dryer, washing machine—it is all there. I stand up and open the door of the office, and Claire is holding two cups of coffee, and under her arm is a stack of paper. She says that I must be bored here with no one to talk to, not right that I have to work so hard. I say that I don't mind, that I like it, that I *am* bored, thanks for the coffee, what has she got, can I see, that's why I brought it, for you to see, my scrapbook from when I was a kid, the pictures were going to be thrown out. She shows me photographs of her childhood. They are extraordinary, documents of a strange tribe, a way of life.

Claire is definitely not a thin little slip of a thing: circus girls are larger than life close up, more to them than meets the eye. I found this in a book, it was written in 1784: 'A young person of sweet and dreamlike appearance, a rope dancer of the abstract school, full of poetry and expression, who danced on a rope with the wings of a sylph and the modest graces sung by Horace.'

101

This was probably Claire's great-great-great-grandmother or similar, back down the line, spinning those mysteries in the air. But Claire, now, sits in the dark night with the cups of coffee, prosaic, frighteningly strong, with a rough edge to her voice and a threatening look in her eye. And in the photographs too, she is a determined, heavy child, learning the secrets of her trade, the lifted chin, the fuck-you superiority. There is Claire doing the splits outside, in a sparkly costume, and you can only just make her out in the dark, the sun is setting, the light is coming in sideways, catching the side of the lorry and throwing a camel into silhouette. There is another picture of Claire on a palomino pony; she says that she really loved that pony, it was the only pony she really loved. She is beside a red lorry and in front of her parent's big top and she is in a cowgirl costume. There is a monkey in a cage and a man with a lion. What is it like, I ask her, growing up in the circus, what does the rest of the world seem like when you are a child? She says that you just have an edge, don't you, you just have an edge. It is a difficult life, carved in wind and disaster and an unearthly picturesque. They don't see that bit; the ongoing visual cliché. But they have an untiring pride in their work, their lives. They just have an edge.

But in any case, Claire adds, I'm only second-generation circus. I ask her what her parents did then, if they weren't in the circus, it is anybody's guess, but she says that they were travelling theatre. She was not circus, she was travelling theatre. I am sure that in this difference lie a thousand implications and prejudices, but it is a language beyond me. She shows me a scrap of brown paper, a little painting to illustrate the structure of the tent for the theatre. It is thin and ripped, a shred of a document, and Claire says it is lovely, she holds it and looks at it and it seems sacred in the dark box office with the light of two bulbs. We drink the coffee and talk, and then Claire goes home to make Jason dinner. She says that they are going to the pub later, do I want to come? And I say that I do.

Claire leaves, and I sit for a bit longer. The rain is hard now, and the wind stronger. I feel that things are slipping away, that I have gone too far to go back. I shut my eyes and can see the green-yellow light of the sunset, and Ernest's trilby blowing off, lifting and flying in the wind, a clown's hat. The office thunders and shakes in the wind, and for a split second I think that it is someone running around upstairs, footfalls from another time.

I can mark out in my head times when I have been forced to defer to this edge. I used to ride an elephant in a circus, an elephant called Beverly. I had always thought that staying on an elephant would be as easy as staying on a wide and gently rocking table. But this is an illusion too. There is a lot of movement to deal with, the elephant sways violently from side to side, and when it runs you are like a rag doll, thrown up and down, and then the elephant heaves on to its back legs and you are thrown up and back, your hand in the strap of the harness, let go and you would crash to the ground, and all the while you have to smile and point your hands, and then climb down off the elephant, skip across the ring, still smiling, trip on to the ring fence, clap with the crowds, skip back over to the elephants, lie down, they walk over you, then you spring up and dance to the front of the ring and curtsy and point your toes and smile all the time. I loved doing it, I had never skipped and shimmied and posed like this before in public, it was exhilarating and hilarious. But as we came out of the ring, folded back through the curtains, I would see my legs running with blood from the rough skin of the elephant, and my knuckles were red with blood too, where they had been ground into the neck underneath the harness. Charmagne, one of the other girls, was blasé, bored, slightly angry, as she came through the curtains on the other side, when I was stage-struck and uncool. Bleeding cow, she would say, dropped me right down then didn't she, the bitch. What was she doing with these complaints and curses? I could see it all. She was setting me outside of the closed circle of circus blood. She was my friend and I loved her, but to Charmagne I was a josser and always will be.

It is Sandra's birthday. Sandra is a trapeze artist on the show, very much a lady in her act, poised, posed and pretty. Her family work on another show and we are going over there this evening, to see her parents and eat cake, and to pick up her sister and some boys to go to a nightclub. Her mum looks like a tiny aggressive bird, her legs are fiercely muscled and she wears high heels all the time. She opens the door of the lorry and hugs Sandra, scolding and chattering in Spanish. The lorry has been converted into a big kitchen. It is beautifully done, with a massive orange copper chimney chute above a substantial cooker, and there is a group of people around a table at the far end of the room eating Chinese takeaway. They finish eating, and the table folds away, and they sit and talk and tease the young people going out. There is a man in the corner, and I recognize him because he is a famous clown. I knew his son, a clown too, I remember him running up and down a scrapyard in Glasgow in his make-up.

There is a loud knock at the door and a boy bounds into the room and talks loudly to the older people, winds them up a bit, makes them laugh. Fools they are, terrible with money! What a voice this boy has, standing in the middle of the room and everyone looking at him. Half-Irish and half-Spanish, he is a juggler. Lovely he is—and moving to Las Vegas next year, Sandra tells me.

Magdalena, Sandra's friend, is a contortionist and hand-balancer, the queen of the tiny costume and thin limb. She wears little white boots with heels and silver studs, immaculate white trousers and white top and her hair in a ponytail, with a curl sexily at the front, and the skin on her face so perfect it will chip if you don't watch out. She is a great artist, Magdalena, perfectly bendy, always in time, and she does a hula-hoop act too, and by the end of it the crowd are going mad, mad for her, clapping without realizing and thinking of discos.

Sandra's granny brings in a birthday cake. Everyone sings and claps and passes the cake round on small pink plates. Sandra hugs her and says that this is her nan, who has taught her everything she knows. The room is very crowded now and Sandra's dad says that we should be off, and her mum talks to her some more in Spanish, and she looks even more like a furious little bird. Perhaps Anita is coming with us and perhaps she isn't. She has recently married a Hungarian boy, and he is ill. He might not let Anita out on her own. Sandra and Magdalena and I run across the ground in the dark to their caravan. There are light bulbs strung above our heads on the main guys and in the light of these shine the backs of some sea lions and they watch us with their glass eyes.

Anita is tiny and Brazilian with big teeth and big eyes and long dark hair and a thin, concave figure. I remember her act, a slow and hypnotic *corde lisse*, a small body in the distance, pulling and stretching on the coiling rope. There are leopard cushions and it is very warm in the caravan. Her husband, Kootchie, is lying on the bed at the end of the room watching television. Anita says, won't you come out Kootchie, come out darling, and he says that he is ill, and Anita leans on the wall and looks at him. She says that she might come out, to us, she'll meet us in the car, it depends on Kootchie. Sandra's dad says that he will give us a lift home after. One of the boys gets his car stuck over the rim of a rut hidden in the long grass, bloody idiot, says Sandra's dad, and he tows him out, and the boys are all whistling and shouting in the dark, we can see them through the rain-flecked windows of the car. Just as we are about to pull away, a figure in a dark coat appears, and it is Anita; she says that she is going to come after all and we budge up and she slams the car door and we are off again, towards the gate that leads from the field to the road. Kootchie is in her mind, though, she thinks of him, what he will do when she is ill, and she asks Sandra's dad to stop the car, she is very sorry and she jumps out and says goodnight, see you later, have a good time, and then she is gone in the dark.

The art of circus showmanship, creating spectacle, muddling the boundaries between art and life, making the lion lie down with the lamb, for real and as a picture. Lord George Sanger was a nineteenth-century showman, and his grandson can remember being picked up from the train station in a coach pulled by twenty Dalmatians. 'I felt like a true Sanger again,' he said. Absurd logistical odds to create a brilliant and equally absurd spectacle. Think of the harness for twenty dogs, the hundred tiny buckles and eighty paws to tangle in the delicate straps, training the dogs, keeping them. Showmanship is about showing off, in the ring, fantasizing about yourself, being sexier, grander, funnier than the last act or the last circus to come to town.

When I was at university, I used to go to travellers' parties, the painted-bus version of travellers. A thousand cultural differences lie between them and the circus. New Age travellers are not showmen, but they are show-offs. Social pageantry is the name of their game, they parade metal-encrusted faces, trail luminous dreadlocks, whirl around on motorbikes and horses and breathe fire. The circus, by comparison, hides. That boy standing at the bar could be anyone: a computer programmer, an insurance salesman, a mechanic. And what does he do? He puts on a costume shining with stones and juggles to a strange audience twice a day. That is all he knows, all he cares about, a transitory and uncompromised life, more interesting and harder, I think, than vain dabbles in roadside culture.

Where I am in all of this, I don't know. I certainly felt like a clown among the girls that night. I was wearing trainers, and the bouncer at the nightclub wouldn't let us in on the grounds that my shoes weren't smart enough. The juggling boy, Lucia, lent me his shoes, he had some others in the car. They were far too big and far from alluring, boys' leather shoes, and I had to shuffle and trip to keep them on. The girls danced in a circle and slow-danced with a boy each at the end of the night, one of their own, that is. Lucia had a go at Magdalena in the corner, and she was soft and nice with him. I felt like an oddity, a bit too butch, a bit too posh; on the outside, looking in.

I liked Lucia, I explained to Eva, but wasn't prepared to compete for him—I didn't know how to. And Eva knew what I was talking about and said that it was hard to find a man these days. She looked out of the window of the box office at the playing field and the boys in shorts playing football.

'Plenty of men here,' she said, 'and not a hero among them.'

I did fall in love with a circus boy once. He was called Pishti and he was a Hungarian ring boy. I was a groom, behind the curtains somewhere, regarded as circus underclass, just very long hours and continual exhaustion. He looked after the elephants, he was tall and blond and quiet, he would just shake his head and whistle to himself when he heard shouting. The family who ran that circus were like that, they didn't talk, you didn't see them much, but you heard them all the time, shouting and shouting. In the morning I would wake in tears, in the night I would sleep with the sound of shouting in my head and hear foreign voices whispering, whispering and shouting and crying, maybe it was my sleep, dreams and nightmares, and after a while I stopped caring. There were a lot of animals in that circus, but it wasn't them that were being exploited, it was the people. The artists sorted themselves out, lived in their own gangs and families, and came and went as they pleased. But the grooms and ring boys were treated as the property of the circus, to be chewed up and spat out at the end of the season. Pishti was one of four Hungarian boys. They had no time for washing clothes, they lived in one caravan and slept on the seats. They couldn't run away as the circus held on to part of their wages.

When we arrived at a new ground, a long drive after a pull-down and a short night's sleep ahead, we would water the horses. I liked this, it was warm in the lorry, and the horses' soft noses and whickering were a comfort. The other groom, Anne, would pass up the buckets, and the boys and I would climb along the partitions, clinging to the roof with one hand and carrying the buckets with the other. The boys loved the horses, and one of them, Toddy, sometimes sat on them like a little jockey in the dark, leaning forwards and putting his arms around their necks.

The boys were my friends and my allies. I used to follow their four lorries with my caravan and trailer. If I broke down they would help me, lashing the caravan together and joking about my incompetence. I loved them and I will never see them again. Joe, Toddy, Pishti and Martin. They were the centre and meaning of my life for a while; then they went away. They had the nastiest time in that circus. They missed their families and their girlfriends. Toddy described the rivers in Hungary, fishing with his friends and the hot summers, his mum who ran a clothes shop, and he showed me a photograph of his girlfriend. They were wild, though. The first week I was with them, we went to a pub on a main road outside Liverpool somewhere. The landlady drew the curtains after closing time, and they danced and drank pints of beer, pushed back the pool table and turned up the jukebox, in the sweat of the dancing the noise of the shouting faded away, it was happy and melancholic at the same time. We didn't know where we were, I didn't know any more, I was starting to lose myself in the circus and they were losing themselves from it. There was a Scottish girl, she had blonde hair and blank, innocent eyes, and she said are you tough, are you tough enough, and I didn't realize how tough she meant, though I thought I was. I danced with Joe, he held me up close and the evening fell away.

Later in the season, in early November, we came back from a bar at about midnight, rolling drunk. We ran along the side of the Mersey, and Toddy went ahead into the dark. I stopped with Charmagne in front of the water, which looked stripped and metallic. Suddenly we saw Toddy in his boxer shorts, climbing down some dark, slippery steps into the water. We did the same, freezing cold and hopping about in the wind. Pishti stood at the top of the darkness, I slid on the steps and went into the water, right under, and Charmagne shouted and Toddy, who was splashing about at the bottom of the steps, pulled me out. That night Pishti stayed in my caravan, the whole night. There were late-night songs on the radio and violet lights outside.

Two weeks later they all drove away in the early morning. It was the end of the season, they had to take one load back to the farm and then they were free. Pishti just drove away in the brilliant early morning sun, without waving. He gave me a boiler suit I had said I liked. After he left, I burst into tears and threw it in the bin. Since then I have steadily forgotten him, though I do think about him sometimes and wonder if he remembers me.

I was supposed to be revising for my Oxford entrance interview but I was fast asleep in bed, and it was ten o'clock. Mum came in and asked me if I wanted to go hunting with her, and I was irritated. I hate remembering this, the adolescent spurning of suggestions. The night before she had asked if I wanted to go to church, to evensong, she was standing at the door, smiling, looking kind, loving me and me hating her because I was eighteen and had decided that the world was all against me. I said I didn't want to go to church. I was proud of my autonomy, the suggestion of atheism, decided alone. No, I didn't want to go hunting either. Philistines, I thought angrily to myself, and me with my exams to do and academia ahead, the pressure, the clever questions and good answers expected, quotes to summon, ideas to develop, understand, undermine, qualify, quantify, they didn't understand this, she didn't understand this. Hunting—as if I had the time.

I did get out of bed to plait her horse for her. It was a thoroughbred, a neat smart little mare, and I am good at plaiting manes. You divide the mane into sections and plait each one and then roll each plait into a little ball. Then the neck looks well-curved and sleek. We put the horse into the trailer and said goodbye. She looked very smart and sweet, she said goodbye, I love you, I love you too, I love you once more. She drove away, down the lane to the road, and I went inside and back to my revising.

The telephone rang when I was downstairs in the kitchen eating toast and jam beside the Aga, a warm kitchen smell. Mrs Crocker said that Mum had had an accident. The memory still stops me in my tracks now, and it will stop me until the day I die.

She was in Cirencester hospital. I was annoyed and a bit worried. She might have broken her leg, or her arm. I wanted to go and see her; a part of me was able to enjoy the drama.

Is she all right though? Not serious, I mean? And the voice said, I'll take you to see her, I'll come and pick you up.

I went to the hospital, and there was a real-life television scene going on outside, flashing lights and white coats. I walked into the hospital, and the nurse put me in a separate waiting room. I didn't know why they were all so formal and worried-looking, I was used to accidents. I had broken two arms falling off ponies. All this was an overreaction, idiotic.

A doctor came in and started to describe what had happened. I didn't understand what he was saying. Then a nurse came in and said that Mrs Stroud was being transferred to Bristol, did her daughter want to see her before she left? And I said that I did, of course, where was she? And I was looking forward to seeing her sitting up in bed and I could say are you all right and we could make a few plans, quickly, before she went. The nurse led me outside and there was more of a commotion than before, more nurses and an ambulance.

It was like a sledgehammer between the shoulder blades. She was lying on a bed and her face was covered in blood. There were huge purple rings under her eyes, and her eyes were shut. She looked as if she was dead. Let her die.

I couldn't breathe and I started to fall over, I was falling, falling right away from it all, it's her daughter, take her away, take her away. Now I think, Let her die, Let her die, in reply, but they wouldn't hear that back then, in the past. The sound doesn't carry.

She went down the motorway to Bristol at a hundred miles an hour, with a police escort—you have seen them go past sometimes, on the motorway, wonder what has happened for a bit. Now you know. A police escort and all the lights. I told my dad this. Were there outriders? he said. He was disbelieving of what was happening to him, to us, to Mum. Will she be all right? he said. It was the first time that I saw beyond him. How very un-all right we couldn't imagine. Death would have been all right.

The house filled up with people quickly. After Cirencester we went to pick Clover up from school, ran into her classroom in tears, with a teacher, the thing she always knew would happen one day. Called from the classroom because your mother is dead. We drove home. Nothing that we could do just yet, said Angela sensibly. Rick, my dad, arrived back in London, and people came back from hunting to help. They made tea, and Clover and I smoked and smoked and shook and smoked.

A friend of Mum's, Dawn, drove us to the hospital. The date was 25 November, and it was freezing cold, and there was thick fog. It was about a forty-minute drive down the M4 to Bristol, to the hospital. As we drove into the car park we saw one of those big signposts that dominate and define the landscape of hospitals—IN PATIENT, OUT PATIENT, MATERNITY, ACCIDENT & EMERGENCY, REHABILITATION. Rehabilitation? Rick read that and winced out loud. We barely knew what it meant. We would know what it meant, or what it didn't mean, soon enough. We waited in the Intensive Care Unit waiting room. We were to become fluent in hospital jargon: ICU, I See You, Rehabilitation. The hospitalscape of tall towers and constant smoke, deep gullies of corridors between buildings and fag-end-strewn yards, televisions in empty rooms and new words to scare you.

The walls were green for calm, and we read magazines and waited and waited and waited. We had tea and we talked together.

The outside rims of Dawn's eyes were red, and her eyes looked shiny. Occasionally Clover and I went outside to the corridor, which stretched to vanishing point on either side, away and away, and the floor was shiny and there were white bundles at various intervals all the way up it, on the ground, and people clicked past with trolleys and some of the people on the trolleys were asleep and some were awake.

The surgeon came to the room after some hours and told my dad that it was very serious and gave us her prognosis.

'We have got a fifty-two-year-old woman who has received a catastrophic blow to the head. The brain has haemorrhaged, and we may have to remove sections of the skull to relieve the pressure as the bruising comes through and the brain swells. She has got a one-in-three chance of surviving the night. If she does recover, then we can say for sure that she will be disabled for the rest of her life.'

I thought of the times Mum had dropped Clover and me off at school on wintry mornings. Clover would put her hand over Mum's mouth and say, fill my hand up with kisses, fill my hand up with kisses, and Mum would kiss into her hand again and again, and Clover would shut her hand and say that she had kisses for all of the day now. Don't let the sun go down on your anger, girls.

'She has lost an eye in the fall. Do you want to see her now, are you sure you want your children to see her at this stage?' And my dad said that he was sure.

I can remember being five or six and sitting on Mum's bed. I can still see the dressing table, the sash windows, the sky outside. Do you love me more than all the money in the world? I asked her. She was standing somewhere to my left, taller than me, the strength of a lion beside me. She said that she loved me more than all the money in the world, of course she did. I didn't quite believe her and I didn't know how to assess this love that I am only now starting to understand. Would you rather have me than a thousand monkeys? She laughed and hugged me, Of course I would rather have you than a thousand monkeys, of course I would, my darling.

Clover and I walked behind Rick into the intensive-care room. The floor was shinier than before; we went through two sets of double doors, and it was quiet. The floor seemed to be sloping this way and that, I couldn't make it out, couldn't navigate it properly. I wasn't even sure if I was moving or the floor was. I didn't know where Mum was at all. She was quite lost. We arrived at a bed and looked at the person lying on it and between us and in silence we decided that it must be her. Her head was twice the normal size, all the slack skin that normally sits on a face was swollen and painfully stretched. She had a bandage around her head. Christ knows what they had done to her, in the operations, what terrible snipping and pulling. Leave her to die in peace. She had the heart of a lion and the strength of a bull and you didn't know what you were dealing with. Her eyes were two purple balloons, but her mouth was still her own. The respirator in her neck breathed slowly in and out for her, and her hands were beside her, still her own hands, still the strength in her arms. In her face she was more herself then, somehow, than she ever would be again. Clover and I sat on either side of her and we held a hand each and what we did was cry and cry and cry and cry. Her hands were her own.

She never came back to us, though she did not die. It is impossible to know what she went through during that time, the battles she fought, the places she went to. She was way out and beyond normal consciousness. Did she feel the wet tears on her hands? Did she hear the voices talking to her? If she did, I don't want to consider too hard the anxiety she must have felt for us all. Much later, when she was on her feet, she would write strange scrawled spidery messages to us. The first word that she wrote was Basingstoke. In a rehabilitation centre in Chippenham, she wrote 'jewels for divers'. She wrote me a message once, on a card or a piece of paper, 'keep eating', it said, and this made more sense than 'Basingstoke'. She was always a bit worried about her daughters being anorexic.

She never learned to talk again. She is confused, and her personality altered. She is disfigured by the accident. Disfigured. She doesn't know who we are, nothing is clear, her world is beyond reckoning. I don't know. I really don't know. I tried. I did try, very hard, Christmas by the inert body in the bed—she was in a coma for two months—and the eye that worked rolling in the socket, watching us, a terrible and reproachful, curious, pained eye. Helping her to sit up, learning all about speech therapy, helping her to the loo, playing games like Scrabble in rehab, always in rehab, in Bristol and Milton Keynes and Oxford. She was physically very strong; she learned to run away, fight, escape. She would try to hitch-hike, try to get control over a life that was changing faster than her ability to comprehend it. She lived at home, home every day, and Clover and I were falling apart at the seams. It was all going wrong. When Mum is better, we kept saying, when Mum is better. But she never did get better.

Before the accident, Clover and I went with Mum to a memorial service. Mum had a very close friend called Elizabeth, whose children were the same age as Clover and me. Elizabeth had cancer and deteriorated very quickly. She wrote to Mum and asked her to look out for Hannah, her daughter, when the time came. I can remember all this very clearly; as with hindsight the event was heavy with symbols. We cried during the funeral: her sister read a letter that Elizabeth had written to be read at the service. It was shockingly defiant of death, declared that this should not have happened, that she should not have died.

Afterwards, everyone walked up the hill to her house. It was a cottage a long way from the road and it had no water or electricity. It was a very strange place and very beautiful. As we walked up the hill, leaning into the incline and then looking back at the other people filling the slope in a little cluster, all enjoying the exertion of the walk, Mum said, The Pilgrimage for Elizabeth. Then we saw Hannah, standing at the top of the slope, looking down at us. She never cried that we saw; she was solemn and withdrawn and did not show pain. Hannah's waiting, girls, Mum said, quick, rush up to meet her. We were not very old, but we understood this pain. We ran up. I can't remember if we hugged, or if we were more cautiously affectionate, but later I saw it all, brittle with significance. She was waiting for us, a still figure of grief. And we joined her without knowing the extent to which we joined her. We three stood at the top of the hill and turned and saw Mum walking the rest of the way across the grass to join us.

And in my mind's eye Mum vanishes, and it is just the three of us and the thing between us that we were too young to understand.

All this was still to come, though, this reckoning. We sat with Mum for a while, a long while, and I can't remember the drive home, the real feel of it. I don't want to. I can remember Clover's blind pain, panic. She was the youngest child, and the closest to Mum, the very closest. We all thought we had it worst, but I think maybe Clover suffered more than anybody. She was so young, her pain so horrible, black, she was as unreachable as Mum. We arrived back at the house in the middle of the night. Nightmares to come and difficult nights. We walked into the study, Emma was standing beside my dad's desk and she caught a hold of us and held us. The world was, at that time, beyond reckoning.

I walk down the hard little lane to the yard where the circus is wintering. The earth is spiked and waterless in the frost. The ground to my right slopes down to the track where I am walking, and there is another path running up the field, along the side of a row of poplar trees. It is a black-and-white line in the landscape. Ahead of me is a pony on its tether. It hears my feet scratching on the ground and it swings its head round to look at me. Beside it there is a trapeze prop. Thin metal, half-against the ground and against the white sky. The search for my horse has begun. I talked to a horse dealer in Cheltenham this weekend, and someone has given me the number of a Cossack rider in Stoke-on-Trent, who breeds Spanish horses. This is the way to be navigated now, people to watch out for and deals to be done. I am thinking about the velvet boots I saw in a shop, and the hard glass stones of a new tailcoat, a flashy silver bridle for the horse waiting in the future; and as I walk, the painted lorries come into view, their white sides and the coloured circus lettering, SANTUS CIRCUS. There is a fire burning on the fields, the flames are orange and there is drifting smoke. The smell of burning comes through the frost, and the flames are orange in a monochrome world. □

IAN PARKER
I WAS BRANDON LEE

Brian MacKinnon with his mother at home in Whitehurst   PATRINA MALONE/HERALD

Brian MacKinnon is thirty-four and he is still waiting for his life to start. Although he always wanted to be a doctor, he is not one; he lives with his mother in a Glasgow suburb, in a small former council flat decorated with many images of pheasants. He reads and he watches comedy on television. He spends time identifying conspiracies among his enemies and he does battle with enraged, vengeful and despairing thoughts. At night he sleeps in a single bed. He rarely goes out and rarely drinks and he does not have a girlfriend. He sometimes lets the phone ring and ring until it stops. He focuses on the future and the past. It's a life both of impatience and idleness—a kind of edgy sloth, like someone at the sour tail-end of a school summer holiday. MacKinnon is a clever man with a sense of humour—he is not, overwhelmingly, gloomy company—but when I talked to him in his neat front room, as his mother nipped in and out with tea and ginger biscuits, it was hard to remember that a proposed film of his life has been written as a comedy.

The joke is this: for nearly two years Brian MacKinnon—a Scot in his early thirties—went out into the world as a Canadian teenager called Brandon Lee. MacKinnon plucked his eyebrows, permed his hair, assumed a Canadian accent and re-enrolled at the secondary school he had left thirteen years earlier. His plan was to start all over again, erasing his age and erasing the hateful fact that he was a medical-school drop-out. He would do one year at school, then go into medicine at university; and then, at last, he would start his life. This is a fraud that you would expect to last a few ghastly minutes; then the police would come—or you would wake up in a panic, thanking God, sweating. But somehow, miraculously, MacKinnon was not challenged. The peculiar contract of seduction made between the conman and the conned held fast for month after month. His disguise was as slight and as effective as a Shakespearean heroine dressed as a man. Brandon Lee made friends, he took a leading role in the school show. He excelled academically and won a place at university. He began to inch his way towards a degree in medicine. Then in the autumn of 1995 the deception fell apart. Brandon Lee was changed back into Brian MacKinnon. Journalists gathered at MacKinnon's door to report a story that seemed borrowed from fiction. Cameras

117

flashed through his living-room window; notes from reporters came through his letter box, offering great riches for a private minute or two. For a few days MacKinnon was a celebrity, a focus of national disbelief, ridicule and respect. Tabloid newspapers told how 'Top-class conman Brian MacKinnon spun an astonishing web of lies . . . ' Columnists delivered their thoughts on Walter Mitty and Peter Pan. On morning television there was banter between a (youthful) presenter and his (youthful) studio crew: 'How old are you?' 'Fifty-six.' 'How old are you?' 'Seventy.' And for the second time in his life MacKinnon was asked to leave a university faculty of medicine.

Eighteen months after his unmasking I went to see MacKinnon in Glasgow. He was waiting for me at Glasgow Central Station, a tall thin man with a thin mouth and a peering, half-smiling expression. He was wearing a suit with a polo-necked sweater—like a teacher or architect who has not forgotten a fashion-conscious youth. He had parked on yellow lines round the corner, and when we got in the car he put his mother's Disabled Parking disc back in the glove compartment, laughing guiltily. He drove west out of the town centre, through the university area—the setting for a humiliation still vivid in MacKinnon's mind after nearly fifteen years. He was chatty; and then apologetic for being chatty: he said I should forgive him for going on, it was a few days since he'd spoken to anyone. He talked softly, with a whistling accent and precise syntax, and with the anatomical formality of a medical student on his first weekend home—a kind of body-part name-dropping. (A boy at primary school 'had a scar from his sternum to his symphysis pubis'; a grieving woman 'grabbed me round the thorax'.) We talked about London and Glasgow and then about *Margin Walker*, his as-yet-unpublished, disjointed, immodest, recklessly libellous and sometimes very moving account of the Brandon Lee story.

In the car, MacKinnon was sharp-witted and relaxed—he is capable of self-mockery—but there were whiffs, too, of various kinds of strangeness that inform *Margin Walker*. By all accounts, MacKinnon carried off his impersonation of a teenager with extraordinary panache; but today, in print and in conversation, his impersonation of an adult sometimes seems less steady. MacKinnon presents a worldly persona (someone is a 'kindly soul', his mother is a 'tough wee woman'), but this can come unstuck when paranoia or fierce personal abuse mess the surface, or when one is reminded of a life snagged in a Glasgow living room, or when his version of events later turns out to be at some distance from the truth. There's an immaturity in his version of maturity; a twelve-year-old swaggering with a cigarette on a street corner. When MacKinnon strives for lofty assurance, he sometimes arrives only at cockiness. He told me that when he worked as a librarian, it had been 'just a piece of nonsense. Easy peasy. Easy cheesy peasy.'

We stopped at a service station and bought fourteen lottery tickets for MacKinnon's mother, then drove to a Mexican restaurant in Milngavie, an area MacKinnon said he preferred to neighbouring Bearsden, which is where he lives. It was the early afternoon, and the restaurant was nearly empty. We ordered hot food that made us choke. 'This is very pleasant,' MacKinnon said, keeping an eye out for chillies, 'but worrying.' Every now and then he apologized for taking the conversation into an unsavoury territory, like human dissection. 'Nothing fazes me in terms of blood and guts!' he would say. Then, looking at the food: 'Sorry.'

We had plenty of time. He is a workaholic with no work. I asked him about the provisional life—a prisoner's life—he now seems to live. 'I don't think there's anything fundamentally wrong,' he said, 'with your work—or your intended work—being your life.' He said there was a Jimi Hendrix song he thought apt, called 'I Don't Live Today'. He said he was still optimistic about qualifying as a doctor, despite Brandon Lee, despite everything. 'I want my education. I'll get it. It's as straightforward as that.'

MacKinnon has a new plan, one 'far more radical' than returning to school with a perm and plucked eyebrows, but it is a secret. 'I would never harm anyone,' he said, 'but I'll go to any lengths—any imaginative lengths—to ensure that by 1999 I'm back at medical school. I'll be there, and no one will know I'm there, and no one will find me. If it becomes necessary, I won't even look the same. There's no length to which I won't go.' I said, 'Plastic surgery?' And he said, 'What's a bit of plastic surgery?' He looked fierce and flushed.

'To fuck with identity,' he said. 'It's just a name. I know who I am.'

Brian MacKinnon gave Brandon Lee, his teenage alter ego, only one living parent. This was a father, whom he made a 'Regius professor of zoology'. Brandon Lee's mother was killed off in a car crash in Canada. She was an opera singer. 'Mezzo-soprano,' said MacKinnon.

Brian MacKinnon's real parents had humbler occupations. His father, Donald MacKinnon, drove fire engines for the Strathclyde fire service; his mother, May, was a nurse. Both came from the island of Mull in the inner Hebrides. May was the daughter of servants—a cook and a gardener—on one of the island's sporting estates, and Donald grew up a farmer's son. He became an expert shot and in later life collected the pictures of pheasants that now survive him in Bearsden. He died of cancer in 1993. Brian speaks of him with pride and reverence, tears welling in his eyes. 'If you saw us together,' he said, 'it would be difficult to imagine that I was his offspring. He was shorter—a wee bit—than I am, but very broad and stocky. Immense, bullish strength. His arms were as thick as my legs, if not thicker.'

His widow, now retired, is an active, attractive woman of seventy-one. She was already thirty-seven when she had Brian in 1963, and she was forty when she had Brian's sister, Dawn. (Dawn, also a nurse, is now married and has a baby daughter.) Brian spent most of his first ten years on a housing estate in Milton in northern Glasgow. He was a bright boy, at the top of his class. With typical fastidiousness, he told me he remembered his exact IQ scores: 183 one year, he said, then 187 the next. 'The average year-on increase was two or three points, and mine had gone up four points!' On holidays, the family would drive north to Loch Fyne, where they had a caravan, and later a holiday cottage. Brian hiked and fished with his father, or more often on his own. (Inspired by a now-forgotten source, he said he used to call sea trout 'margin walkers', because of their habit of springing from the water, 'dancing between air and water': hence the title of his manuscript.)

In the mid-1970s May MacKinnon was offered a job as a warden in a council-run sheltered-housing scheme in Bearsden.

Brian MacKinnon as Brandon Lee with fellow pupils at Bearsden Academy   PA NEWS

The job came with a house. Bearsden is a hilly middle-class suburb of Glasgow: more than ninety per cent of the housing is owner-occupied, and a preponderance of bungalows gives the place the vague feel of an English seaside town. According to MacKinnon, his mother would have thought Bearsden a sufficiently 'good area to get into' to give up nursing. The family moved, and Brian joined Bearsden Academy, a large state secondary school with 1950s buildings and a strong academic record. His father was not a lawyer, his accent was wrong, and he lived in council housing, but Brian remembers no sense of social discomfort. Rather, fellow pupils made the happy assumption that he was as hard as nails. He played football, he acquired the nickname China (narrow eyes), and he wrote at least one science-fiction story for the school magazine (he calls it 'some arrant piece of nonsense'). Academically he did well, although he now had to content himself with being close to the top of the class, rather than at the very top. He said that he was happy at school—'You know, a happy kid'—and then terribly bored: 'Like any other sixteen-year-old, I wanted to get on to do other things.'

He just wanted to get out, get to university. He wanted to go to medical school.

Why medicine? In MacKinnon's own explanation of this now intense and unquenchable ambition (he thinks surgery, in particular, would suit him), he talks of a 'primordial' desire, of which he became fully aware in adolescence: 'I remember when I was thirteen to fourteen, the adolescent thing was just starting— greasy hair and spots. And I remember I'd been home at lunchtime to wash my hair—I had the impression it had gone into greased spikes'—he laughed as he told me—'and I came back and I was standing in the corridor, out of breath, and this girl came along and she was banged up quite badly—she had cuts, plaster, she was making her way along. That was a point of realization, thinking, I'd like to do something about that. I didn't like seeing people suffer. I never liked that. Even animals suffering. I remember my father killing a rabbit one time, and a seagull another—both its legs had come off at the knee and he realized it wasn't going to survive, and I wanted to do something for it; I didn't understand the killing.'

MacKinnon is satisfied with the drama of the girl in the corridor. He places no significance on childhood visits to hospital to have lipomata—tumour-like fat deposits—removed from his arm. And he is at great pains to say he was never pushed by his parents. May MacKinnon, agreeing, said, 'I'd never tell my family what to do—never, ever.' She told me she merely gave support to Brian's own ambitions. I heard this disputed several times by those who know the family and think they saw something more powerful passing from mother to son. I was told: 'She was determined above all things, from when he was a wee boy.' 'She seems to run every aspect of his life.' 'She wants the best for him, more than any normal mother would.' I was advised to remember that May MacKinnon was born into service and that she was a nurse: 'You look up to doctors when you're a nurse.' I was told that although Brian had friends around the house as a boy, they tended to be other boys: 'It's difficult to have girlfriends if your mother doesn't want you to.' Later, when the grown Brian MacKinnon impersonated a seventeen-year-old, his movements seemed more restricted than those of a true seventeen-year-old:

'He always had to be in. The guy's thirty-two years old and he's told his mother he'll be in at ten o'clock and he has to go.' I heard the half-serious suggestion—for which there is no supporting evidence—that May MacKinnon choreographed the entire Brandon Lee episode.

Brian MacKinnon is an unusually self-contained man who seems to need few relationships other than that with his mother. (Quoting Jerry Seinfeld, and apologizing for the 'arrogance' of the sentiment, MacKinnon told me, 'Once you get to thirty you don't want to meet new friends. You're not even interviewing.'). May MacKinnon perhaps has more distractions, including a daughter and granddaughter, but she seems similarly bound into this relationship. (When Brian-as-Brandon went to Dundee University three years ago, she went with him.) She likes to quote a Scottish paraphrase of the Marquise de Sévigné: 'The more I see of other folk, the more I love my dog.' I asked MacKinnon if he was looking after her, or if she was looking after him; he said neither was true. In the flat I witnessed a curious scene between the two, when Brian described to me a complicated (and, as I later established, non-existent) conspiracy among his supposed enemies. His mother said: 'Yes, a conspiracy.' Her tone was flat: a mirror of approval in which her son was invited to take a glance.

Donald MacKinnon, it is said, would not have guided his son into any particular career and was usually content to let mother and son 'make their plans'. But it's tempting to consider his unintended influence. In 1978, at around the time of the girl-in-the-corridor, Donald MacKinnon retired injured from the fire brigade. At a fire, he had half-fallen into an uncovered manhole; one leg had gone into the hole, and he had done terrible damage to his hips. (For the rest of his life, he walked with a marked limp.) Mr MacKinnon looked for less strenuous work. And—this is not something one learns from his son—he found it in Milngavie, as a lollipop man.

One would hardly dare mention it to Brian, but the Freudian disciple Helene Deutsch once reported on a case that looks peculiarly relevant: the case of Jimmy, a conman. Janet Sayers describes it in her book *The Man Who Never Was*:

Ian Parker

Jimmy initially founded his self-esteem on identifying with an idealized image of his businessman father. But when Jimmy was seven, his father became a chronic invalid. Jimmy's belief in himself, based on idealizing his father, would have been in danger of collapsing, if Jimmy had not defended himself by conning others into crediting him in a succession of impressive male guises—as gentleman farmer, great writer, movie producer and inventor.

We can guess about Brian's levels of self-esteem, but he was certainly anxious to get to university. The usual route to university in Scotland is via six years of secondary school. Brian wanted to be there after four years, stayed for a fifth—when he passed his ultimate school examinations, his Highers, with three As and two Bs—and in the autumn of 1980 started a degree in medicine at Glasgow University. He was seventeen.

When he talked to me about university, MacKinnon became angry and then apologized. 'Usually,' he said, 'I get on in quite a cheery way with folk, but it's just the subject matter . . .' And for a while we talked about other things: he is something of an authority on British comedy (*The Fast Show*, Eddie Izzard, Spike Milligan); he likes rather stern, bedsit-depressive guitar music and Vaughan Williams (he kindly made me a tape that included both). He goes climbing—without ropes, he said, and without fear. He reads P. G. Wodehouse and Conan Doyle.

According to Brian MacKinnon, things went wrong at Glasgow University almost immediately. He began to feel ill early in the first year. He said he couldn't concentrate. He thinks he may have contracted glandular fever (although none of the doctors who examined him made that diagnosis). He pressed on with his work. 'I was trying to keep my head down. Still turning up.' Unwisely, MacKinnon sat exams without declaring an illness—'I was worried,' he said, 'it being the first year'—and failed all three of his first-year subjects, including anatomy, which he describes as his favourite.

He passed the resits and was allowed into the second year. He told me he collapsed in an anatomy class in the first week. 'I got

124

out. I phoned my dad and he took me home.' By this stage, according to MacKinnon, he was so ill, his mother feared for his life. He said that in the months that followed he seldom got out of bed; he was delirious and subject to night sweats, and his weight dropped drastically. He was missing classes and exams, and in January 1982 he had the first of several meetings with Professor Bryan Jennett, then dean of the medical faculty and now the man he regards as his life's great adversary. 'He was like no one I'd ever met before,' MacKinnon said. 'He had these cold blue eyes. He had a murderous look about him.'

Professor Jennett is now retired. He seems an approachable man, not murderous, though when I went to see him in Glasgow, a medical journal lay open on a table at a photograph of someone pulling at the freakishly elastic skin covering their knee. There was also a typescript of *Margin Walker*, and an accompanying letter in which MacKinnon hoped Jennett would 'be moved by both the eloquence and the veracity of my account of the trials to which I was subjected by you and a few of your colleagues'.

Jennett remembered that on this first meeting, MacKinnon asked for compassionate leave. 'I remember his saying, "I've got illness at home." Usually when you say, "What is it?", they say, "Father's just died," or "My sister's been run over in front of the house," or something like this. And he said, "My sister's got a cold and is coughing—it's keeping me awake at nights." I immediately smelt a rat.'

MacKinnon's version of this meeting is vague: he said he cannot remember most of what happened in this period. He can only recall a terrible lack of sympathy. His version does not rule out the possibility that he neglected to talk about his own illness, and tried to find other mitigating circumstances for his absences and failures. He now says it would have been 'obvious' he was ill (although one can imagine that MacKinnon, the great impostor, could have seemed well if he had wanted to, and thus, perversely, managed to act his way out of safety). This meeting seems to have set a pattern in MacKinnon's dealings with the faculty: he was failing in his studies, but was too panicked—or indeed unwell—to put forward a coherent case, or to cooperate in planning some kind of rescue. He wanted to be left alone.

MacKinnon missed more exams. Because notes from his GP referred only to 'debility', Jennett sent MacKinnon first to the student health service and then to a consultant clinician at Gartnavel Hospital. No physical illness was found, and MacKinnon was asked to see the student psychiatrist, Dr Cheynne, who diagnosed marginal depression. MacKinnon was prescribed a low dosage of antidepressants, and within a week, Cheynne was noting an improvement in his patient (although MacKinnon said he did not take the drugs).

By now, more than halfway through his second year, MacKinnon was hopelessly behind in his studies. He was encouraged to do something to avert the disaster of 'exclusion'. Professor Jennett's advice was that MacKinnon should transfer to another, easier, course. Or MacKinnon could withdraw from medicine, and reapply when he felt more capable. (In MacKinnon's version of these negotiations, Jennett was screaming: 'You are failing! You are failing!') Reluctantly MacKinnon withdrew. Three months later, he reapplied, asking to restart the second year straight away. MacKinnon claimed he was now well, and Cheynne supported that claim. (MacKinnon says he was under pressure to reapply so soon, and Jennett says he was not.) He was accepted. 'We gave him a second chance,' said Jennett.

But the same happened again. In March MacKinnon failed his anatomy and biochemistry exams. Again he was advised to consider another course. In June he failed his physiology and pharmacology. He had now failed all of his second-year exams twice—many of them with very low marks. On resits in September he managed to pass only one of the four, and now—in accordance with the rules—he had to leave the course; he was 'excluded'. He appealed, saying that—despite former claims—he had been ill when he applied to rejoin the second year. His appeal was rejected. It's a simple rule: you must declare ill health before sitting an exam, not afterwards.

One could cast MacKinnon as a gambler betting madly to recover irrecoverable losses. He would say he was well, then fail, then claim illness, then say he was well, then fail. Now he was out. A clever seventeen-year-old, who seems to have defined himself through his medical ambition ('It's my purpose,' he still says), found he could not get through the course. If he found himself intellectually incapable—in this new world of unstructured learning and in a class filled with brilliant fellow students—that is not how he sees it now. He said he did not feign illness to hide his failure, and nor did he make himself ill through anxiety. He was genuinely physically ill and was punished for being ill. He was set upon by 'hyenas'.

One could also say that in Professor Jennett and his colleagues, MacKinnon discovered adults who were not infinitely indulgent of his ambition, and who did not regard medicine as something to which he was entitled. Although Brian's mother twice paid visits to Professor Jennett, the university could not be led to understand that Brian should and would become a doctor. (It's easy to see how Jennett's behaviour—recommending another course, challenging him to pin down his illness—could have looked like desperate cruelty.) Both men's versions are probably true: Jennett behaved with perfect decency; MacKinnon was tortured by Jennett. From this point on, MacKinnon's medical 'purpose' was to be joined by something more savage and single-minded. Perhaps not uniquely in the history of medical education, that part of MacKinnon's ambition that was to do with helping sick girls in school corridors now seems to have lost ground to something similar but different: a desire to be acknowledged as a man up to the task of helping sick girls in corridors. MacKinnon wanted this to be known, and he wanted Professor Jennett, in particular, to know it. In *Margin Walker*, MacKinnon quotes Nietzsche: 'What is the strongest remedy?—Victory.'

For two years after leaving Glasgow University, MacKinnon worked at The Athenian, a now-defunct health club in Bearsden. He sold exercise classes on commission and claims to have made a lot of money. (This later helped fund his continuing education.) He was good at his work; it scares him to think how easily he could have drifted into a life as a successful small businessman, his purpose forgotten.

It was not forgotten. MacKinnon talked to his Member of the European Parliament, Hugh McMahon, and he considered an appeal through the European Court of Human Rights. In the spring of 1986, now aged twenty-two, he found a way of inching back towards the life that had been taken from him. MacKinnon took a temporary clerical job in the library of Glasgow University. At the library that summer, MacKinnon's campaign continued: he wrote to all three hundred members of the university senate.

By the end of the summer MacKinnon had realized that he would not be allowed back into medicine by the direct route. He would have to approach it indirectly, an idea which filled him with shame and disgust, for this was 'whoring'. He applied to Glasgow to do a four-year course leading to a Bachelor of Science degree. He was accepted, started that autumn, and within a few months was talking to the new dean of medicine about transferring. In December of his second year he applied formally and was turned down.

He stuck with the course. The plan now was to finish, and then apply to medical school as a graduate student. (He would need a first or a 2:1.) He was as resolute as ever. But halfway through his degree, there was a sudden challenge to his determination: he met the love of his life. 'I don't particularly feel any need for another,' he told me. 'Maybe I've got a swan gene in me.' (Today, he claims to have no romantic life: 'It just doesn't figure. Work's what I want.' He also volunteered the information that he is not gay—although fond of the company, he has noticed, of camp gay men, including the hairdresser on Bath Street who used to do his Brandon Lee perm.)

MacKinnon's new love distracted him from his lifelong purpose. She showed him another way. 'And that worried me. Because at the time I met her I was trying so hard to get back into medicine . . . I suppose she stilled the rage that I had, she had that quality. And I got frightened sometimes that I would settle in that, and I would accept that I was that guy—a failure as a medical student. I would go on with my BSc, go and do a PhD or something and end up doing research for ICI or whatever . . . ' So he ended the relationship. 'I just walked away from it. Since then I've gone out with people, but it's just been because they asked.'

In his BSc finals, to his disbelief, MacKinnon got a 2:2. He believes he was deliberately marked down and he refused to graduate. It was better to have nothing. 'I knew I'd got—I'd been

YES I would like to subscribe for
- ☐ 1 year (4 issues) at £24.95 *(saving 22%)*
- ☐ 2 years (8 issues) at £46.50 *(saving 27%)*
- ☐ 3 years (12 issues) at £67.00 *(saving 30%)*

(*Granta* sells for £7.99 in bookshops.)

Subscribe for yourself

Please start my subscription with issue no

NAME & ADDRESS *(please complete even if ordering a gift subscription)*

POSTCODE

97F5S58B

Total* £

☐ Cheque (to 'Granta') ☐ Visa, Mastercard/Access, AmEx

Card no:

/__/__/__/__/ __/__/__/ __/__/__/ __/__/__/ __/__/__/__/

Expire date /__/__/__/__/ Signature

* POSTAGE: NO ADDITIONAL POSTAGE REQUIRED FOR UK SUBSCRIPTIONS. FOR EUROPE PLEASE ADD £8 PER YEAR. FOR OVERSEAS SUBSCRIPTIONS, PLEASE ADD £15 PER YEAR.

☐ Please tick this box if you would prefer *not* to receive promotional offers from compatible organizations

or for a friend.

I would like to give a subscription to the following. My name, address and payment details are above.

NAME AND ADDRESS: Mr/Mrs/Ms/Miss

Return, free of charge if posted in the UK, to: Granta, Freepost, 2-3 Hanover Yard, Noel Road, London N1 8BR

Postcode

NAME AND ADDRESS: Mr/Mrs/Ms/Miss

Or use our

UK (free phone and fax):
FreeCall 0500 004 033
OUTSIDE THE UK:
Tel: 44 171 704 0470
Fax: 44 171 704 0474

Postcode

told that I'd got—a first.' He can understand scepticism about this—he is not lost to paranoia—but he is convinced that he was the victim of university corruption: 'Oh, absolutely. I saw evidence of it every day. They're just a nasty lot. You offend one, you offend another.'

He had now spent seven years at university, had no degree, and was still living at home. That summer, MacKinnon and his mother visited his grandmother on Mull. One evening, their car was in an accident with a drunk driver. MacKinnon and his mother were injured, and his ninety-six-year-old grandmother was badly hurt, lost an eye and died ten days later in hospital. MacKinnon was shaken, and 'rested for the next six months to a year'. He became, he said, quite agoraphobic. During this same period, he 'got religion' (his phrase), of an 'inward-looking' kind. He gave up fishing, now thinking it morally indefensible.

It is as if he had drunk too deeply of 'Never Say Die' self-help propaganda—as if he had taken it too literally: he would not give up his goal. An insurance pay-out—he got £5,000, and his mother got £9,000—kept doors open. The University of Edmonton in Alberta, Canada, had a science course from which MacKinnon might be able to transfer to medicine. He was accepted on the understanding that he would first do one year of a biological-sciences degree course (Edmonton had been told nothing of MacKinnon's seven university years). Fudging his academic past, he applied to Glasgow Polytechnic (later Glasgow Caledonian University) and so started his third degree course since leaving school—a man doomed to live in a Groundhog Day of freshers' weeks. (Since leaving school the first time MacKinnon has rarely been far removed from the company of people in their late teens.) He finished the year and flew to Canada in the summer of 1992; he said that only once there did he realize quite how hard it would be for a foreigner to transfer into medicine. (In MacKinnon's colourful manuscript, the bad news was brought home to him when a fellow student said: 'Well, like I say, dude, gettin' landed immigrant status and a place in med school ain't goin' to be the easiest thing in the world for you.') He decided to cut his losses and fly home.

Iis father had cancer. And as Brian now helped his mother nurse him, the famous plan was hatched. He realized that time had run out: even if he could wipe from his CV the two incomplete Glasgow courses, he was becoming too old to apply to medical schools—they are reluctant to take students over thirty. 'It was either lie down and fade away,' he told me, 'or do something positive.' Resentment was stacked on resentment. His own continuing rage was bolstered by what he saw as indignities suffered by his father: an alleged delay in the cancer's diagnosis, and Strathclyde Regional Council's 'inhuman' attempts to rehouse the family while Donald MacKinnon was ill (May MacKinnon had retired that year, and they had had to leave their accommodation at the sheltered-housing complex).

Donald MacKinnon died in April 1993. MacKinnon put his plan into action. ('Too much *Mission: Impossible* as a child, or something,' he said to me.) Shortly after the funeral, May and Brian had to move into a new flat in a street called Whitehurst, in Bearsden: a rare street of two-storey council houses in the middle of a thousand privately owned bungalows. (They later bought the flat.) In the process of the move, Brian had the new place to himself for a few days and he had a fax machine. Through an ad he found in *Private Eye*, MacKinnon set up a temporary mailing address for a Professor William Lee in London. Mail and phone messages for Professor Lee would be accepted here and forwarded to Brian at Whitehurst.

Then he looked for a school. Sitting on the floor of the unfurnished, uncarpeted flat, he rang Douglas Academy in Milngavie: 'Hello,' he said, 'this is Professor Bill Lee. I'm calling from London.' He asked if his son, Brandon, could join the fifth year to sit Highers. It was not possible: the school had a policy of sixth-year exit (Brian would have had to do two years). He made the same call to Boclair Academy in Bearsden, but the school did not take students from outside its catchment area. There was one other possible school, and MacKinnon 'wasn't going to let a little bit of weirdness get the better of me'. He rang Bearsden Academy, his old school. He spoke to Mrs Holmes, a deputy rector, and then sent her a fax:

Dear Mrs Holmes

This is to introduce my son, Brandon, who is currently staying with his grandmother, Mrs M. Maclean, at 11 Whitehurst, Bearsden.

He is a very bright young man, with excellent analytical powers, great perseverance and disciplined study habits. His ambition is to win a place at a University Medical School and to become a doctor. To these ends, he is eager to undertake the Scottish Higher study courses and examinations in: English, Mathematics, Chemistry, Physics and Biology. It is my hope that you can thus accommodate him.

Please find included with this letter, a report on Brandon's recent progress, from Ms Marsha Hunt, BSc, his former Science tutor.

Yours sincerely,

William Lee

MacKinnon thinks that the death of the actor Brandon Lee, a few weeks before, might have brought that name to his unconscious attention. (Lee—the son of Bruce Lee—died while making *The Crow*, in which he played a rock musician who returns from the dead in a vengeful mood.) But he swears he had never heard of Marsha Hunt, the novelist and former girlfriend of Mick Jagger. Nor, it seems, had Mrs Holmes. She asked Professor Lee if his son would come and see her.

MacKinnon is a confident, nippy driver. At some point after we had eaten our Mexican lunch, he took me for a little tour of north-west Glasgow. We passed Bearsden Academy: an ordinary-looking school in a vaguely collegiate style, with modern outbuildings and, behind, sloping playing fields. I asked him how he felt on seeing it. 'I've no emotional reaction at all,' he said, laughing. 'Mr Bland. Sorry.'

Four years ago, when MacKinnon first went through the gates as Brandon Lee, when he went to see Mrs Holmes with his new perm and Canadian accent, he said he felt no great lurch of emotion, no turmoil as memory was made solid. 'I was so preoccupied with the mechanics of getting by, there was no time for that. I just wanted to get through it.' He said he was 'anaesthetized' to the strangeness. 'I was kind of on a mission. It was clinical and automatic.' If, at the school gates, there was confusion, it was a kind of moral confusion. 'As I walked through, I was arguing with myself: "Can this possibly be right?"' And then the argument was settled. He said to himself: 'Right, I'm going to do this.' Mrs Holmes could not have been more helpful. At the end of his meeting, she asked to see a birth certificate—and then said, 'No, I'll believe you.'

The following term MacKinnon went back to school. His first responsibility on his first day was morning registration: he joined the other pupils of 5C—sixteen- and seventeen-year-olds—waiting to be called into a classroom by their registration teacher, Gwynneth Lightbody. He had not tried hard for a youthful look. He carried a briefcase and wore an anorak with a drawstring waist. He looked shy. Mrs Lightbody put her head round the door. And—although MacKinnon does not remember this (he tends to overplay his *Mission: Impossible* invisibility)—she took him to be a fellow teacher. 'I assumed he was waiting for the first class after registration,' she said. 'I said, "If you'd just like to wait, the registration will only take a short time." He said, "Oh, I'm one of your pupils."'

Gwynneth Lightbody was surprised, but hoped she did not show her surprise. 'I said, "Well—in you come."' She told me that 'He did not look like your typical teenager. I assumed he was an adult, but when you're presented with facts . . . I mean, in teaching, you see all sorts of strange sights. It could be he had some illness that made him age rapidly—or something.'

On that first day she met some fellow teachers mid-morning. 'We were all saying, "Have you got a pupil that looks old?" We'd all thought he was an adult. But we assumed everything had been done, and he was just a bit of an oddity.' Pupils were doing the same, trying to make Brandon fit his own story—by reminding themselves, for example, of the wide range in teenage body types. 'I had a boyfriend who was over six foot then,' one pupil said to me; another said: 'I could think of boys with beards and hairy chests. If someone says they're seventeen, you're not going to turn round and say no, no you're not.' By lunch, it seems, MacKinnon had been accepted as an old-looking, odd-looking teenager—an alien from Canada—rather than an adult who looked his age.

Last year the Bearsden Academy magazine gave satirical advice on 'How to return to school without getting caught'. Its recommendations: 'Pick a really inconspicuous name, not the name of a movie star. Don't take the lead role in the school play. Appear to be broke. Be into the same bands as your adopted peers, like Blur. Don't talk about the perils of drinking, as teenagers don't think there are any!' This is all hindsight. MacKinnon can remember no real close calls, even with teachers who had taught him thirteen years earlier. Disbelief, once suspended, refused to be reinstated. 'We used to see him driving about, and that was quite strange,' said a Bearsden contemporary, laughing. Another said, 'He always seemed to know more about physics than we did.' Nicola Walker, with whom he went on holiday the following year, said, 'He was really into older music. He was into totally weird stuff, like Joy Division. He gave me a Joy Division CD. Joy Division is not something people our age are into.'

An impostor does not need an unshakeable story: the Tichborne Claimant, a celebrated nineteenth-century conman, was twice the size of the man he claimed to be, knew nothing about dogs or the French language, as he should have done, and remembered none of the names of his boyhood friends.

MacKinnon heard some younger pupils joke that he looked forty; and someone called out 'Brian McKinnon!', which gave him a start (Brian McKinnon was a fellow pupil). But no one guessed; no one seemed to want to guess. To fellow pupils he was no threat—he was known to be immensely clever and quite funny, if a little distant and nerdy. ('He liked *Star Trek*; I liked *Star Trek*; he told a lot of jokes,' said Gordon Barron, typically, who despite being from California was fooled by the North American accent.) To the teachers, he was a dream: bright, interested and studious— his hand flying up to answer every question. In registration, while most pupils sat as near to the back as possible, MacKinnon sat alone at the front, holding conversations with Mrs Lightbody about events of the day. 'He was like another adult,' she said.

133

'You got an adult response from him'. When he was absent, he was unusually scrupulous about bringing a note from home. Even after MacKinnon's cover had been blown, Bearsden's headmaster, the late Norman MacLeod, called Brandon Lee a 'polite, well-spoken gentlemanly young man' and an 'ideal pupil'—managing to leave aside the fact that he did not exist.

MacKinnon seems to have kept extraordinarily calm. Photographs show him looking relaxed and happy. After his exposure, there was some newspaper talk about method acting. MacKinnon himself makes a more macho comparison: to the psychology of the tortured prisoner: 'I'm the last person in the world to compare myself to Steve McQueen [in *The Great Escape*], but I kind of went in cooler zone, if you like.' (He put on a German accent and said, laughing: 'Cooler! Ten days! Twelve days!') He seems almost never to have slipped. The story in which Brandon Lee remembered where he was when Elvis Presley died—at roughly the time Class 5C was being born—was invented by a Bearsden boy to please a reporter. On just one occasion, he forgot to be Canadian and had to pretend that he was mimicking a Scots accent. After meeting MacKinnon, I read a thriller he had recommended, called *The Chameleon*. As a prisoner subjected to torture in Vietnam, the Chameleon learns great skills of adaptation: 'To straighten or stretch was too painful to bear if he was going straight back into the cage. By staying in one position, he was allowing his body to adapt to its circumstances . . . ' Once out of Vietnam, the Chameleon follows a career in assassination. His powers of impersonation allow him to mimic—and thus make a patsy of—a friend or associate of the victim. I could see why MacKinnon might have liked this.

Although many people find it impossible to believe, MacKinnon told me that his mother knew nothing about Brandon Lee until much later: she believed he was attending Bearsden Academy in his own name, as an extramural student. School friends never came to the house, he explained, and nor did they have his phone number. Whatever the exact truth here, it was important to MacKinnon's mission that he never had to explain himself to anyone but his mother. The mission required money, nerve, a slim build and a supportive mother; but also a fairly empty social landscape. Brian had few friends, and most of those few lived away from Glasgow—in Canada (where he had been on a number of holidays) and in Germany. There was no one around to tease him about the new hairdo, no one to catch a glimpse of him as he slipped in and out of the school gates just a few streets from home. 'Friendship, even close friendship, only runs so deep with me. If that suggests superficiality, I don't know. Maybe I haven't found the right friends,' he said.

In his first months at Bearsden, his ambition was to remain as inconspicuous as possible. He could hide behind his Canadian accent; and the knowledge that his opera-singing mother had recently died in a car crash was bound to inhibit close questioning about his home life. (In a continuing family carnage, Brandon's father, too, died in the course of the year.) But he was under an obligation not to appear hopelessly unsociable. Universities would want to see a good school report as well as good Highers. MacKinnon had, in the end, to mix. And in this role, it seems, he was as accomplished as any other. He agreed to play football, he joined a school trip to see a production of *Macbeth*, he wrote a story for the school magazine, 'Perils of Drinking', about a young man's relationship with his mother's boyfriend. Perhaps surprisingly, he also took a lead role in the school play, *South Pacific*. This was high-risk: exposing himself to an audience of parents, older brothers and older sisters; MacKinnon said he was 'press-ganged' into it. Tim Perman, a Bearsden pupil to whom MacKinnon later confessed the truth of his identity, said he clearly enjoyed it and wonders if MacKinnon took pleasure in having his acting ability—previously known only to himself—given public acknowledgement. 'I don't think he'd done acting before'—a pause—'except for his whole life. He took it on reluctantly, but once he did it, I think he really loved it.' There was one awkwardness: the script called for a kiss between MacKinnon—a man playing a boy playing a man—and Valerie Douglas, one of his teenage co-stars. MacKinnon felt understandable awkwardness, and in rehearsal after rehearsal put off the moment with comically feeble excuses. Val Douglas took no offence, but was a little puzzled. 'He had to build up to it,' she told me. In the end, 'It wasn't what you'd call a great snog. It was the kind of kiss you'd give your dad.'

The rehearsals for *South Pacific*, in the spring of 1994, brought MacKinnon into contact with students he had not known before—Tim Perman, Nicola Walker—and he was drawn into a new sociability. Gaining confidence, MacKinnon would tell stories and pursue lines of thought with an unusual intensity and maturity. He was deep. At moments he could appear to be almost a hybrid—half-student, half-teacher; a boy-sage. Nicola Walker said: 'Sometimes he'd seem to get a bit ahead of us all, go into detail about some intellectual idea he had, and we'd be: "Whoa! Wait a minute!"'

Tim Perman was impressed. He is now studying law at university and has not talked to MacKinnon since the story broke, when May MacKinnon unfairly accused him of speaking ill of her son to the press. He is at pains to set the record straight. 'He's just one of the most worldly, intelligent, nice, generous people. He was so kind to everybody—all through school, he had such an effect on everybody. Anyone who had any intelligence and wasn't narrow-minded, anyone who spoke to the guy, who got to know the guy for who he was, fell in love with him. It wasn't because he was older, it wasn't because he was thirty . . . OK, that had something to do with it. But he just had an amazing effect on students and teachers.'

To no one's surprise, MacKinnon got five As in his Highers, and a place to study medicine at Dundee University. In the autumn of 1994 he and his mother drove east and rented a chilly house in Tayport, across the Tay Bridge from Dundee. Brian started his course: Dundee students assumed he was a mature student. It was noticed that he tape-recorded his lectures. MacKinnon said: 'I didn't drop a single mark in that first term.' At weekends mother and son would drive back to Bearsden. MacKinnon insists that his mother was still ignorant of his fraud, now more than one year old.

Before the first term had finished, MacKinnon had asked to defer for a year, citing—those accident-prone Lees—the death of a grandmother. He told me the real reason was financial; a planned sale of the Loch Fyne holiday cottage had fallen through. But MacKinnon also conceded that he was beginning to tire of Brandon Lee's company. His plan had been to declare his true

Brian MacKinnon (far left) in South Pacific   ALAN HAYWARD/HERALD

identity on graduation, and see what kind of medical work—if any—he would then have been allowed to do. But by the time MacKinnon left Dundee, his story was already beginning to come apart; or he was letting it come apart. ('I don't know if you can passively precipitate something . . . ' he said softly.) In a mishap that he could have prevented, a medical dictionary addressed to Brandon Lee was sent to Whitehurst while the MacKinnons were in Dundee. It was taken in by a neighbour who then questioned May MacKinnon about the name. Only at this point, MacKinnon said, did he have to confess to his mother. (According to one of the stranger pieces of reconstructed dialogue in *Margin Walker*, she asked: 'You acknowledge a facet of absolute law and then you proceed to rationalize your lack of adherence to it?') A little later, two Bearsden Academy girls paid an unannounced visit to Whitehurst, and the same neighbour, out on her step, told them

137

there was no Brandon Lee in that house, only a Brian MacKinnon, an adult.

When Brian came back to Glasgow, this peculiar news had already circulated among the Bearsden friends. He tried to shrug it off: the neighbour was confusing him with a cousin. This was only half-accepted. The Bearsden Academy group—the same friends who, when the story broke, wrote an affectionate letter of support for MacKinnon in the Glasgow *Herald*—made an agreement among themselves not to press Brandon about his secret, and not to pass it on: 'We knew he was a nice guy,' Nicola Walker said, 'and he hadn't done anything really horrendous, like murdered someone—or we hoped he hadn't.' With this indulgence, Brian started going out a little, giving himself the freedom to lead an ordinary city life of pubs and clubs and parties. He found himself with friends, and they seemed to mind, for example, when he let them miss his eighteenth birthday. (He had decided to have been born on 4 June 1977, which replaced 3 June 1963.) When he talks today, he does not mention this sociability—it does not sit with his self-image to have once sought out and enjoyed the company of teenagers.

Tim Perman had been travelling in China while Brian was at Dundee and made contact as soon as he returned. 'Brandon said he was saving up for six months and he was going to start again the next year. He said he had a job as a carpet fitter or something. I got to see him quite a bit that year, and we got quite close. We used to go to the Beefeater [a Bearsden pub] most Mondays, and towards the end, towards summertime, we went into town and went nightclubbing a few times, normally as a group, once or twice we went just me and him.' Again, Perman told me of 'deep conversations' and, in pub quizzes, of Brandon's spooky success in the field of Seventies pop music. It was a sign of a new kind of openness that MacKinnon invited Perman into the house. 'I met his mother,' he said, 'and she seemed quite friendly. She certainly didn't stay around long. I came in, we sat down in the living room, she disappeared into the kitchen.'

One night that spring or early summer Perman and MacKinnon went to a club, the Garage, on Sauchiehall Street in central Glasgow. Brian had a drink, but was not drunk: 'He didn't drink much, but I got the impression that when he did drink—which was rare—he wouldn't really handle it very well.' They were upstairs in the club when Brian leaned towards Perman and said, 'Would you be able to keep a secret that was really important to me, and if it were ever to get out could put my life in danger?' MacKinnon put his hand in his pocket and brought out his passport. Perman saw his name for the first time, and saw the date of birth. MacKinnon, amazed that he had told someone, started laughing. He explained how he had been tortured at Glasgow University.

In MacKinnon's own recollection of events that year, he said he told only one person: Gillian McCallum, a Bearsden Academy girl he had met through her best friend, Nicola Walker. He and McCallum had gone out a few times after he had come back from Dundee, and on one occasion, in a vegetarian restaurant, he told her the truth of his identity. It is generally agreed that Brandon Lee was not a sexual predator. Nicola Walker told me, 'He had flirted with Gillian, but they weren't sexual feelings. And I think she cared about him.' Brian accepts that he may have flirted, but thinks he found her company 'sensuous' rather than 'sensual'. ('I don't woo,' he said, 'or let myself be wooed, or any nonsense like that. It's just not part and parcel of what I do.') He admired what he saw of her 'psychic' skills, and tells a curious story about her coming to the psychic rescue of a hedgehog about to be run over in the dark.

Gillian McCallum and her friend Sheila Louden had planned a fortnight's holiday in Tenerife for the end of the summer, and they asked MacKinnon to join them. (Gwynneth Lightbody, the Bearsden teacher, said, 'You would have worried about Brandon's safety in their hands, rather than the other way round.') In late August the three of them flew out to an apartment complex in Playa de las Americas. MacKinnon told me now he was there to keep an eye on his enemies. He said he was suspicious of Sheila Louden and her family, and wondered if they were implicated in a letter he had received from Dundee in June, which asked all enrolling (or re-enrolling) students to show evidence of their age. In this version, Tenerife was reconnaissance—and it rather cleverly marries two contradictory self-images: someone in control and someone mistreated: it's the victim-sleuth. But MacKinnon also half-accepts that he might have been implicated in the crime; he might have been looking for somewhere suitable to bump off Brandon Lee, somewhere away from Glasgow and away from Whitehurst.

The girls slept in the only bedroom, and MacKinnon slept on the sofa in the main room. The girls went out, ate, danced, found boys and on one occasion persuaded Brian to join them in a club. 'It was too loud. It's hellish! It crushes you. If people want to have sex, why don't they just make an appointment, instead of all that rigmarole!' Nicola Walker came out to join her friends for her first holiday without her parents; and she too was let into the secret of Brian's identity. Brian was now talking with a Scottish accent.

Nicola Walker could feel some tension in the air—a build-up of 'niggly little things'—and this soon came to a head. There had been a kind of flirtatious skirmishing with the four British boys in the next-door apartment; one night, when MacKinnon and the girls came back from dinner, they saw that something had been sprayed in shaving foam on their patio window. 'Something stupid,' Nicola said, 'probably something with a sexual connotation.' Gillian, Sheila and Nicola decided to go over and retaliate. 'We were going to get them back. Just a laugh.' And Brian suddenly lost his cool.

'He shouted something like, "Don't you dare fucking do that!"' Nicola said. 'He could have started by saying, "I don't think you should do that," but he sort of blew up, just suddenly, he snapped, he started shouting. It was scary, especially as he was meant to be our friend. It was like our dad or something shouting at you.' On reflection Nicola could see his point; he was worried for them and he was worried they might drag him into something. But at the time he seemed terrifying and unreasonable, as Brandon Lee had suddenly become someone else.

When term started at Bearsden Academy, people already knew about Brandon and Brian. The story was out. Nicola Walker assumes that calls were made between Tenerife and

Glasgow—friends learned, parents learned. In early September Brian received a recorded-delivery letter from Norman MacLeod, Bearsden's headmaster, who politely asked Brian if he could call the school, 'regarding a discrepancy in school records'. Brian arranged to see MacLeod the following Monday.

Tim Perman spent an evening with MacKinnon in these last few days. He tried to reassure him about the letter and about his future at Dundee. 'We went to the cinema in the centre of Glasgow. As we were driving back, he suddenly got incredibly nervous and sweaty. It was like something out of a thriller; like we were running away from the Mafia. He said, "Tim, get the wheel, get the wheel, I've just got to pull over." I said, "What's the matter, Brandon?" He said, "I feel like I'm about to have a heart attack." His face went red in three seconds. I was worried that he was about to die. He suddenly went completely off the rails. We pulled over, and he undid the seat belt: he was breathing really heavily, just incredibly scared. That was the very first time I'd ever heard him speak with a Scottish accent.'

Mr MacLeod had received an anonymous telephone call: 'Brandon Lee is Brian Lachlan MacKinnon, who attended Bearsden Academy in the late 1970s.' MacLeod had looked up the old Brian MacKinnon file and found a photograph of MacKinnon aged thirteen. At the Monday meeting MacLeod did not force a confrontation. But he showed MacKinnon the photograph: 'There's a resemblance,' he said gently, 'don't you think?' MacKinnon kept his cool, admitted nothing, and offered to bring in his birth certificate a few days later, after he had returned from a holiday he was about to take in Germany.

He flew off to a 'Healthy Vacation Week' in a clinic in Wurzburg in Bavaria. MacKinnon said he had friends who worked there; he was not a patient. On 18 September, on his second night abroad, his mother rang. 'I've just had the most terrible shock,' she said. The story had broken, on the BBC's Scottish news.

MacKinnon offered to come home, but his mother told him to stay put. The next day, a stern letter arrived at Whitehurst from Dundee University, asking Brandon to explain reports of 'false information' in his application. His mother read him the letter over the phone. By now, Whitehurst was full of news crews. The story was in every newspaper. Reporters were cruising the streets of Bearsden, looking for teenagers.

MacKinnon flew back on 23 September and arrived at Whitehurst by taxi in the dark and the rain. It was a 'gruesome' scene. Cars were parked everywhere, and their doors all opened as he approached. A journalist said in his ear: 'People have a right to know.'

On 25 September he replied to Dundee at length, through the pages of the *Herald*, the newspaper that he thought most likely to be read by the Scottish medical establishment. It was a defiant and aggrieved letter, but it included a confession. 'I did supply Dundee University with false information.' The dean of the medical school replied: 'I have to inform you that I am not willing to readmit you to the medical course in October 1995.' The Dundee switchboard was overrun with calls from aspiring medical students asking to take MacKinnon's place.

When I went to Whitehurst, Brian MacKinnon's mother was friendly. 'We're so overcrowded in this small house,' she said. 'Father died just as we were coming up right enough, so we had more space, but still . . . It was such big rooms in the last place.' She was wearing a bright, jaunty scarf.

MacKinnon has a small bedroom off the living room: a single bed, a globe, another pheasant print. He explained that the living room is his 'domain'. So we sat there, under many photographs of Dawn and her family and none of Brian. 'I don't like my picture showing,' he said. May MacKinnon went elsewhere, saying: 'I'll let you get on with your business.'

'I'm nearly thirty-four,' MacKinnon said to me, 'and I still haven't done anything with my life. That's the reality.' I asked him if perhaps he didn't want to do anything with his life; if an impossible ambition was a certain way of making sure he didn't have to do anything. I asked him if he was afraid of growing up. 'I've no fear,' he said softly. 'I don't fear anything. I fear damnation. That's why I wouldn't put a bullet in anyone. I'm certainly not frightened of the future. I'm just driven by that one idea.' I wondered if he ought to forget that one idea and . . . 'And do something else? There's nothing else that interests me. I wouldn't be living—and I'm fed up with not living.'

'Brandon Lee' did not disappear overnight. His old Bearsden friends still use the name, and some don't correct themselves. For a while, MacKinnon hung on to part of Brandon's sociability. After his exposure, he organized a trip to see a comedy show and he was seen at parties. Nicola Walker, who found it difficult to think of Brian as older than Brandon, kept in touch and wrote a generous foreword for an earlier version of *Margin Walker*. She also talked to Peter Broughan, the film producer who made *Rob Roy* (with Liam Neeson, Jessica Lang, Tim Roth) and who—in advance—bought rights to the MacKinnon manuscript. But more recently, she has lost touch. He has slipped away into Whitehurst. 'I think he's trying to get away from all his school friends,' she said. 'The younger people. I haven't heard of him making contact with any of them for a long time.' I asked MacKinnon when he last went to a party, and he said he had gone to an eighteenth last year—he had stayed twenty minutes, blown up some balloons, and then left. He is now focused on his task—this means keeping an eye on his case, and trying to contain his annoyance at the discourtesy and ill will of others. He is not always successful: lawyers' letters get sent out, enemies pursued. All of Brian's dealings with the media have left him unhappy: he fell out with the *Herald*; he has been through two literary agents; and because he refuses to change a word of his manuscript, he is without a proper publisher.

The people who had liked Brandon Lee found it hard to dislike Brian MacKinnon. He hadn't murdered anyone. 'He wasn't beating up wee old grannies,' as one Bearsden parent put it to me. There was fascination but there was little real resentment. 'I think he made everyone look a bit of an arse,' said Ian McFarlane, a school friend, but he smiled as he said it. The teachers were annoyed to have wasted time and sympathy on a non-existent orphan, but were also annoyed with themselves. 'We were a right crowd of dopes,' said Gwynneth Lightbody. 'He stood out like a sore thumb.' Another friend from school, Sarah Cobbe, wrote to MacKinnon to apologize after a newspaper wrongly quoted her. 'My main hope,' she wrote, 'is that this doesn't break you and that . . . you can

143

begin living again. I always thought "Brandon" was a kind, intelligent person and thought highly of him. I am convinced this person wasn't entirely fictional.'

It is not quite clear whether he was or not. Brandon was born of Brian's obsession, but he was also something of a relief from it. Brandon got Brian out of the house, like an agoraphobic's chaperone. Brandon had to get things done; Brandon had to find other things to talk about than Professor Jennett. But now Brandon has been dismissed, and MacKinnon wants nothing more to do with him. So, while Bearsden pupils still speak well of their former classmate, MacKinnon is finding it hard to return the favour. (It does not help, perhaps, that three of them are studying medicine.) He tends to talk of the Bearsden pupils as shallow and silly: 'They somehow seemed lighter,' he said, 'than the people I was at school with originally.' And in a discussion about his possible sexual curiosity, he crosses a line into meanness: 'OK,' he said, 'so young girls have young bodies, and older men who are stuck in that rut like young flesh, but they've also got young girls' mentalities. It doesn't even figure to talk to them.'

He is still sure he will return to medicine. He is considering a new, bespoke identity, built to last; and we should probably take MacKinnon at his word when he talks about plastic surgery. But his real hope is that this will not be necessary; on a good day, MacKinnon imagines his book catching the imagination of people in positions of power in the medical establishment in Britain and abroad; the injustice he has suffered would be acknowledged, and the hurdles that stand between him and his purpose would be brought down.

He knows that the highest of many high hurdles is his reputation as a cheat. (His letter from Dundee pointed out that 'The public expect the medical profession to demonstrate both knowledge and integrity . . . ') There are some professions where his ingenuity might have been forgiven, or even commended, but this is not one of them. And, unhelpfully, MacKinnon is not interested in a nice resprayed degree from a Third World source—he wants the real, western, accredited thing; he will only join the club that's determined not to have him. 'I want the knowledge. I want to know what's happening at the forefront of medicine. I won't be one of those doctors who get their degree and then don't bother reading a research paper for the rest of their lives,' he said. 'There is nothing else I want to do. I can't waste all my life.'

In the flat in Whitehurst, May MacKinnon came back into the living room to watch the midweek lottery draw on television. 'Have you had anything on the lottery?' she asked me. 'I've won £140 in tenners . . . ' MacKinnon interrupted her; and when she started talking again, he turned up the volume on the television: it was done quite subtly, and she seemed to take no offence. 'I just want him to do what he's going to be happy with,' she said. 'As long as you're happy doing it, that's all we ever said.' □

HAWTHORNDEN CASTLE

INTERNATIONAL RETREAT FOR WRITERS

Fellowships for Creative Writers

Spring, Summer and Autumn Sessions 1998

Applications are invited from novelists,
poets, dramatists and other creative writers
of any nationality who have published
at least one book or similarly substantial
piece of work. Four-week fellowships
are offered to those working
on a current project.

Application deadline:
30 September 1997

For further details and an application form contact:
The Administrator
Hawthornden Castle
Lasswade
Scotland
EH18 1EG

GEORGE STEINER
HERALDRY

Rain, particularly to a child, carries distinct smells and colours. Summer rains in the Tyrol are relentless. They have a morose, flogging insistence and come in deepening shades of dark green. At night, the drumming is one of mice on or just under the roof. Even daylight can be sodden. But it is the smell which, after sixty years, stays with me. Of drenched leather and hung game. Or, at moments, of tubers steaming under drowned mud. A world made boiled cabbage.

That summer was already ominous. A family holiday in the dark yet magical landscape of a country condemned. In those mid-1930s, Jew-hatred and a lust for reunification with Germany hung in the Austrian air. My father, convinced that catastrophe was imminent, the gentile husband of my aunt still blandly optimistic, found conversation awkward. My mother and her fitfully hysterical sister sought to achieve an effect of normality. But the planned pastimes, swimming and boating on the lake, walks in the woods and hills, dissolved in the perpetual downpours. My impatience, my demands for entertainment in a cavernous chalet increasingly chill and, I imagine, mildewed, must have been pestilential. One morning Uncle Rudi drove into Salzburg. He brought back with him a small book in blue waxen covers.

It was a pictorial guide to coats of arms in the princely city and surrounding fiefs. Each blazon was reproduced in colour, together with a brief historical notice as to the castle, family domain, bishopric or abbey which it identified. The little manual closed with a map marking the relevant sites, including ruins, and with a glossary of heraldic terms.

Even today I can feel the pressure of wonder, the inward shock which this chance 'pacifier' triggered. What is difficult to render in adult language is the combination, almost the fusion of delight and menace, of fascination and unease I experienced as I retreated to my room, the drains spitting under the rain-lashed eaves, and sat, hour after entranced hour, turning the pages, committing to memory the florid names of those towers, keeps and high personages.

Though I could not, obviously, have defined or phrased it in any such way, that armorial primer overwhelmed me with a sense of the numberless specificity, of the minutiae, of the manifold

149

singularity of the substance and forms of the world. Each coat of arms differed from every other. Each had its symbolic organization, motto, history, locale and date wholly proper, wholly integral to itself. It 'heralded' a unique, ultimately intractable fact of being. Within its quarterings, each graphic component, colour and pattern entailed its own prodigal signification. Heraldry often inserts coats of arms within coats of arms. The suggestive French designation of this device is a *mise en abyme*. My treasures included a magnifying glass. I pored over the details of geometric and 'bestiary' shapes, the lozenges, diamonds, diagonal slashes of each emblem, over the helmeted crests and 'supporters' crowning, flanking the diverse arms. Over the precise number of tassels which graced a bishop's, an archbishop's or a cardinal's armorials.

The notion which, in some visceral impact, tided over me and held me mesmerized was this: if there are in this obscure province of one small country (diminished Austria) so many coats of arms, each unique, how many must there be in Europe, across the globe? I do not recall what grasp I had, if any, of large numbers. But I do remember that the word 'millions' came to me and left me unnerved. How was any human being to see, to master this plurality? Suddenly it came to me, in some sort of exultant but also appalled revelation, that no inventory, no heraldic encyclopedia, no *summa* of fabled beasts, inscriptions, chivalric hallmarks, however compendious, could ever be complete. The opaque thrill and desolation which came over me in that ill-lit and end-of-summer room on the Wolfgangsee—was it, distantly, sexual?—has, in good part, oriented my life.

I grew possessed by an intuition of the particular, of diversities so numerous that no labour of classification and enumeration could exhaust them. Each leaf differed from any other on each differing tree (I rushed out in the deluge to assure myself of this elementary and miraculous truth). Each blade of grass, each pebble on the lake shore was eternally 'just so'. No repetition of measurement, however closely calibrated, in whatever controlled vacuum it was carried out, could ever be perfectly the same. It would deviate by some trillionth of an inch, by a nanosecond, by the breadth of a hair—itself a teeming immensity—from any preceding measurement. I sat on my bed striving to hold my breath, knowing that the next breath would signal a new beginning, that the past was already unrecapturable in its differential sequence. Did I guess that there could be no perfect *facsimile* of anything, that the identical word spoken twice, even in lightning-quick reiteration, was not and could not be the same (much later, I was to learn that this unrepeatability had preoccupied both Heraclitus and Kierkegaard).

At that hour, in the days following, the totalities of personal experience, of human contacts, of landscape around me became a mosaic, each fragment at once luminous and resistant in its 'quiddity'—the scholastic term for integral presence revived by Gerard Manley Hopkins. There could be, I knew, no finality to the raindrops, to the number and variousness of the stars, to the books to be read, to the languages to be learned. The mosaic of the possible could, at any instant, be splintered and reassembled into new images and motions of meaning. The idiom of heraldry, those 'gules' and 'bars sinister', even if I could not yet make it out, must, I sensed, be only one among countless systems of discourse specifically tailored to the teeming diversity of human purposes, artefacts, representations or concealments (I still recall the strange excitement I felt at the thought that a coat of arms could hide as well as reveal).

I set out, as many children do, to compile lists. Of monarchs and mythological heroes, of popes, of castles, of numinous dates, of operas—I had been taken to see *Figaro* at the neighbouring Salzburg Festival. The wearied assurance of my parents that such lists already existed, that they could be looked up in any almanac or work of standard reference—my queries about anti-popes and how to include them visibly irritated my somewhat ceremonious and Catholic uncle—brought no solace. The available indices of reality, be they a thousand pages thick, the atlases, the children's encyclopedias, could never be exhaustively comprehensive. This or that item, perhaps the hidden key to the edifice, would be left out. There was simply too much to everything. Existence thronged and hummed with obstinate difference like the midges around the light bulb. 'Who can number the clouds in wisdom? Or who can stay the bottles of heaven . . . ?' (How did Job 38: 37, already know

George Steiner

about rains in the Salzkammergut?) I may not have cited the verse to myself in that drowned August, though the Old Testament was already a tutelary voice, but I did know of those bottles.

If the revelation of incommensurable 'singleness' held me spellbound, it also generated fear. I come back to the *mise en abyme* of one blazon within another, to that 'setting in the abyss'. Consider a fathomless depth of differentiation, of non-identity, always incipient with the eventuality of chaos. How could the senses, how could the brain impose order and coherence on the kaleidoscope, on the perpetuum mobile of swarming existence? I harboured vague nightmares at the fact, revealed in the nature column of some newspaper, that a small corner of the Amazon forest was habitat to thirty thousand rigorously distinct species of beetles. Gazing at, recopying with watercolours, the baronial or episcopal or civic arms, pondering the unlimited variations possible on formal and iconic motifs, I felt a peculiar dread. Detail could know no end.

How can a human voice cast a huge sickening shadow? On short waves, the wireless chirped and often dissolved in bursts of static. But Hitler's speeches, when broadcast, punctuated my childhood (whence, so many years later, *The Portage to San Cristobal of A.H.*). My father would be close to the wireless, straining to hear. We were in Paris, where I was born in 1929. One of the doctors assisting at my awkward birth then returned to Louisiana to assassinate Huey Long. History was always in attendance.

My parents had left Vienna in 1924. From meagre circumstances, from a Czech-Austrian milieu still in reach of the ghetto, my father had risen to meteoric eminence. Anti-Semitic Vienna, the cradle of Nazism, was, in certain respects, a liberal meritocracy. He had secured a senior legal position in the Austrian Central Bank, with fiacre (the use of a carriage and horses). A brilliant career lay before the youthful Herr Doktor. With grim clairvoyance, my father perceived the nearing disaster. A systematic, doctrinal Jew-hatred seethed and stank below the glittering liberalities of Viennese culture. The world of Freud, of Mahler, of Wittgenstein was also that of Mayor Lueger, Hitler's exemplar. At their lunatic source, Nazism and the final solution are Austrian rather than German reflexes. Like his friend out of Galicia, one Lewis Namier, my father dreamed of England. For the East- and Central-European Jewish intelligentsia, the career of Disraeli had assumed a mythical, talismanic aura. But he suffered from rheumatic fevers, and medical sagacity of the day held France to be the milder climate. So Paris it was, and a new start under strained circumstances (my mother, Viennese to her fingertips, lamented this seemingly irrational move). And to the end of his days, my father never felt at home among what he judged to be the arrogant chauvinism, the frivolities, the myopia of French politics, finance and society. He would mutter under his breath and unjustly that all nationals will sell you their mothers, but that the French delivered.

Of fragile physique, my father was compounded of formidable will and intellect. He found a surprisingly large portion of mankind unacceptable. Sloppiness, lies, be they 'white', evasions of reality, infuriated him. He lacked the art of forgiveness. His contributions to the skills of international investment banking, to the techniques of corporate finance in the period between the wars are on record. His Zionism had the ardour of one who knew, even at the outset, that he would not emigrate to Palestine. His bookplate shows a barque, a seven-branched candelabrum at its bow, approaching Jerusalem. But the holy city remains on the far horizon. Papa embodied, as did every corner of our Paris home, the tenor, the prodigality and glow of Jewish-European and Central-European emancipation. The horrors which reduced this liberal humaneness and vision to ashes have distorted remembrance. Evocations of the Shoah have, tragically, privileged the remembrance of prior suffering, particularly throughout Eastern Europe. The proud Judaism of my father was, like that of an Einstein or a Freud, one of messianic agnosticism. It breathed rationality, the promise of the Enlightenment and tolerance. It owed as much to Voltaire as it did to Spinoza. High holidays, notably the Day of Atonement, were observed not for prescriptive or theological motives, but as a yearly summons to identity, to a homeland in millennial time.

By virtue of what was to become an unbearable paradox, this Judaism of secular hope looked to German philosophy, literature,

153

scholarship and music for its talismanic guarantees. German
metaphysics and cultural criticism, from Kant to Schopenhauer and
Nietzsche, the classics of German-language poetry and drama, the
master historians, such as Ranke, Mommsen, Gregorovius,
crowded the shelves of my father's library. As did first editions of
Heine, in whose mordant wit, in whose torn and ambiguous
destiny, in whose unhoused virtuosity in both German and French,
my father saw the prophetic mirror of modern European Judaism.
Like so many German, Austrian and Central-European Jews, my
father was immersed in Wagner. During his very brief spell under
arms in Vienna in 1914, he had ridden a horse named Lohengrin;
he had then married a woman called Elsa. It was, however, the
whole legacy of German-Austrian music, it was Mozart, Beethoven,
Schubert, Hugo Wolf, Mahler who filled the house. As a very
young child, at the edge of bedtime and through a crack in the
living-room door, I was sometimes allowed to hear chamber music,
a lieder recital, being performed by musicians invited into our
home. They were, increasingly, refugees in desolate plight. Yet even
in the thickening political twilight, a Schubert song, a Schumann
study could light up my father's haunted mien. When concessions
had to be made to encroaching reality, my father gave them an
ironic touch: recordings of Wagner were now played in French.

Only in the posthumously published letters of Gershom
Scholem have I come across the same note of helpless clear-
sightedness and warning. Over and over, even prior to 1933, my
father laboured to warn, to alert, to awaken to refuge not only
those whom he and my mother had left behind in Prague or in
Vienna, but the French political-military establishment with which
his international dealings had brought him into contact. His
'pessimism', his 'alarmist prognostications' elicited only officious
dismissal or hostility. Family and friends refused to move. One
could come to reasonable terms with Herr Hitler. The
unpleasantness would soon pass. The age of pogroms was over. In
diplomatic and ministerial circles, my father was regarded as a
tedious Cassandra, prone to well-known traits of Jewish hysteria.
Papa lived those rancid 1930s like a man trapped in cobwebs,
lashing out and sick at heart. There was also, however, a more
private and constant regret.

His own studies in law and economic theory had been of exceptional strength. He had published monographs on the utopian economics of Saint-Simon and on the Austrian banking crises of the later nineteenth century. The absolute need to support various less qualified members of his family, the collapse of the dual monarchy and the aftermath of world war had thrust him into finance. He respected the importance, the technical ingenuities of his craft, but cultivated scant regard for most of those who practised it (one of the few contemporaries he acknowledged as pre-eminent, also in integrity, and whom he came, in certain outward gestures and tone, to resemble, was Siegmund Warburg). My father's innermost passions lay elsewhere. His uncertain health had barred him from medical studies. He turned to intellectual history, to the history and philosophic aspects of biology. His learning was extensive and exact. His appetite for languages remained unquenched to the very end (he was systematically acquiring Russian at the time of his death). Investment banking occupied the main of his outward existence. At the core, it left him almost indifferent. From this tension came his uncompromising resolve that his son should know next to nothing of his father's profession. This partition could reach absurd lengths: 'I would rather that you did not know the difference between a bond and a share.' I was to be a teacher and a thorough scholar. On this last point, I have failed him.

Why this elevation of the teacher-scholar rather than, say, the artist, the writer, the performer in a sensibility so responsive to music, literature and the arts? There was scarcely a museum in Paris and, later, in New York, to which he did not take me of a Saturday. It is in this instinctive preference for teaching and learning, for the discovery and transmission of the truth, that my father, in his aching stoicism, was most profoundly Jewish. Like Islam, Judaism is iconoclastic. It fears the image, it distrusts the metaphor. Emancipated Judaism delights in the performing artist, especially the musician. It has produced masters of stage and film. Yet even to this day, when it informs so much of American literature, when it can look to a Kafka, a Proust, a Mandelstam or a Paul Celan, Judaism is not altogether at ease with the poetics of invention (*fabulation*), with the mustard seed of 'falsehood' or fiction, with the rivalry to God the creator inherent in the arts. Given the limitless wonders of the created universe, when there is such wealth of actual being to be recorded and grasped by reason, when there is history to be untangled, law to be clarified, science to be furthered, is the devising of fictions, of *mimesis* a truly responsible, a genuinely adult pursuit? Freud, for one, did not think so. Fictions were to be outgrown as man ripened into the 'reality principle'. Somewhere in my father's restless spirit a comparable doubt may have nagged. Even the most Voltairean, perhaps atheist—I do not know—of Jews knows that the word *rabbi* simply means 'teacher'.

Only later did I come to realize the investment of hope against hope, of watchful inventiveness, which my father made in educating me. This, during years of private and public torment, when the bitter need to find some future for us as Nazism drew near, left him emotionally and physically worn out. I marvel still at the loving astuteness of his devices. No new book was allowed me till I had written down for his inspection a précis of the one I had just read. If I had not understood this or that passage—my father's choices and suggestions aimed carefully above my head—I was to read it to him out loud. Often the voice clears up a text. If misunderstanding persisted, I was to copy the relevant bit in my own writing. At which move, it would usually surrender its lode.

Though I was hardly aware of the design, my reading was held in balance between French, English and German. My upbringing was totally trilingual, and the background always polyglot. My radiant mama would habitually begin a sentence in one tongue and end it in another. Once a week a diminutive Scottish lady appeared to read Shakespeare to and with me. I entered that world, I am not certain why, via *Richard II*. Adroitly, the first speech I was made to learn by heart was not that of Gaunt, but Mowbray's farewell, with its mordant music of exile. A refugee scholar coached me in Greek and Latin. He exhaled an odour of reduced soap and sorrow. □

JOYCE CAROL OATES
LOVER

Y*ou won't know me, won't see my face. Unless you see my face.
And then it will be too late.*

Now the spring thaw had begun at last, now her blood, too,
began to beat again. The earth melting into rivulets eager and
sparkling as wounds.

Since the man who'd been her lover would have recognized
her car, she acquired another.

Not one you know, or would expect but of a make she'd never
before owned, never driven nor even ridden in—an elegant yet not
conspicuous Saab sedan. It was not a new model but appeared, to
the eye, pristine, newly minted, inviolate. In bright sunshine it
gleamed the beautiful liquidy green of the ocean's interior and in
clouded, impacted light it gleamed a subtler, perhaps more beautiful
dark, steely gunmetal grey. Its chassis was strongly built to
withstand even terrible collisions. It had a powerful transmission
that, as she drove, vibrated upward through the soles of her
sensitive feet, through her ankles, legs, belly and breasts; through
her spinal column, into her brain. *This is a car you will grow into*,
the Saab salesman was saying. *A car to live with.* She felt the
reverberations from the car's murmurous hidden machinery as of
an intense, fearful excitement too private to share with any stranger.

It was the weekend of Palm Sunday.

So now in the thaw. Miles of puddled glistening pavement,
staccato dripping. Swollen, bruised clouds overhead and a
pervasive odour as of unwashed flesh, a fishy odour of highway
exhaust, gases like myriad exhaled breaths of unspeakable
intimacy. In this car that responded so readily to her touch as no
other car she'd ever driven.

She was patient and she was methodical. Taking the route her
former lover took on the average of five evenings a week from his
office building in the suburb of Pelham Junction to his home in
the suburb of River Ridge; three miles along a highway, Route 11,
and five-and-a-half miles along an expressway, I-96. Memorizing
the route, absorbing it into her very skin. *Unless you see my face.
And then it will be too late.* She smiled, she was a woman made
beautiful by smiling. Gleam of perfect white teeth.

And her ashy pale hair dyed now a flat matt black. Swinging
loose about her face. And sunglasses, lenses tinted nearly black,

159

disguising half her face. Would she be willing to die with him? That was the crucial, teasing question. She'd kick off her shoes in the car, liking the feel of her stockinged feet, the sensitive soles of her feet, against the Saab's floor and pedals.

Sometimes, pressing her foot against the gas pedal, feeling the Saab so instantly, it seemed simultaneously, respond to her lightest touch, she experienced a sharp, pleasurable stab in her groin, like an electrical current.

How many times she would drive the complete route, exiting for River Ridge and returning on southbound I-96, like a racing driver preparing for a dangerous race, rehearsing the race, in full ecstatic awareness that it might be the final, lethal race of his life, she would not know; would not recall. Sometimes by day, but more often by night, when she could drive unimpeded by slow-moving traffic, the Saab like a captive beast luxuriating in release, yearning for higher speeds. Like one transfixed, she watched as the speedometer needle inched beyond seventy-five toward eighty, and beyond eighty, risking a traffic ticket in a sixty-five-mile zone. *At high speeds, unhappiness is slightly ridiculous.*

It was in the second week of her preparation, near midnight on Saturday, that she passed her first serious accident site in the Saab. On southbound I-96, near the airport exit, four lanes funnelled to one, traffic backed up for a mile. As she approached, she saw two ambulances pulling away from the concrete, glass- and metal-littered median, sirens deafening; saw several squad cars surrounding the smoking wreckage, revolving red lights, blinding red flares set in the roadway. Yet, as soon as the ambulances were gone, an eerie silence prevailed. What had happened, who had been injured? Who had died? The Saab, sober now, was one of a slow and seemingly endless stream as of a funeral procession of mourners. Strangers gazing in silence at the wreckage of strangers. Only death, violent and unexpected and spectacular death, induces such silence, sobriety. She did not believe in God, nor in any supernatural intervention in the plight of mankind, yet her lips moved in prayer, as if without volition. *God, have mercy!*

The Saab's driver's window was lowered. She hadn't recalled lowering it but was leaning out, staring at the wreckage, sniffing, her sensitive nostrils stung by a harsh yet exhilarating odour of gasoline, oil, smoke; she was appalled and fascinated, seeing what appeared to be three vehicles mangled together, luridly illuminated by flares and revolving red lights. Two cars, of which one appeared to have been a compact foreign car, possibly a Volvo, and the other a larger American car, both crushed, grilles and windshields and doors shoved in; the cars looked as if they'd been flung together from a great height with contempt, derision, supreme cruelty by a giant-child. The third vehicle, an airport limousine, was less damaged, its stately chrome grille crumpled and discoloured and its windshield cracked like a cobweb; its doors flung open crudely, like exclamations. She was disappointed that the accident victims had all been taken away, no one remained except official, uniformed men sweeping up glass and shattered metal, calling importantly to one another, taking their time about clearing the accident site and opening the expressway again. The Saab was moving forward at five miles an hour, a full car length behind the car that preceded it, as if reluctant to leave the accident site, though a police officer was brusquely waving her on, and, behind her, an impatient driver was tapping his horn.

The sleek black stretch limo was one of a kind in which her former lover frequently rode on his way to and from the airport, on the average of three times a month; several times, in the early days of their relationship, she'd ridden with him, the two of them intimate and hidden in the plush back seat, shielded by dark-tinted windows, whispering and laughing together, breaths sweetened with alcohol, hands moving freely over one another. How eagerly, how greedily touching one another. *If it had happened then. If, the two of us. Then.* She could have wept, that opportunity lost.

Next day she slept late, waking dazed at noon. Bright and chill and fresh, and the sun glaring in the sky like a beacon. It was Easter Sunday.

The man who'd been her lover, and whom she had loved, was an executive with an investment firm whose headquarters were in a corporate park off Route 11. Beautifully landscaped, like a miniature city, this complex of new office buildings glittered like amber Christmas-tree ornaments. It had not existed five years before. In the bulldozed, gouged and landscaped terrain of Route

11, northern New Jersey, new lunar-looking cities arose every few months, surrounded by inlets of shining, methodically parked automobiles.

She'd visited her former lover in his office suite on the top, eighth floor of his gleaming glass-and-aluminum building; she'd memorized her way through the maze of the corporate park, past clover leaves, past a sunken pond and Niobe willows—she could not attract the unwanted scrutiny of any security guard. For in her beautiful sleek Saab, in her good clothes, styled hair and sunglasses, with her imperturbable intelligent face, her poise, she looked the very model of a female inhabitant of Pelham Park, a young woman office manager, a computer analyst or perhaps an executive. She would have her own parking space, of course. She would know her destination.

Her former lover's reserved parking space was close by his office building. She hadn't had to worry that, like her, he might have acquired a new car, for his car was identifiable by the reserved space; in any case, she'd memorized his licence-plate number.

His telephone number, too, she'd memorized. Yet had never once dialled since he'd sent her away. Pride would never allow her to risk such hurt, guessing he'd changed the number.

You won't see my face. But you will know me.

Weekdays he left his office sometime after six-fifteen p.m. and before seven p.m., crossing briskly to his car, which was a silvery-grey Mercedes, and departing on his north-northwest drive to River Ridge. (Except for the days he was travelling. But she could tell at a glance when he was away, of course.) The Mercedes aroused in her a wave of physical revulsion; it was a car she knew well, had ridden in many times. The sight of it made her realize, as she hadn't quite realized until then, that he, her former lover, had not felt the need to alter anything in his life since sending her away; his life continued as before, his professional life, his family life in River Ridge in a house she had never seen, and would not see; nothing had been altered for him, above all nothing had been altered in his soul, except the presence of her from whom he'd detached himself like one shrugging off a coat. A coat no longer fashionable, desirable.

Circling the parking lot, which was divided into sectors, each

Lover

sector bounded by strips of green, bright and fine-meshed as artificial grass though in fact it was real, and vivid spring flowers. Waiting at a discreet distance. Knowing he would come, must come. And when he did, quite calmly following him in the Saab, giving herself up to the instincts of the fine-tuned motor, the dashboard of gauges that glowed with its own intelligence, volition. *You will know me. You will know.* The first time she followed him only on Route 11, as far as the exit for I-96; she was several cars behind him, unnoticed by him of course. The second time she followed him on to I-96, which was trickier, again keeping several vehicles between them, and on the expressway the Saab had quickly accelerated, impatient with holding back; moving into the outer, fast lane and passing the Mercedes (travelling at approximately the speed limit, in a middle lane) and continuing on, at a gradually reduced speed, past Exit 33 where he departed for River Ridge; again he hadn't noticed her of course, for what reason could he have had to notice her? Even had he seen her in the swift-moving Saab he could not have identified her in her new matt-black hair, her oversized dark glasses.

The third time she followed him was in a sudden, pelting April rain that turned by quick degrees to hail, hailstones gaily bouncing on the pavement like animated mothballs, bouncing on the silver hood and roof of the Mercedes, bouncing on the liquidy-dark hood and roof of the Saab. She'd wanted to laugh, excited, exhilarated as a girl, daring, on the expressway, to ease up behind him, directly behind him in a middle lane, following him unnoticed for five-and-a-half dreamlike miles at precisely, teasingly, his speed, which was sixty-nine miles an hour; when he exited for River Ridge, the Saab had been drawn in his wake, and she'd had to tug at the steering wheel to keep from following him on to the ramp. *You never knew! Yet—you must know.*

Sometimes cruising the expressway after he'd left. For she was so strangely, unexpectedly happy. Strapped into the Saab's cushioned dove-grey seat, a band across her thighs, slantwise between her breasts, tight, as tight as she could bear, holding her fast, safe. It was at the wheel of the Saab, passing a second and a third accident site, she'd understood that there are no accidents, only destiny. What mankind calls accident is but misinterpreted destiny.

163

Naked inside her clothes, now the days were warmer. Now the thaw had come at last, the earth glistened with melting, everywhere shining surfaces, oil-iridescent puddles like mirrors. *So happy! You can't know.* She surmised that her former lover might be thinking that she'd disappeared or was dead. He'd expressed concern that she was 'suicidal'—with what disdain he'd uttered the word, as if its mere syllables offended—and now he would be thinking, quite naturally he would be thinking she was dead. If he thought of her at all.

Naked inside her clothes, which were loose-fitting yet clinging, sensuous against her skin. Her buttocks pressed into the cushioned driver's seat, her thighs carelessly covered by the thin, silky synthetic material of her skirts. (For always she wore skirts or dresses, never trousers.) And her legs bare, pale from winter but smooth, slender and graceful, like the sleek contours of the Saab's interior. She kicked off her high-heeled shoes, placed them on the passenger seat, liking to drive barefoot, liking the intimacy of her skin against the Saab's gas and brake pedals. Sometimes at night truckers pulled up alongside her, even if she was travelling in the outer, fast lane, these strangers in their high, commanding cabs, not readily visible to her, maintaining a steady speed beside her for long tension-filled minutes, peering down at her, at what they could see of her slender body, her bare ghostly-glimmering legs in the dashboard light of the Saab, they were talking to her of course, murmuring words of sweet, deranged obscenity which she could not hear and had no need of hearing to comprehend. *Not now, not yet! And not you.*

Once, sobbing in the night. Her knuckles muffling the sound. And the pillow dampened with her saliva. And she'd felt his hands on her. In his sleep, his hands groping for her. Not knowing who she was, perhaps. Her exact identity, as in the depths of sleep, in even the most intimate sleep, lying naked beside another we sometimes forget the identity of the other. Yet he'd sensed her presence, and his hands had reached for her to quiet her, to subdue. To cease her sobbing.

Weeks after Palm Sunday and the Saab entering her life. A mild, misty evening of a month she could not have named.

By this time she'd memorized the route, every fraction of

every mile of the route, absorbed it into her brain, her very skin. The precise sequence of exit ramps, the succession of overhead signs she might have recited like a rosary, stretches of median which were made of concrete and stretches of median which were weedy grass; how beyond Exit 23 of I-96 there was, on the highway's shoulder, a litter of broken glass like fine-ground gems, part of a rusted bumper, twisted strips of metal that looked like the remains of a child's tricycle. And in a railroad underpass near Exit 29 a curious disfigured hubcap like a skull neatly sheared in half. By day you could see secreted on certain stretches of pavement, on both Route 11 and I-96, hieroglyphic stains, a pattern of stains, oil or gasoline or blood or a combination of these, baked into the concrete, discernible as coded messages to only the sharpest eye. And there was Exit 30 where you turned in a tight hairpin, scary and exhilarating as a carnival ride if your car was moving above twenty miles an hour, circling a marshy area of starkly beautiful six-foot reeds and cat's-tails, at its core pools of stagnant water, black and viscous as oil on the sunniest days. How drawn she was, how unexpected her yearning, to such rare remaining pockets of 'nature'—relics of the original landscape where, in theory, perhaps in fact, a body might be secreted for years; a body quietly decomposing for years, never discovered though passed each day by hundreds, thousands of people. For in such a no man's land, at the very core of the complex highway system, no pedestrians ever ventured.

From six p.m. onward she waited until, at six-fifty p.m., her former lover appeared. Carrying his attaché case, walking quickly to his car. Unseeing. As she sat in the Saab, motor off, some fifty yards away, calmly smoking a cigarette, betraying no agitation, nor even alert interest; knowing herself perfectly disguised, her sleekly styled matt-black hair covering part of her face. Her make-up was flawless as a mask, her mouth composed, eyes hidden by dark glasses. Her nails were filed short but fastidiously manicured, polished a dark plum shade to match her lipstick. Calmly, in no haste, turning the key in the ignition, feeling the quick, stabbing response of the Saab's motor waking, leaping to life.

Yes, now. It's time.

An insomniac night preceding, a night of cruising I-96, and

yet she felt fully rested, restored to herself. Tightly strapped into the passenger seat like a pilot at the controls of a small plane, yet controlled by the plane; secured in place, trusting to fine-tuned, exquisitely tooled machinery.

At a careful distance she followed her former lover through the winding lanes of Pelham Park. Waited a beat or two to allow him to ease into traffic on northbound Route 11. Then following, with utter casualness. Once on the highway, a mile or so after entering, the Saab demanded more mobility, more speed, so she shifted into the outer, fast lane; she'd lowered both the windows in the front, her hair whipped in the gassy, sulphurous air, and she'd begun to breathe quickly. Now there was no turning back, the Saab was aimed like a missile. The Mercedes was travelling at about sixty-five miles an hour in a middle lane; her former lover would be listening to a news broadcast, windows shut, air-conditioning on. It was a hazy evening; overhead were massed, impacted storm clouds like wounds; at the western horizon, brilliant shafts of fiery, corrupt sun the colour of a rotted orange; the industrial-waste sky was streaked with beauty of a kind, as a girl living elsewhere, she'd never seen. By degrees the misty air turned to a light feathery rain, the Saab's windshield wipers were on at the slowest of three tempos; a caressing, stroking motion; hypnotic and urgent. Now she was rapidly overtaking the Mercedes and would exit close behind it for I-96; once on I-96 she would swing out again into the fast lane to pass slower vehicles including the Mercedes, one of a succession of vehicles, at which she need not glance. She had five-and-a-half miles in which to make her move.

How many times she'd rehearsed, yet, on the road, in the exhilaration of the Saab's speed and grace, she would trust to instinct, intuition. Keeping the silvery, staid-looking car always in sight in her rear-view mirror even as she maintained her greater speed; hair blowing about her heated face, strands catching in her mouth. Her eyes burnt like headlights; there was a roaring in her that might have been the coursing of her own fevered blood, the sound of the Saab's engine. *At high speeds, unhappiness is not a serious possibility.*

He hadn't loved her enough to die with her; now he would pay. And others would pay.

The glowing speedometer on the Saab's elegant dashboard showed seventy-two miles an hour; the Mercedes, two cars behind, was travelling at about the same speed. She would have wished a higher speed, eighty at least, but hadn't any choice; there was no turning back. Pinpoints of sweat were breaking out on her tense body, beneath her arms, in the pulsing heat between her legs, on her forehead and upper lip. She was short of breath as if she were running or in the throes of copulation.

Switching lanes, shifting the Saab into the next lane to the right, so abruptly she hadn't time to use her turn signal, and the driver of a car in that lane protested, sounding his horn. But she knew what she meant to do and would not be dissuaded, allowing two cars to pass her in the Mercedes's lane; then moving back into that lane, so that now she was just ahead of the Mercedes, by approximately two car lengths. Rain fell more forcibly now. The Saab's windshield wipers were moving faster, in swift, deft, percussive arcs, though she didn't recall adjusting them. In sensuous snaky patterns rain streamed across the curved glass. In the rear-view mirror the Mercedes was luminous with rain and its headlights were aureoles of dazzling light, and staring at its image she felt a piercing sensation in her groin. She believed she could see, through the rain-streaked windshield, the pale oval of a man's face; a frowning face; the face of the man who'd been her lover for one year, eleven months and twelve days; yet perhaps she could not have identified the face; perhaps it was a stranger's face. Yet the Saab propelled her onward and forward; she could almost imagine that the Saab was propelling the Mercedes forward as well. She was bemused, wondering: how like high-school math: if the Saab suddenly braked, causing the Mercedes to ram into its rear, with what force would the Mercedes strike? Not the force of a head-on collision, of course, since both vehicles were speeding in the same direction. Would both swerve into another lane, or lanes? And which other vehicles would be involved? How many individuals, at this moment unknown to one another, would be hurt? How many injuries, how many fatalities? Out of an infinity of possibilities, only one set of phenomena could actually happen. The contemplation of it left her breathless, giddy; she felt as if she were on the edge of an abyss gazing blindly out—where?

It was then that she saw, in the rainwashed outside mirror, another vehicle rapidly approaching at the rear. A motorcycle! A Harley-Davidson, by the look of it. The cyclist was a hunched figure in black leather, his head encased in a helmet and shining goggles; he seemed oblivious of the rain, weaving through lanes of traffic, boldly, recklessly, now cutting in front of a delivery van, provoking an outraged response of horn-blowing, now weaving out again, into the lane to the Saab's right, just behind the Saab. She pressed down quickly on the gas pedal to accelerate, to allow the cyclist to ease in behind her if he wished; there was no doubt in her mind he would do so, and he did; bound for the outer, fast lane in a breathtaking display of driving skill and bravado. And in the rain! *Because he doesn't care if he dies. Because there is no other way.*

She felt a powerful sexual longing for him, this hunched, bearded stranger in his absurd leather costume; this stranger she would never know.

Acting swiftly then, intuitively. For Exit 31 was ahead, with its two exit-only lanes; many vehicles on I-96 would be preparing to exit, shifting their positions, causing the constellation of traffic to alter irrevocably. Within seconds the cyclist would have roared ahead, gone. In the dreamy space of time remaining she felt a rivulet of moisture run down the left side of her face, like a stream of blood she dared not wipe away, gripping the steering wheel so hard her knuckles ached. She saw admiringly that the Saab was free of human weakness; its exquisite machinery was not programmed to contain any attachment to existence, any terror of annihilation; for time looped back upon itself at such speeds and perhaps the Saab and its entranced driver had already been annihilated in a multi-vehicular crash involving the Harley-Davidson, the Mercedes and other vehicles; perhaps it was a matter of indifference whether the cataclysm had happened yet, or was destined to happen within minutes; or, perversely, not to happen at all. But her bare foot was pressing on the brake; her toes that were icy with fear, pressing on the Saab's brake as a woman might playfully, tauntingly press a bare foot against a lover's foot; a quick pressure, but then a release; and another quick pressure, and a release; jockeying for position, preparing to move into the left lane, the cyclist might not have noticed, for a low-slung sports car was approaching in that lane out of a tremulous glimmer of headlights, quite fast, possibly at eighty miles an hour, lights blinding in the rain; the cyclist was rapidly calculating if he had time to change lanes, or had he better wait until the sports car passed; he was distracted, unaware of the Saab's erratic behaviour only a few yards ahead of him; and a third time, more forcibly, she depressed the brake pedal, unmistakably now, the Saab jerked in a violent rocking motion, and there was a shriek of brakes that might have been the Saab's, or another's; the Harley-Davidson braked, skidded, swerved, seemed to buckle and to right itself, or nearly; she had a glimpse of the bearded man's surprisingly young face, his incredulous eyes widened and wondering inside the goggles, in her rear-view mirror, in the very fraction of an instant the Saab was easing away, like a gazelle leaping away from danger. Within another second the Saab was gone, and in its wake a giddy drunken skidding, swerving, a frantic sounding of horns; faint with excitement she held the gas pedal to the floor racing the Saab to eighty, to eighty-five, the car's front wheels shuddering against the rain-slick pavement yet managing to hold the surface, while behind her it appeared that the motorcycle had swerved into the outer lane, and the sports car had swerved to avoid a direct collision yet both vehicles careened on to the median, and there they did collide and crash; at the same time the Mercedes, close behind the motorcycle, had turned blindly into the lane to its right, and what appeared to be a delivery van had narrowly managed to avoid hitting it. The Mercedes and the van and a string of dazed, stricken vehicles were slowing, braking like wounded beasts, passing the flaming wreckage that would be designated the accident site. She saw this spectacle in miniature, rapidly shrinking in her rear-view mirror and in her outside mirror; by this time the Saab itself was exiting the expressway, exhausted, safe; she was trying to catch her breath, laughing, sobbing, finally rolling to a stop in a place unknown to her, near a culvert or an underpass smelling of brackish water and bordered by wind-whipped thistles, and her spinal cord was arched like a bow in a delirium of spent pleasure and depletion; her fingers rough between her legs trying to contain, to slow, the frantic palpitations.

Next time, she was consoled. Next time. ☐

MANUEL BAUER
TIBET

Isabel Hilton

When I first visited Lhasa, in 1995, the little village of Shol still lay at the foot of the great Potala Palace, the empty residence of the Dalai Lama. The village had been there since the eighteenth century; the sixth Dalai Lama, a notorious barfly and womanizer, used to visit it in thin disguise to drink and to pen the lyrical love poems that are still sung in Lhasa. But when I returned a year later, Shol had gone. On its site is a giant plaza, an empty space created, appropriately enough, to commemorate the thirtieth anniversary of the creation of the Tibetan Autonomous Region, the Chinese colonial administration which rules what were once the provinces of Outer Tibet, the old political domain of the Dalai Lamas.

Until the 'liberation' of Tibet by China in 1951, the number of Chinese who lived there could be counted in handfuls. Even in the border provinces of Inner Tibet (so-called because they were closer to Beijing), the population was overwhelmingly Tibetan. In the nineteenth century, feeling the pressure of British and Russian imperial ambitions, the Tibetan government had effectively closed the borders, and it became a matter of law as well as custom that few foreigners lived there. The last imperial house to rule China was a Manchu dynasty whose Buddhist emperors owed the Dalai Lamas of Tibet a spiritual allegiance in return for which they offered temporal protection. But the new secular empire that emerged from the Chinese revolution had harder attitudes to borders and the peoples that lay within them. Tibet became imperial territory to be brought under central control. By 1951, after a brief and hopelessly one-sided military encounter, a treaty had been signed: the Seventeen Point Agreement for the Peaceful Liberation of Tibet. In 1959, after the Tibetan rebellion, the treaty was torn up, and the occupation became direct.

Today two-thirds of the territory—the old Inner Tibet—has been divided between neighbouring Chinese provinces, and the Tibetan population is counted as a minority. In Outer Tibet, the Tibetan Autonomous Region, the Chinese population has grown steadily over the past ten years.

In the early days the occupiers were troops and bureaucrats. Now they are also civilian settlers. Each category has contributed to the destruction of Tibetan culture in the past four decades. The

172

troops built the roads that now carry Chinese goods and immigrants into Tibet, and Tibetan natural resources out. There are an estimated quarter of a million of them in the Tibetan Autonomous Region, and they provide an unbreakable corset of security.

The Chinese bureaucrats are numbered in thousands. Few of them desire to settle—they live in ghettos, heavily subsidized by the central government and show little inclination to integrate with a population whose language many do not speak, whose customs and beliefs they despise and whose food they find repellent. The Chinese civilians, who are arriving in ever-increasing numbers, come because Tibet has been sold to them as a land of opportunity, a Klondike from which minerals, gold and carbon can be extracted, where trade can be pursued against little competition, and fortunes made. They offer the Chinese government the prospect that Tibet can be assimilated through colonization.

The obliteration of the past is not unique to Tibet: most Chinese cities have been razed to the ground and rebuilt in the latest wave of modernization. But in Tibet the process is also political. To destroy a culture, you have to destroy its memory, a memory carried largely in the Buddhist church. The religious establishment is now heavily restricted in numbers and closely controlled politically. Last year it was officially decreed that 'patriotism'—loyalty to Beijing—is the prime requirement for religion, and it is the stated objective of the government to remove the influence of the Dalai Lama from the religion of which he is head. Secular education, which has now largely replaced monastic education, is controlled by the government and in its higher levels conducted in Chinese. History, of course, is taught from the point of view of the occupier. Lhasa university, which until last year was the only institution of higher learning that used the Tibetan language, has now been told to teach in Chinese.

The city of Lhasa is being destroyed at a devastating rate. More than half of the old city has been demolished, its traditional buildings replaced with breeze-block pastiche. The municipal plan envisages the demolition of the rest of the city by the end of the century. What was once the holy city of Tibetan Buddhism will become a monument to the new Chinese barbarism. □

ISABEL HILTON

Buddhist novices on a pilgrimage to Jokhang, the holiest temple in Tibet

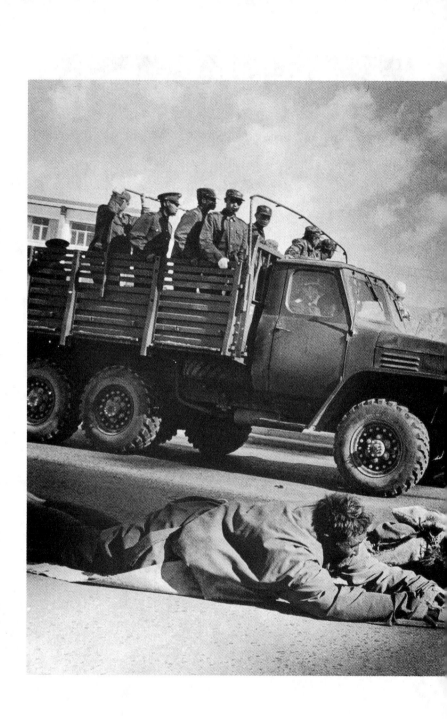

Buddhists on a pilgrimage to Jokhang prostrate themselves on one of Lhasa's new ring roads as Chinese soldiers look on

Prayer flags. The TV mast in the background stands on the site of the Menpa Trantsang, the old Buddhist medical school demolished by the Chinese

A Tibetan pilgrim performing 'khora'—or encirclement —of the Chamdo monastery in the now-Chinese city of Kham

A lute-player in Chamdo, the Tibetan part of the Chinese city of Kham

A Chinese woman passes a group of Khampas, Tibetans from the eastern province in Bayi

*A goldmine
at Renmai,
near Kham.
Tibet is rich
in minerals,
which the
Chinese
are keen
to exploit*

*Chinese
soldiers and
Tibetan
woman
(right)*

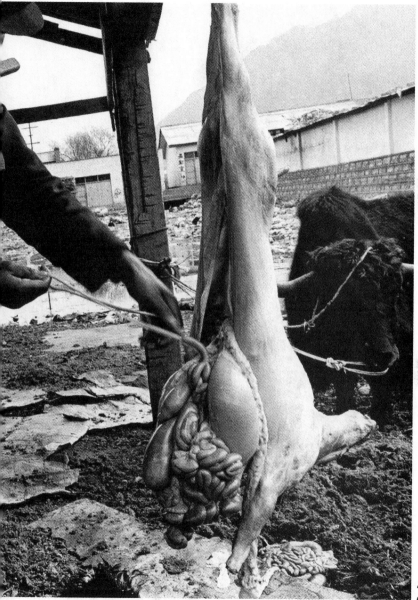

*Slaughterhouse
at Bayi*

*The market
at Bayi,
where ninety-
nine per cent
of the
population is
now Chinese*

The Erlang pass, one of two main routes from Tibet into China

unknown public
the journal you listen to

we elucidate

Unknown Public's unique editorial approach guides you through the multidimensional world of creative music by bringing together outstanding recordings from many genres, styles and idioms.

we surprise

UP brings you music you may have heard about but haven't heard. Hard-to-find recordings; debut tracks from new talents; rare radio broadcasts; work in progress; preview tapes; contemporary classics. Music that defies categorisation.

we stimulate

UP takes a thematic approach. Each issue is built around a different aspect of music-making or musical thought. Each title is a starting point for cross-references and connections with literature, the visual arts, theatre, dance, film and television.

we entertain

Each issue of the award-winning journal contains 75 minutes of music mastered to the highest standard, accompanied by intelligent editorial and innovative design and packaging.

volume i
UP01 points of
    departure
UP02 common ground
UP03 pianoFORTE
UP04 musical
    machinery

volume ii
UP05 voicebox
UP06 eclectic guitars
UP07 the netherlands
    connection
UP08 sensuality:
    essence and nonsense

forthcoming issues
volume iii
UP09 all seeing eye
UP10 bloody amateurs
UP11 naked
UP12 talking drums

UP has included works by more than 150 creative musicians, including John Adams ○ Louis Andriessen ○ Django Bates ○ George Benjamin ○ Carla Bley ○ Gavin Bryars ○ Sheila Chandra ○ Robert Fripp ○ Tod Machover ○ Alex Maguire ○ Ensemble Modern ○ Michael Nyman ○ Seigen Ono ○ Steve Reich ○ Howard Skempton ○ David Toop ○ Mark–Anthony Turnage ○ Kevin Volans ○ Errollyn Wallen ○ Frank Zappa

unknown public
we deliver

Four issues of the most stimulating new music for only £55 a year. For free information leaflet, index and subscription details, write, fax or call:
unknown public, dept.GR58,
FREEPOST (RG 2558), P.O. Box 354,
Reading RG2 7BR, UK
[no stamp required if posted in UK]
fax: +44 (0)118 931 2582 tel: +44 (0)118 931 2580

PETER WALKER
MAORI WAR

My friend Spencer, a New Zealand Maori, is what people used to call a good-time Charlie. He is famous, in a small way, for the number of parties he goes to and the way they liven up when he gets there. When I first met him, six years ago, he was running a restaurant near Charing Cross in London. The quick drink he had with his staff after work became a minor legend. People would cross the city at midnight to be there. If they were lucky, they might get away at four in the morning. Not everyone appreciates Spencer's gregarious streak. The Syrian who owned the restaurant, for instance, called in the police when he inspected his depleted cellar. But Spencer believes in the value of a good time. He has faith in the party.

However, when I ran into him in New Zealand, in the summer of 1996, he wore a look of puzzled embarrassment I had not seen before. We were driving around Wellington harbour and he was describing, not for the first time, a trip he had just made to the South Island with his flatmate, Hughie. Fantastic hospitality down south, he assured me. Terrific wines—Cloudy Bay, Moa Ridge—great local beer, seafood, wild pork . . . 'the works'.

He paused. 'But things got a bit tricky down there,' he said. 'I was staying with Hughie's family; and we were having a party. There were about a dozen of us; everyone was getting along fine.

'Then I went to the toilet. And while I was in there, there was a knock on the door. And then this voice said: "You fucking Maoris . . . get out of our area."'

'What did you do?' I asked.

'I didn't *know* what to do,' he said. 'I was stunned. I just stood there. But I had nowhere else to go, so I went back to the party. I pretended nothing had happened.'

'But who'd done it?'

'It was weird. I went back into the room, and everyone was all smiles. "Cheers, Spence," and all that. I talked to all of them over the next couple of hours. And I still don't know which one of them it was.'

I was eleven years old before I ever saw a Maori. I grew up in Christchurch, a stolid, flat, prosperous town with, historically, only a tiny Maori population. Indeed, the marked absence of

199

natives was one of the factors that inspired the Canterbury pilgrims to settle there 150 years ago. Their intention was to build an Anglican utopia, and in a way they succeeded. Christchurch was 'the cathedral city . . . the Garden City of the Plains . . . the most English city outside England'.

There was little sign that we were in the South Pacific, and none at all that we were on the edges of Polynesia. English elms and willows bent in the hot summer nor'westers and in winter stood leafless in fogs penetrated by the headlights of Ford Prefects and Morris Oxfords. The tolling of Big Ben for the evening news on the BBC ('This is London') woke us (in a weird twist we barely noticed) every morning. Gilbert Scott's cathedral and the university, the schools, the courts, the clubs, the council chambers had all been built in the proper nineteenth-century Gothic Revival manner, though the Catholics and the banks preferred the classical style. One night in 1868 the great Waimakariri river to the north rose and swept down on the town, leaving the frumpy Gothic buildings up to their bustles in water. But it sank back again, was embanked and channelled and has never since made an appearance in the drawing rooms of Christchurch; even its name, sprawling, like the river itself over a mile-wide shingle bed, was usually reduced to a curt Anglo-Saxon 'Why-Mack'.

And of course there were no Maori. There was one on the shilling, and one on the twopenny stamp—depicted, I think, running through a swamp, carrying a parcel—but his business there, on the stamp and the shilling, and for that matter in the swamp, was unclear to me. There was the occasional article in our school journals on the Ancient Maori, but he meant no more to us than the Roman boy, with his tutor and slave, in our blue-covered *Everyday Life in Rome*.

Then one summer we went to Picton and there on the grass between the hotel and the sea I saw a group of about thirty Maori in traditional costume—a concert party. I can still remember my surprise at the sight of the red lipstick on the women's dark faces and the unfamiliar harmonies of Maori plainsong, and recall how sharply the outlines of the hills seemed to stand against the sky. I was shocked, as children are, by this first incursion of otherness into my life.

But there was another feeling. For the first time I realized that even the solid Anglican city of Christchurch, with its fogs and elms, had not risen upon a vacancy. It was a superimposition. There had been something here before us, and—remarkably—it was still here.

When I was fourteen, my family moved to Hawkes Bay on the North Island. Here the question of race was not so remote. The Maori population in and around the twin cities of Napier and Hastings numbered several thousand. Oddly, this had very little effect on the community's self-image. We were, we believed, a little Britain of the south, which just happened to contain two races living side by side. Maori and Pakeha (the Maori term for white people) worked together, played rugby together, inter-married and shared the same rights and interests. It was true that there had once been a war over land and sovereignty, but this was a century ago, and had simply proved our splendid and complementary qualities. The Maori distinguished themselves with their gallantry: their warriors leapt over parapets to take water to dying British soldiers and—in the same battle, or was it a different one?—sent ammunition to the British when they ran out, so that the fight could continue. The whites, in turn, were generous victors, enfranchising the Maori and setting aside seats for them in parliament. The colour bar erected everywhere else in the British Empire was unknown in New Zealand. We were proud of the fact that we, unlike any other white community in the world, called ourselves by the name given us by the indigenous people—Pakeha. No one even troubled to ask what this word meant; today a Maori is likely to tell you it means 'rats' or 'fleas' or some other troublesome pest, but it is probably a contraction of *pakepakeha,* a mythological pale-skinned people in Maori legend, heard singing as they float on driftwood down rivers in flood. We were even proud of the fact that our national rugby team always began their matches with a Maori haka, or war dance. It was another sign that we were, in the official phrase, 'one people'.

The trouble with this ideology was that it did not quite fit the facts. Maori were not quite so carefree and happy-go-lucky as we imagined. On the contrary they seemed, to my newcomer's eyes,

201

to be aloof, tense and ill at ease. And they were poor—you saw them in town and immediately recognized the broken grilles and rusted mudguards of a 'Maori car' (old wrecks were always called that), the back seat crammed with kids. Most of all, they were elusive. Maori boys began secondary school in the third form but by the fifth had vanished; probably into some unknown Maori world of seasonal labour, or into the menacing gangs that had started to form in the state-housing blocks of Hastings.

Nor did we live 'side by side'. Whites lived among Maoris (back then everyone added the English 's' to the word) only in the poorest areas, or if they happened to be in Napier Prison. In any case, most Maori lived in their own settlements—Paki Paki, Bridge Pa or Fernhill—not far away, but just out of sight. Perfectly good roads led to these places, but no one I knew ever went there, and I could not think of a reason that would ever take me there either.

When I was seventeen, I had a summer job in the abattoir at Whakatu, near Hastings, where up to thirty thousand lambs were slaughtered each day. The workers, seven or eight hundred of us, were mostly Maori, though the foremen and the staff in the administration block were white. I was set to work on the 'bung bench' with a gang of five others, all Maori. Our job was to sluice the lamb intestines, which would then be made into sausage skins, or, I was told, condoms—a lowly occupation in this hierarchy of blood and knives and flaying.

I became quite friendly with one of my workmates, Teddy Rau, a boy of about my own age. For four weeks we worked together, and, with our hands full of still-warm intestines, we talked—mostly about sex. He could never tell whether girls liked him or not and was in a state of stifled envy of his cousin, who had several girlfriends at the same time and had even had sex with one of them, on the Gisborne railcar while it was crossing the Mohaka Viaduct.

One night, at the end of summer, some weeks after I had left the abattoir, I went to a dance in Napier with my new girlfriend. We were out on the dance floor, and suddenly there was a terrific blow on my back, just below the shoulder blades. I staggered and

NORTH
ISLAND

Waitangi

Hauraki Gulf

Auckland

Coromandel
Tauranga
Taneatua
Whakatane

Waitemata

Otahuhu

Waikata

Te Kuiti

Rotorua

North Taranaki Bight

Gisborne

Ruapehu △

Hawke Bay

South Taranaki Bight

Wanganui

Hastings

Tasman
Sea

Nelson

Pacific
Ocean

Wellington

SOUTH
ISLAND

Waimakariri River

Christchurch

| 0 | 100 Miles |
| 0 | 160 Kms |

nearly fell, but turned to find myself face to face with Teddy Rau.
There were two other Maori standing behind him. He stared at
me with a blank expression. I looked back, too surprised to speak.
I had a momentary notion that the blow started out as a friendly

slap on the back, but somewhere in the air between us the open palm changed into a fist. Neither of us knew why; nor did we say a word. Teddy left the dance, and I never saw him again.

A second memory, from that same summer. It was a routine afternoon at Whakatu, but I had missed the bus home after work. The slaughterhouse—a grimy five-storey brick building—stood in a small township of mostly Maori inhabitants, and the narrow horizons of life there, the stench of meat and tallow, and the thought of the surf crashing on the beach at Napier, made the heat oppressive. While I waited, a Maori woman and a young child came past. She had a handsome face, but looked furious, as a sixty-year-old woman well might after a long walk in the hot sun. The child—probably her grandson—was no more than four and was dawdling behind, poking a stick into a ditch. Ignoring my presence, though I was only a foot away, she turned and snapped out three words, like the flick of a whip: 'Come on, Nigger.'

Nigger! A word I no more expected to hear than I thought to see a cross burning on a lawn. I could not tell whether it was a nickname or a casual term of abuse, nor which was worse. Back in the 1850s the word put in a brief appearance, and as tensions rose over land it began to crop up in settlers' diaries and letters. During the wars in the 1860s and 1870s it flourished openly across newspaper columns and in public speeches. But then it edged out of sight, out of the national vocabulary. Despite the casual condescension of whites—every schoolboy had his fake Maori accent and his Maori jokes—I had never heard it used by a white New Zealander.

These two incidents—the blow on the back, the ugly word overheard—were too fleeting and cryptic to cast any shadow over my acceptance of the received version of race relations. We were an example to the rest of the world, right? Two races, one people, hard-working whites, happy-go-lucky Maori, a tapestry of light and shade . . . we all believed that. But received versions often have deeper functions—as alibis, perhaps, or spells. As an alibi, this one told us that there were no dark secrets in our past; as a spell, it gave us a pleasant sense of superiority over other white communities—Australians, South Africans, Americans.

In the early 1970s, I went abroad for the first time. Most New Zealanders, leaving school or university, suddenly open their eyes and see where they are—in a small country at the edge of the world. Then they leave as fast as they can. I did the sort of things we all did on this mandatory world trip: helped build a house in Colorado, fell ill in Benares, fell in love in London, where I served gin to glum businessmen in a pub near Victoria, taught French in a riotous and dingy school off the Caledonian Road. After two or three years overseas, most of us return, and so did I. But not for long. Eighteen months later, I was away again, this time to Australia and California. Antipodeans can spend years like this, wavering between hemispheres, unsure where to settle.

During these years away I became aware that racial changes were afoot. Maori protests began, mostly over specific pockets of land that had been seized by the authorities in the recent past or were under threat. Thousands of Maori marched from the far north to the capital, Wellington, five hundred miles away, demanding an end to land appropriation. Later, when I happened to be back in Auckland, I watched in amazement as army trucks rumbled across town, carrying hundreds of police to evict local Maori from a site which seemed not only to be lawfully theirs, but to be the tiny remnant of what had once been promised them in perpetuity.

At the same time, new books appeared that completely rewrote the history of the wars. They argued that Maori had never actually been defeated in battle, but were tricked into surrender, or simply swamped by more and more British soldiers, many sent straight from service in India. After the Indian Mutiny, the attitude throughout the empire towards its subject peoples became much harsher. Even the Maori briefly became 'black vermin'. By the mid-1860s, there were more imperial soldiers in New Zealand than in England or any other British territory.

Suddenly, a hundred years later, the Maori wars began to look very different to us—they became a tale of broken treaties, land invasions, burning churches and tortured prisoners. One settlement of two thousand unarmed, pacifist Maori was attacked and sacked, the men sent into exile, women raped, lands forfeited. The New Zealand ideology of race—our alibi and spell—appeared to be cracking. Even the most hallowed national legends were now embarrassments. At school we had heard of the Maori chief Te Ori Ori who was wounded taking water to a dying British soldier. We were not told that after the battle Te Ori Ori was flung into a prison hulk in Auckland harbour for six months, or that the New Zealand minister of war made a point of forbidding straw mattresses for the wounded.

In 1981 I left again, and this time I did not return for fifteen years, except on occasional flying visits. From the vantage point of a London newsroom, I watched more radical changes unfold. New Zealand became a global byword for the spirit of free enterprise: even more strikingly than Thatcher's Britain or Reagan's America, it grasped the free-market nettle. The welfare state was dismantled, and most state assets—transport, banks, post offices, forestry—were auctioned off. A huge disparity in wealth began to open up.

Not surprisingly, race relations grew worse. National day celebrations of the founding Treaty of Waitangi were disrupted. Huge claims for reparation were put forward by Maori: after all, if national assets were being sold off, why should they be excluded? By 1995 the country was in an interracial uproar. Flags were trampled, buildings occupied, courts disrupted. Children who set fire to a school were described admiringly by their Maori elders as 'warriors of our people'. There were threats of terrorism, of burning forests and bombing dams. The Queen herself was manoeuvred into making an unprecedented apology for historic wrongs. New Zealanders I met in London would debate whether the country would turn into another Bosnia or merely an Ulster. A hundred and twenty years after the colonial conflict had ended, the little word 'war' was heard once more in the land.

The Maori demands for reparation and decolonization and sovereignty were conventional enough; the burning flags and barricades a predictable symptom of unrest. Yet when I read the reports (and even, back home on flying visits, when I wrote them) there always seemed to be something missing. It was as if, after each outburst, a silence fell and people thought: 'That's not what we really meant. That isn't really what we want.'

What we do know—the salient facts—can be marshalled quite easily. New Zealand has a population of 3.4 million people, of whom 400,000 are Maori. They are part of the Polynesian race that emerged from South-East Asia three or four thousand years ago and spread across the Pacific Ocean, reaching their furthest outpost, Aotearoa (the Maori name for New Zealand) between AD1000 and 1350. There they formed about fifty *iwi* (tribes) which were frequently at war with one another.

The first European to sail into view was a Dutchman, Abel Tasman, who departed hastily after a bloody encounter in 1642. The inhabitants, he thought, had 'rough voices and strong bones, the colour of their skin being between brown and yellow, they were full of verve, and wore their hair pulled back in a bun in the Japanese manner'. He called the country Staten Landt, wrongly believing it to be part of a greater southern continent, and it was an Amsterdam map-maker who later named these mountainous islands after a muddy Dutch province in the North Sea.

Then, in 1769, came Captain Cook. And in the following fifty years, shoals of other whites came in his wake—whalers, traders, missionaries and finally settlers. The islands were recognized as an independent nation in 1835, but only five years later, when five hundred or so Maori chiefs signed the Treaty of Waitangi, New Zealand became a British colony.

Under the treaty, the chiefs conceded 'sovereignty' to Britain, and Britain guaranteed something called *tino rangatiratanga* to the chiefs. It seems probable that neither side knew what the other was talking about. To the Maori, 'sovereignty' meant, at best, some remote principle that might protect them from invasion by the French. But to the British, the Maori concept *tino rangatiratanga*—'the full power of chieftainship'—meant little more than authority within the tribe.

Despite the variety of interpretations—and they pour out today faster than ever—a few fundamentals are clear. One of the purposes of the treaty was to save the Maori from the calamities that had swept over other peoples ruled by Europeans. A humanitarian mood reigned in the Colonial Office in London: it was the heyday of abolition, and the bullying and butchery that had taken place elsewhere were not going to happen in New

Zealand. At Waitangi, the British came ashore with promises they meant to keep.

Twenty years later, these promises were all broken. Instead, the British brought invasion, war and the confiscation of land. The treaty was abandoned, remembered only as a curious, romantic frontispiece to the country's history. The idea that anyone should feel bound by it scarcely entered people's heads. It was, said the chief justice in 1877, a 'simple nullity'.

And then, surprisingly, a century later, it came back to life.

At first no one could make it out. It was Waitangi Day 1971—and the usual ceremony was being held in the far north. Naval vessels fired a salute to honour the accession of the Queen; there was a ceremonial Maori challenge and then the usual speech praising the 'tapestry of light and shade', the two races side by side. A bugler sounded Sunset Call, and, in an unconsciously accurate piece of symbolism, the lights on the Treaty House were extinguished, and the naval vessels were lit up in the bay.

At these 131st anniversary celebrations the then finance minister, Robert Muldoon, 'Piggy' to the nation at large, was in the middle of his speech when there was a disturbance. A woman stood up behind him, shouting, waving her arms and repeating a phrase again and again. Muldoon faltered. People craned to see what was happening. Even among the naval guard of honour, standing rigidly to attention around the flag, eyeballs rolled sideways slightly—far enough for the guard to be taken by surprise when a group of young Maori rushed the flagstaff, hauled down the naval ensign and set fire to it. A scrum of police, navy cadets and Maori tussled over the flag, which was eventually rescued and returned, scorched, to its proper place. The young Maori, wearing green wreaths and black clothing, began a slow handclap that drowned out further speeches. Then a squall swept in, and the rest of the ceremony was cancelled.

Nobody really understood what had happened; no one was even sure what the woman was shouting. 'Honour and freedom!' some newspapers reported. 'Honour the treaty!' said others. Apart from that, there was a puzzled silence in the press. It was as if this was the first time anyone had actually shouted in New Zealand: no one knew what to make of it. Only Muldoon got the message.

He turned and glowered at the protester. 'That,' he grated, 'is a very dangerous woman.'

Twenty-five years later, there can be no one in the country in doubt as to what was shouted that day ('Honour the Treaty!'). Everything has changed. The dangerous woman has been listened to. A ministry and tribunal have been set up to ensure the Treaty is honoured. Hundreds of millions of dollars have been paid in compensation. Maori now enjoy new rights in property, forestry, fishing, mining, education, broadcasting and culture. And yet the anger has not abated. Maori spokesmen are demanding more than a billion dollars' worth of land reparations. The Treaty of Waitangi has become a weapon in the struggle to turn New Zealand back into Aotearoa—Land of the Long White Cloud.

I felt the full depth of the Maori grievance quite by chance, when I went back to Christchurch last year. I had not been there for twenty-five years, but I wanted to see the country from the flat, stolid, white city of my childhood.

'Twenty-five years?' people said. 'You'll find it terribly changed.'

But when I arrived, late on a rainy Sunday afternoon, it seemed eerily unchanged. A few shiny high-rise buildings had touched down in the centre, but otherwise there was the same deep sabbath calm, the same sense of razor-keen snobbery in the better suburbs—Fendalton and Merivale—and the same magical wood of English oaks and Scots pines near the centre of town. Scenes from childhood are generally supposed to seem smaller when revisited in later life, but this rule does not apply to woodland, for the trees quietly keep pace with the years. The avenues and copses of Hagley Park and St James Park seemed, if anything, deeper, taller and darker than I remembered.

On my second day there, I went with friends to see an exhibition of late nineteenth-century portraits of Maori. Some of these were rather fine paintings, but the tone was valedictory. The chiefs and the women of rank were depicted as noble, stoic, resigned, the senators of a dying race. It was widely believed at that time that the Maori, whose numbers at one point sank to thirty thousand, were doomed to extinction.

Leaving the gallery I walked across the lawn and found myself in a part of the Botanical Gardens I did not remember. And there I found a circle of standing stones: a cromlech, a henge. It made me laugh at first—it was not very impressive, although a circle of black pines added a kind of Caledonian sternness to the concept. But then I wondered how such a monument, twelve thousand miles from Britain, in a country in which such things had never been built, must look to Maori eyes.

We had brought our laws and institutions and planted them in the country. We had introduced our trees, grasses, thrushes, blackbirds—even the English hedgehog snuffled in Christchurch back gardens. But until I saw the henge of yellowish stones, I had not realized how deeply driven into the turf were the claims of Englishness. Not only had we taken over the present and rewritten the immediate past, we were ready to annex the part of the landscape where imagination and prehistory touch. This circle of stones, no more than a garden folly in one light, seemed also to be another way of telling the Maori, absent-mindedly and as if without malice, that they were not really there.

From Christchurch I went, on a bright day in midsummer, to Wanganui, a town on the west coast of the North Island. It was late morning—some Maori teenagers were hunkered down on benches in the main street; a few whites drifted from shop to bank and bank to shop. A wide brown river flows through the town, and I went down to a small park on the river bank, between the courthouse and the rowing club. Moutoa Gardens is just an acre or two of mown grass shaded with old trees and studded with war memorials. So it would be easy to miss the one oddity that it had to offer—a stone pedestal about six feet high, inscribed with the word BALLANCE, but supporting the remnants of a pair of marble boots.

John Ballance was an obscure colonial premier, and his broken marble boots were the only sign that for seventy days in 1995 Moutoa Gardens was the centre of New Zealand's growing racial conflict. That May, hundreds of Maori occupied and barricaded the park. The streets nearby echoed to the sound of haka, the Maori war challenge. Cars driven by whites were threatened and sometimes attacked. At first, the Maori demanded

210

Maori protesters performing a haka in Wanganui   POPPERFOTO/REUTER

simply that the park be returned to them; then the demands grew wilder. All public land in the district must be handed over. Whites must pay rates to Maori. Maori sovereignty must be established over the region, indeed over the whole country.

Hundreds of Pakeha cheered outside the courthouse when the eviction order was granted. But on the eve of a massive police operation to break up the demonstration, and breathing defiance till the last, the occupiers slipped away, taking the statue of John Ballance with them. The old colonialist had been visible throughout the siege, a twelve-foot hostage looming above the cooking fires and haka groups. For the first few days the statue remained unharmed, but then it was decapitated; the head was replaced with a pumpkin—not a round orange pumpkin, which might have transformed it into a friendly Hallowe'en ghoul, but one of those grey varieties the same colour as the stone. This gave the figure an air of sinister inanity.

This idiot moonface appeared in all the newspapers, and came to symbolize both this occupation and all the others which sprang up across the North Island at the same time. On the night

211

before they struck camp, the rebels, under the eyes of the police surrounding the park, managed to chop Ballance up and cart him away with them.

I wondered what he had done to deserve this special treatment. Or was he just unlucky to be caught behind enemy lines? Ballance, a Maori leader in Wanganui told me, was a mass-murderer. She said he had sent flour laced with arsenic to the tribes living upriver. He had committed genocide.

This was a terrible charge, and I was not inclined to believe it. It did not seem to fit in with even the darkest facts of the country's history.

'How do you know this is true?' I asked.

'We just know.'

'But how?'

'Well,' she said reluctantly, 'it's in the Taylor diaries.'

Taylor was a clergyman in Wanganui in the mid-nineteenth century, and his diaries survive in the town library. But when I read the manuscript that afternoon, there was no mention of Ballance at all.

'What do you think?' I asked a white man sitting on a bench beside the river. 'Ballance and his arsenic—it sounds like a bad business.'

'Oh, no,' he said. 'Ballance was a good man. He did a lot of good for the Maoris.'

This was a phrase guaranteed to make my antennae twitch. A lot of people—old family doctors, big landowners, magistrates, local policemen—are said to have done 'a lot of good for the Maoris'. It is one of those phrases that is invariably followed by a denunciation of Maori ingratitude, sloth, stupidity . . .

I did not have to wait long.

'Oh,' he said artlessly, when I asked what he thought of the occupation. 'We're all racists in Wanganui now. The Maoris are just a pack of lazy, black—well, no, we don't mind the local ones protesting and what have you, but the outsiders coming in and stealing, making trouble and giving the town a bad name . . . '

He fixed me with a wounded expression: 'Write something good about Wanganui,' he commanded. 'Write about our lovely new velodrome in Cook's Gardens.'

He gazed over at the park and its war memorials.

'We used to get along fine with the Maoris,' he said. 'We never saw any difference between them and us. My boy, he had a Maori pal when he was a kid, and one day his gran said to him: "How's that little black friend of yours?" And he didn't know who she was talking about. That's how colour-blind we were!'

In Auckland I went to a wedding, a Maori–Pakeha wedding. It's worth emphasizing that ever since the two races encountered each other, there has been one constant: sexual attraction. Even the war years were marked by alliances and marriages, from the governor and the household of the Maori king downwards.

The wedding was a smart affair. There were a Maori bishop and a knight on the bride's side, and the groom, a middle-class Pakeha, had friends from the art world and advertising. Actresses turned up at the church in racy convertibles; I even glimpsed a top hat or two. The reception was held in rooms at Cheltenham Beach, soft, buttery lighting inside and, outside, the Hauraki Gulf with its necklace of islands and mountains. Just as the champagne corks began popping, a cruise liner emerged from behind the nearest headland, as if part of the general ebullience, and sailed past, filling the windows.

Then the speeches began. After the first, from the bride's side, five or six middle-aged Maori women, dressed in purple and wearing the sort of hats that aunts wear to weddings, were suddenly on their feet in different parts of the room, singing a song, a *waiata,* their hands moving in time. The Pakehas' eyes gleamed: the Maoris were being marvellous!

This is what Maori do, have always done: the women sing after a speech. There is something Attic about Polynesian culture: following a significant action or address, a chorus springs up and comments in song. There is nothing portentous or self-conscious about the performance. On the contrary, it is charmingly perfunctory and usually ends in laughter. Later, I asked one of the women what that first song had said.

'Oh, I don't know what we sang . . . I don't remember,' she said. But a typical wedding *waiata* might praise the speaker or marriage or life in general:

> Love is not only
> a thing of today—
> from our ancestors
> it has been passed to us, to *us*!

Further speeches from both sides followed. One of the speakers, a tall Maori of about forty, with a brilliant, slightly condescending smile, broke into English as he finished: 'For the benefit of our Pakeha guests, I have just greeted this house, those who have lived here before and who are now dead. And I acknowledge that body of water, the Waitemata, and I greet the mountain behind us, Rangitato . . . '

This is something that Maori also do, the *mihi,* the tribute to the house, the dead, the landscape. It certainly provided a sharp contrast to the speaker before him, a young Pakeha friend of the groom's. This man's speech went as follows: 'Er, good on ya, mate. You've got yourself a pretty good sheila there. Aw . . . I'm no good at this. But, anyway, you know, er . . . love ya both [gives the thumbs-up]. Yeah, nice one!'

The speeches continued. A surprising number of the groom's friends wanted to put in a word, but it seemed they had nothing to say. They stumbled for the most part towards the facetious, a sort of boastful inarticulacy. Why, I wondered, did the white New Zealanders, well educated and well travelled, want to prove that they had no store of words to draw on?

It is often said that a sense of inferiority vis-à-vis the Pakeha has fuelled Maori grievances. But so has its opposite—the hauteur of a people who have lived in a country for a thousand years and can overlay every part of the landscape with names in their genealogy; a people who can address mountains. The first time I ever set foot in a Maori household (I was twenty-one, visiting a student friend out in the country), I mentioned a sheer table-topped mountain we had passed a few miles back.

'Does it ever get snow on the summit?' I asked.

'Not often,' my friend's mother said. 'And when it does, the people around here say, "Look, Rangitawaea has put on his cloak."'

I must have looked blank. 'Rangitawaea?'

'Oh, his great-great-great-grandfather,' she said, nodding towards her son.

This seemed to me impossibly grand, a five-thousand-foot mountain becoming, under certain dispositions, one of your forefathers, and I assumed that I had stumbled on an unusual shard of family pride embedded in that remote and sandy corner of the country. But most Maori know their past and their surroundings in this way. When I looked out the window from the wedding party across to Rangitato, the low symmetrical volcano beloved of Auckland's tourist brochures, for a moment it looked more solemn and grave than it ever had on the postcards.

On the morning after the wedding I went to the district court in south Auckland, a suburban sprawl of about half a million people, predominantly Maori and Polynesians living in state housing. In the rest of the country, south Auckland is a byword for wickedness and squalor. I had been there before, late one night, riding in the back of a police car cruising the streets of Otara and Otahuhu. Two hours passed before the police radio crackled into life: 'Male Maori teenager wearing Bugs Bunny T-shirt being pursued: has assaulted complainant at Mobil service station and stolen his leather jacket.' That was the sole outrage against law and order committed in south Auckland on a hot Friday night in midsummer.

In the courthouse, I watched the weekend harvest coming in. The nation's coat of arms hung on the wall: a cloaked Maori and a white maiden with a marked resemblance to Britannia gazed at each other across emblems of toil and prosperity—fleeces, anchors and so forth. Below this image sat their modern equivalents: a stout woman, in judge's robes, looking impassively at the stream of young brown faces in the dock.

Their crimes are mundane. X has stolen a packet of chicken breasts from Pak N' Save. Y has kicked over a motorbike parked in Otahuhu's main street. Z has stolen a car from a dealer's yard (his explanation: 'I wanted a car'). The New Zealand police force was established in the land wars in the 1860s as the Armed Constabulary, and its main function was to catch Maori. Looking around Otahuhu District Court today, it seemed it still was.

Yet something was wrong. For a start there was a surprising number of no-shows.

'Call Samson Kerepa.' A pause . . .

'No appearance, Ma'am.'

'Charles Putai?'

'No appearance, Ma'am.'

'Ricky Ngatai?'

'No appearance, Ma'am.'

'Aotolo Patolo?'

'No appearance, Ma'am.'

'Jason Bolter?'

'No appearance, Ma'am.'

Even those who have turned up do not seem to be fully present. Some stare rigidly into space; others wave and grin at friends in the gallery. One young man of about twenty with a dark, vulpine face is in a peculiar state which I cannot quite read. He is gazing round from the dock like someone who has just joined a party, but he is also hyperventilating—sucking in air through his teeth and breathing out fast, with a sound like 'faarrrck'.

'I *beg* your pardon!' says the judge.

'Yeah, yeah,' he says, as if to say, if that's what you want.

Trembling on the brink of revelation here is the belief that has penetrated Maoridom, right down to these jobless teenagers—that all of this, from the coat of arms to the majestic operation of the law, is a con-trick. The words hang unsaid in the air: 'OK. I pinched a packet of chicken breasts, or maybe a Ford Fiesta. But you stole our *country*.'

I left Auckland and drove through the Waikato, the heartland, the centre of New Zealand's huge dairy industry. I must have been on this road thirty or forty times in my life, but today, in the light of what I now know happened here, it had taken on a different appearance. This is the place where the worst aggression and confiscations took place, acts for which the Queen herself has apologized—perhaps the first time in a thousand years of English monarchy that a sovereign has signed a document that refers to 'the crimes of the Crown'.

Property known to be stolen looks different from that which has been lawfully acquired. The handsome farmhouses, the endless green paddocks stocked with black-and-white cows are outwardly the same, but they have also now been translated to the uneasy region between right and wrong. They are, in police parlance, 'the proceeds of a robbery'.

The value of these proceeds is still being debated. It was a strange experience to sit in the office of the minister of justice in Wellington and ask what he thought of the main front-page story in the evening paper. This outlined compensation claims by local Maori for the greater part of the capital city itself. Eighty per cent of the suburban areas, where most of the city's 400,000 people live, and many important sites in the centre, had, it was said, been wrongfully acquired.

The minister became testy. 'People get excited,' he said, frowning at the phenomenon of public emotion. 'But these claims will be dealt with in the normal way. There's nothing unusual about this at all.'

There did seem to be something unusual to me. Here we were, in the heart of a modern law-based state—beyond the minister's windows rose the pillars of parliament; the Supreme Court was over the way, the US embassy down the road, the Dominion Museum, the stadiums and schools around the capital—and all of it, every stone, stood on shaky ground.

I was driving to Gisborne, to see the replica of Captain Cook's barque, the *Endeavour*, which was circumnavigating the country. In Auckland and the Bay of Islands thousands of people had lined the wharves eager to pay twelve dollars for a tour of the ship, but now a controversy had blown up. Gisborne is a town of about thirty thousand people, half of them Maori. The more radical among them were demanding that the vessel leave the country. It was not welcome, they said. Attempts might be made to sink it. The crew would not be safe if it came ashore.

The grounds of the Maori argument were predictable: Cook was not, in their eyes, the disinterested, stargazing navigator fondly memorialized by whites, but the first robber-colonialist. As soon as he struck land, where Gisborne now stands, he started shooting Maori—a fact overlooked in commemorations of this moment.

'We're sick of you Pakeha jumping for joy every time Cook's name is mentioned,' one activist was quoted as saying in a newspaper.

When I reached Gisborne at about noon, the *Endeavour* had not yet arrived, so I went to the Maori settlement below Kaiti Hill. There I had a friend I had met in Auckland, an economist named Nicky Searancke who had spent years researching her tribe's land and fishing claims and who was about to go to Oxford to do a doctorate. She explained that the situation had grown more complicated. A dispute had broken out between Maori who wanted to welcome the ship and those violently against it. A compromise had been reached. The crew would be welcomed on the *marae*—the traditional Maori meeting place—at Kaiti, but at the same time would be confronted with the Maori perception or memory of Cook's landing.

The *Endeavour* was due to dock at about one-thirty p.m.; while we were waiting, Nicky showed me around the *marae* and led me into the meeting house itself. There are about a thousand of these *wharenui*—'great houses'—scattered across the North Island, some little more than bare halls standing in a paddock, but others immense: carved or darkly painted cathedrals of Maori life. The one at Kaiti is the largest and one of the most famous in the country. Inside, out of the midday glare, there was a meditative gloom. Nicky pointed out the main features, the carved ancestral figures lining the walls, intersected with flax panels woven in a kind of calligraphy that recorded the lives of certain local women and families; the rafters were painted to signify important Maori constellations. We were in a room of words and stars, and, most importantly, of ancestors.

It would be hard to overstate the importance of genealogy in Maori society. The more recent ancestors were gathered in rather reduced circumstances, in oval-framed sepia photographs clustered on the end wall. But the further back they receded, the greater and more glowering the carved figures along the side walls became. This geometry of the past is almost the exact opposite to ours. Our parents and perhaps grandparents may loom over us, but then there is a sharp dwindling into anecdote and anonymity. Maori ancestors, in contrast, grow larger and more important the further back they are, ending up in solid immensities—a range of hills or a constellation of stars. The two geometries never converge, and this is one source of difficulty between the races. Pakeha quite simply do not believe that Maori really care about the past in this way, just as they don't feel responsible for the actions of their own, indistinct forefathers.

Lost among the stars and ancestors, I missed the arrival of the *Endeavour*. This was a pity—I had meant to go to the top of Kaiti Hill and see its sails appear on the horizon, to think of it drifting towards an unknown eighteenth-century coast, or perhaps even succeed in imagining it through Maori eyes—as a great bird that had detached itself from the clouds, or a mobile island manned by goblins. But by the time I reached town, the barque was already on its way up the river, sailing, as it were, past its own consequences—fish factories, car parks, the Millburn cement silo.

There was a big crowd on the wharves, though scarcely a Maori to be seen. The ship docked, and a brief municipal welcome followed. There was a flash of mayoral chain, a town crier in bright blue knee-breeches rang a handbell and shouted 'Oyez', waved his tricorne hat and gave the crew the freedom of the port. Then they were all marched off to the *marae.*

Cook had arrived at almost that exact spot on a Monday afternoon in October 1769. He departed three days later, leaving six or seven Maori dead. He had wanted to load the inhabitants with presents and 'all imaginable kindness' but he could hardly let his crew be attacked or robbed with impunity. The Maori for their part could not allow the newcomers—even if they were goblins—to come ashore and ignore the essential rituals of approach. The result was a strange confusion of uneasy embraces and panicky gunfire.

Two hundred years on, watching those same rituals unfold at the *marae* (and with the memory of the town crier still fresh in mind) it seemed amazing that the two races had ever managed to communicate at all. The twelve thousand miles that once separated them were weirdly compacted in the fifty yards that lay between the sailors off the replica *Endeavour*, held up at the gateway to the *marae,* and their Maori hosts, watching them from in front of the meeting house.

First came the challenge, the *wero*, in which three men chosen for their agility and fearsome appearance advanced towards the gate, uttering hoarse, single cries, their faces contorted. The best description is by Cook himself: 'His gait was singular,' he wrote, 'nor can I compare the manner of his lifting his legs to any thing better than that of a cock sideling to his Antagonist on the Sod.' Then followed a tense business with a green branch and a spear being laid down before the visitors, after which the challengers retreated, with the same gestures and strangely lifted steps, in reverse.

Then came the *karanga*, the call to the visitors to approach, made by an old woman on the porch. This is a call not only from the living to the living, but also between their respective dead. No one I know has ever heard it without the hairs on the back of their neck standing up.

Finally the visitors were ushered forward and seated on one side, and the Maori speeches began. The order of ceremony here, as at the wedding, required that after each speech a song or *waiata* would be sung. But when the second speaker had finished and sat down, a swarm of young men came forward. A frisson went through the crowd.

'It's *Ruaumoko*!' Nicky said in my ear.

'What is *Ruaumoko*?' I asked.

'One of our haka,' she said. 'The big one.' Most people will know the haka, if at all, as the war dance performed by the All Blacks before a rugby international. But that is only fifteen footballers, mostly Pakeha, scattered in a hasty arc over the lush turf of Twickenham or Cardiff Arms Park, performing a manoeuvre they've been practising for a week or two in their hotel car parks. A real haka, done by forty or fifty Maori on their home *marae,* as well as being fierce and 'horrid'—the word invariably used by the first European witnesses—is a set of violent and minutely synchronized actions which accompany a chanted poem, perhaps three or four hundred years old and susceptible to several levels of interpretation, sacred and profane.

Ruaumoko, composed in the eighteenth century, is a classic haka of the East Coast. It invokes the power of the earthquake god—someone never far from one's thoughts in this part of the island. It is performed only on special occasions. As the Maori men advanced, stamping their feet and chanting, the crew of the *Endeavour* looked rather shaken.

'Actually, it's all about sex,' said Nicky. 'Phallic superiority. "We are better men than you. This is our country. Watch how you behave," is what it's saying.' From her tone, I understood that it is both an insult and an honour to have *Ruaumoko* unleashed on you.

It took me some time to find an English text of *Ruaumoko*. It couldn't be translated, I was told; it was not for publication. Eventually I tracked down a translation published in 1943. This turned out to be the sacred—and bowdlerized—version. 'This,' said a prim footnote, 'should satisfy all but deceased Maori elders who held the key to this old masterpiece of the phallic cult.'

> Hark to the rumble of the earthquake god!
> 'Tis Ruaumoko who stirs and quakes!
> Au! Au! Au e ha! . . .

> It is the rod of Tungawerewere,
> The sacred stick given by Tutaua to Uenuku . . .

> Cleaving the twin peaks of Hikurangi . . .
> A gift of the gods! The wonder of men!

I showed the Maori text to a Pakeha scholar of the language. 'Ah,' he said, adjusting his glasses. '*Ruaumoko*! Let me see . . . "Over whose hips does the seminal fluid splash?" . . . Golly . . . "The orgasm like the shudder of the biting dog". Do you know, I really think it might be better to get an elder from the tribe to do this for you . . .'

I left it there. I was interested in the words primarily as a contrast with what had happened next on the *marae,* after the haka was finished and it was time for the visitors to reply.

There were various speakers—the Mayor of Gisborne, the captain of the *Endeavour*, a spokesman for the ship's corporate sponsors and so on. Between the second and third of those, something unexpected happened. There was a shuffle of feet and then some of the crew, grinning and elbowing one another, came forward. Some bright spark among them had thought of a riposte. They began to sing:

What shall we do with a drunken sailor?
What shall we do with a drunken sailor?
What shall we do with a drunken sailor,
Early in the morning?

The protocol on a *marae* is strict, and the order of speakers and choice of songs are the subject of endless discussion. That day in Gisborne we were gathered to exorcise a grievance generations old—*Ruaumoko* was a sign of the solemnity of the occasion. And in wandered the Drunken Sailor with his silly grin.

It is easy for Pakeha to make mistakes on a *marae*, especially if they are trying to do things in a Maori way. These solecisms are generally forgiven and, judging from the wintry smiles on the faces of the Maori hosts, 'The Drunken Sailor' would be forgiven, or at least overlooked. Yet I was struck, once again, by the gulf in language and ceremony that yawned between the two races. It is an odd kind of gap: it is not caused by indifference, or contempt or ignorance, although Maori often accuse whites of all three. In the next speech that afternoon, I came closer to understanding its real nature.

The speaker—the corporate spokesman—was nervous, and stumbled over his words: 'Speaking as a New Zealander of, of European distraction,' he said, his voice quavering, 'this afternoon I feel the pain of . . . the shocking things . . . that happened to your ancestors . . . ' And in that quaver, I thought I heard the faint, strange, background radiation that hovers through this whole story.

'The fact is,' a lawyer had told me over lunch a week before, 'we *love* the Maoris.' I was startled: this was the sort of thing people used to say thirty years ago but never say today. Not because it is a lie, but because it might be true. And if it *is* true, then it puts us in a worse light than ever. For it is one thing to attack and dispossess a people you dislike or fear—the impenetrable Aborigines, for example, or the Zulu—but quite another to do the same to a race whom you profess to 'love'.

Is it possible even to speak of 'racial love' in the twentieth century? Only with some discomfort, although its opposite, 'racial hatred', makes a sprightly entry into any conversation. Yet in the 1840s it was possible: 'You are the very counterpart of

Englishmen,' said Governor Grey to Maori chiefs in 1848. 'In love and mutual trust, the two races will be lost in one.' Most early Pakeha observers concur: the Maori were brave and chivalrous, but also industrious and clever. In the mid-1840s Maori literacy rates were as high as in any country in Europe. In 1842 a missionary wrote: 'Their cry was the same in almost every place we staid at—"Books, books! Give us books, lest we perish!"'

This was the race we entered a treaty with, then attacked and stripped of its heritage.

I was struck by the number of Pakeha, from the minister of justice down, who insisted that they did not feel any guilt for the past. It was like a mantra: 'We don't feel guilt, we won't feel guilt, we mustn't feel guilt.'

That night I slept in a motel a few yards from the beach where Cook and the Maori first encountered each other and I found an image forming briefly in my mind. I saw two figures, a Maori and a Pakeha, locked together in what from one angle was a loving embrace, but from another was a wrestler's grim stalemate. The white's hands covered the Maori's eyes, a Maori hand was thrust across the white's mouth. One was unable to see, the other unable to speak. This ambiguous dream-embrace seemed to sum up much of the past contact between the two races. It has been a long clinch, from which they are only now, with difficulty, disengaging.

In Wellington I went to see Doug Graham, the minister of treaty settlements. He is the man in charge of one of the most detested policies towards Maori, the 'billion-dollar cap', a take-it-or-leave-it, full and final settlement for all the wrongs, great and small, that Maori have suffered. A billion dollars, it turns out, is not enough: four days' worth of the Gross National Product cannot erase a century and a half of deep wrong. Oddly enough, among Maori, his standing was higher than that of most white ministers. He is a rare bird among politicians, a Pakeha who has learned his way around a *marae* and can call on rhetoric equal to the occasion. I wanted to see him not so much about compensation but about another issue agitating Maori minds—the second great asset they lost, their own political power, *tino rangatiratanga*.

Nobody today is quite sure what this means. At a gathering of thirty thousand Maori in Rotorua, it seemed to mean picking up litter and taking lost children to the lost children's tent. At the other end, it means wild visions of a separate Maori state—even proposals to disenfranchise all Pakeha, allowing them to stay on, taxed and policed, as guests of Maoridom. Between these extremes are some perfectly sober propositions. Tribal control of expenditure is one—at present, a tribe or *iwi* needs ministerial approval to spend more than two hundred dollars. New constitutional models are being devised, setting up, for example, a separate Maori lower house to propose legislation to a bi-racial upper house. What all the exhortations and plans have in common is a determination for the Maori to regain some control over their lives. New Zealand can no longer remain a little Britain in the south. In some explicit way it must become a Maori nation again.

'We've taken all the power and kept it for a hundred years,' I said to the minister. 'When are you going to give some back?'

'If you mean tribal control of spending—of course, it's absurd they haven't got it. If you mean a national body that can speak for all Maori—excellent. But if you mean an upper house with a power of veto—it's never going to happen.'

'Why call it a power of veto? Why not think of it as a power of approval?'

'We're not even thinking about it.'

'But it's not going to go away, this question. Every Maori I talk to says the same thing. They want their own source of power.'

'It'll never happen.'

I persisted: 'What about the meeting at Hirangi in April? Five thousand Maori—chiefs, conservatives, radical separatists. They called it a constitutional convention.'

'Never happen,' the minister said.

A state's first instinct is to preserve itself entire. But there are tricky calculations to be made. Give them too little autonomy, and they will fly off in anger; give them too much, and the game is up.

As it happens, there once was an independent Maori state within white-ruled New Zealand. It was about ten thousand square miles of wild country in the central North Island. Its 'capital' was a place called Te Kuiti—the inverted commas represent the poverty and hopelessness of the people who, defeated and impoverished by Pakeha confiscations, had gathered in Te Kuiti around the Maori king. One of these was a guerrilla leader called Te Kooti. He was not a very successful general—he never won a battle, although he did escape about fifty ambushes and for years led government troops on a ludicrous dance around the country. But he was also a great poet, a prophet and a builder of dozens of *wharenui,* the 'great houses' in which Maori found a redoubt as their old world disappeared under the grass of white farmers.

One evening at sunset, I stopped at Te Kuiti, now a farming town on the main trunk line, and went into the grounds of the first great house he built. An old red van pulled up and the Maori driver watched me with, I thought, some suspicion (over the past few years there have been sporadic arson attacks by Maori and whites on one another's property) but then he drove away. As he left, I saw in the back of the van the same row of little dark heads that I remembered in the rusty old cars of Hastings in the 1960s. While I stood before the locked door, admiring its carved lintel in the dusk, I had a presentiment: that the Maori were going to win their fight to reassert themselves and reshape the country.

I was not sure where this conviction came from: it may have simply been the glimpse of the big family in the old red van. Maori are younger and more fertile than the rest of the population, and as their numbers grow, they will wield more power. On some projections, they will constitute nearly half the population by 2045. As the Maori population climbs, the argument goes, so it will be better represented in the legislature, and the demand for separate chambers—for autonomy—will simply fade away. There have already been a few Maori cabinet ministers; and at present a party dominated by Maori has a powerful but junior role in the coalition government. It has already used its new power in surprising ways: it pushed, for instance, to retain the historic links with Britain, preventing moves to end New Zealand's judicial connection with the Privy Council in London. It is a firm snub to the Pakeha that the Maori should feel that five old men, driving from the House of Lords to Downing Street, should be a better guarantor of their rights than New Zealand's own Court of Appeal.

But Maori power, according to radicals, is not just a matter of counting votes. Some Maori are eager for confrontation on a wider front (witness this year's assault on the America's Cup, when a Maori student took a hammer to a yachting trophy). One of the most chilling moments of my time in the country was talking to a gently spoken, silver-haired lawyer, Moana Jackson, about Hastings where we had both grown up in the 1960s. He agreed that race relations then were bad.

'What's your definition of good race relations?' I asked.

'When the two races never meet,' he said.

He paused. 'There's no need to be scared,' he said. 'We are not vindictive people. We'll treat you better than you treated us.'

There is undoubtedly a strong tide running in favour of the Maori at the moment, before which the white New Zealanders are strangely acquiescent. But it is full of ambiguous currents, and is driven by goodwill as well as aggression. The old saying—that over time a country assimilates its conquerors—still applies. If violence and death did come, both sides would surely draw back shocked, like swimmers colliding, because many Pakeha want to see the country change, and are drawn to the Maori world for the qualities their own seems to lack. Whites used to boast about a fraction of Maori blood in their veins; now they are learning to speak Maori and proudly recount their visits to a *marae*. Even the most reactionary white will stop in his diatribe and tell you how well he personally gets on with Maori. Not getting on with the Maori suggests you are uptight, stiff, unnatural, and the Maori are seen as the opposite of all that. They are thought to be at home with themselves, and at home in the country.

A friend of mine, an actor called Bruno Lawrence, died not long ago. He was not buried in the local cemetery; the Maori allowed him to be buried in theirs. This was an unheard-of distinction, whispered in tones of awed envy. Bruno Lawrence to lie among the Maori dead! How much better could you get on with Maori than that?

Semi-darkness, an hour before sunrise. A crowd of people, some shivering, are standing in a belt of pine trees. A scythe of rain cuts out the hill across the fields, and a single dark shadow moves along the road towards us and gradually takes shape as a second crowd. The two crowds converge, pause, then come through the gate towards us, one man calling, the others giving the refrain. This is the opening of a new *marae,* on the wild east coast of the Coromandel Peninsula.

Perhaps a thousand people have gathered here this morning; pinpricks of headlights are still coming down the hill towards the coast. As the procession reaches the new meeting house, the crowd sheltering under the pines comes forward to watch the proceedings, and I am surprised at how many Pakeha are among them. The ritual lifting of the *tapu* commences; the house is circled, then ministers lead the way inside, with hundreds pressing in after them, while hundreds more stand outside listening in the rain to the prayers, haka, speeches and *waiata* that follow in the usual order. Most of the Pakeha have no idea what is being said or sung. A thousand people will soon eat breakfast—cereals, sausage rolls, club sandwiches, chops, pineapple, melon—in a huge marquee which billows upwards and outwards in the wind.

Race relations in this area are not especially good. Over the hill in the town of Coromandel there are two pubs: 'Maoris in the bottom pub, rednecks in the top pub' was the formula I was given. Here in the marquee that seems hard to believe. It is now broad daylight, and a red ensign raps in the wind above the meeting house, where speeches and singing are starting again. The cooks are coming outside for a smoke; the teenagers are heading down to the beach. The opening will last three days, and hundreds of people will come and go as they please during that time. As we leave the tent and make our way back to the paddock where the cars are parked, another question occurs to me. What would be an equivalent event in my own community? Where would you find this easy exchange among complete strangers, the palpable sense of feeling at home in a place you have never seen before? It seems absurd, but the only thing that comes to mind is a radio talk show. On Friday evenings there is a nationwide phone-in on a single subject: rugby. Rugby and any topic pertaining thereto. When did screw-in studs replace nail-on studs? Are the Waikato Chiefs swinging the ball out wide enough? Why aren't any Super Twelve games being played in Timaru? Should the national

227

anthem be played in provincial games against Northern Transvaal?

The switchboard is always lit up. The voices pour in, animated, happy to be together on safe ground. I'm not all that interested in rugby but in the stark farmhouse where I'm staying I tune in too because I like the show's atmosphere of community.

Yet there is something unreal and diminished about the voices coming through the night. This is not really the community, but an escape from it. There is something over-eager and hopeful, something almost childish about them. Something is missing in the Pakeha community: when today's Maori offer visionary models of society, white New Zealanders can no longer point confidently to a superior model. The civic imagery of modern New Zealand is almost comic: here and there across the landscape rise gimcrack images, dopey colossi. At Te Kuiti, opposite the ancient carved meeting house, a huge concrete shearer fleeces a huge concrete sheep. Near the volcanic cone of Mount Ruapehu stands a giant fibreglass vegetable (THE WORLD'S LARGEST CARROT!). Elsewhere you can see a massive cow, a lobster, a salmon and an apple; there is even a four-storey-high kiwi fruit.

By contrast, the new Maori *marae*, with its red gable and figurehead, seems solid, four-square and mature. It is a strange twist in the tale, I think, as we go through the shelter belt of pines, that to such a place as this—in one sense a redoubt against the victorious invaders—so many Pakeha should now be making their way, if only to see what, in winning, they have lost. □

JOHN BIGUENET
THE VULGAR SOUL

It began as a chafing, a patch of dry skin, in the palm of his left hand. He ignored it at first, though at odd moments he found himself absent-mindedly rubbing the chapped flesh.

It persisted. After a week or so, he appealed to the pharmacist in the old-fashioned drugstore and soda fountain near his house. The druggist, a young man whose diploma on the wall behind him was as fresh and white as the medical frock he donned before counselling customers about their minor complaints, asked the man to extend the hand with the rash.

'It's not a rash, exactly,' he said, opening his palm over the counter. 'It's just sort of scaly.'

'Well, Mr Hogue—'

'Tom,' the man interrupted.

'Well, Tom, I think we've got what you need.' The pharmacist led him down an aisle of ointments. Reaching for a purple box, the druggist explained that a simple moisturizing lotion would probably suffice. 'But,' the young man added gravely, 'if itching develops, we may have to consider a hydrocortisone cream.'

Sitting in his car in front of the drugstore, Hogue unscrewed the top of the bottle and coaxed a dab of the lotion on to his hand. Massaging the raw flesh with the mineral oil, he saw deeper cracks in the skin than he had noticed before. He poured more lotion into his palm.

That night, peeling off his socks as he undressed for bed, he thought his right foot seemed blistered. 'Damn new shoes,' he told himself, though a sly doubt vaguely tormented him as he rubbed moisturizing lotion into his hand. He restrained himself from looking more closely at the blister.

Work preoccupied Hogue for the next few days. The lotion seemed to soothe his chafed hand. The blister, which had engorged itself, burst and filled again, required some attention though. He bandaged his foot to prevent infection and waited for his body to heal its own wounds. He smiled at his overblown worries and let them drift away down the broad boulevards of a busy life.

It was with the startled panic of one who suddenly remembers a forgotten obligation that he felt the dampness on the bottom of his sock when he unlaced his shoe a few evenings later. Slipping the sock off his foot, he was shocked to see the bandage soaked with blood. He hopped into the bathroom and sat on the edge of the tub with his ankle resting on the other leg. Holding his breath, he gingerly peeled back the tape of the dressing. As the bandage came off, he glanced at the sore and quickly looked away. Taking another breath, he bathed it in peroxide. He was surprised that he could find no open wound beneath the cotton ball with which he wiped the blood, only a deeply chapped bruise the size of a quarter.

By the time Hogue fell asleep hours later, he had convinced himself that there was really nothing all that strange in what had happened. Rushing from meeting to meeting that day, he had done more walking than usual, and that must have opened the blister. Tomorrow was Saturday. He would try to keep off his feet over the weekend and give the blister a chance to heal.

Despite two days on the couch with a pillow beneath his foot, by Monday he was hobbled by a tenderness on the bottom of both feet. The blistering had spread to the other foot.

He was embarrassed by the expressions of concern offered by his colleagues as he limped to his office. Though he wore bandages, his gait was deformed by the ache of the two raw bruises on his feet. He tried to stay at his desk all day.

Driving home, he passed the drugstore but thought better of conferring with the young pharmacist; he imagined how ridiculous he would look, tottering on one leg as he laid a bare foot upon the counter. And what if it started to bleed? He often ran into his neighbours at the little store.

Hogue decided to wait. Except for the soreness, he was perfectly healthy. He felt sure nothing was wrong, or so he told himself.

The tenderness eased over the next few days, although there were a few incidents of bleeding. He began to use the moisturizing lotion on his feet. Religiously, he continued to apply the lotion to his hand, but, while the dry skin did not worsen, neither did it improve. In fact, it was while rubbing his palms together with a dollop of lotion that he first felt the roughness on his right hand.

He was surprised to find himself almost resigned to his discovery, as if he had been waiting, unknowingly, for this last extremity to exhibit the chafing of the other three.

But there was nothing foreseen in the revelation he received as he undressed one night. Naked before a mirror, he saw a pink circle glowering at him just below his ribs. He watched in the mirror as his fingers inched over his body towards the chapped skin. His hand recoiled as it brushed the intensely painful spot. Suddenly blood began to ooze from it. Hogue lifted his hands to his face; each expressed, drop by drop, thin streams of blood. He did not have to look down to know that his feet were bleeding too.

It seemed a contradiction to him even as he felt it, but a horror somehow calm and deliberate took hold of him. He held out his hands and watched himself in the mirror quietly bleeding. The terror that rose in him had matured so slowly over the last few weeks, had teased him so often with its acrid taste, that he felt no panic. But he did feel absolutely lost.

The next morning Hogue convinced the nurse who answered the phone to schedule an immediate appointment with his doctor. He would have to hurry right over, she told him, to meet with the doctor before the regular appointments began at ten o'clock.

He bandaged himself as well as he was able and made himself drink a glass of orange juice.

The doctor was in a jolly mood when he entered the examining room. Hogue tried to think how to begin.

'Something's happening to my body,' he said haltingly.

'Tell me about it,' Dr Lowy nodded, dragging a stool closer to the examining table on which Hogue sat.

The doctor didn't interrupt until near the end of the story. 'And all five irritations began to bleed simultaneously?' he asked with a tone of surprise that worried Hogue.

'Simultaneously,' he assured the doctor, 'and for no reason.'

'Show me,' Dr Lowy instructed.

Hogue removed his shirt as well as his shoes and socks. He let the doctor loosen the five bandages.

Switching on a flexible lamp, the old man examined each area carefully. 'I suppose you've tried some kind of lotion? Yes, you told me you did, didn't you?'

Finally pushing aside the neck of the lamp with his arm, the doctor looked up at Hogue. 'It looks like some kind of eczema. But just to be safe, perhaps we should get a dermatologist's opinion.'

'And the bleeding would be consistent with eczema?'

233

'It would be unusual,' the doctor admitted. 'That's why I think we should call in a specialist.'

'It couldn't be something more serious, could it?' Hogue asked.

The doctor sighed. 'It can always be something more serious. Maybe we'll do a little blood work on you, see what the numbers say.' He buzzed for his nurse. 'Let Maggie draw a few samples, and then give me a call Friday afternoon around four. I'll let you know what we turn up.'

As he opened the door to leave, he added, 'By the way, don't bandage them unless they start bleeding again. Maggie will give you the name and number of a dermatologist I work with. I'll give him a call this morning and get him to see you this week, OK?'

Neither the dermatologist nor the lab results shed light on his condition. Everything was 'within normal ranges', Dr Lowy assured him when they spoke on Friday, but he asked Hogue to set up another visit for the next week. 'I want to do a little research over the weekend,' the doctor said enigmatically.

When he arrived for his appointment on Tuesday, the nurse ushered him into Dr Lowy's private office rather than an examining room. 'The doctor will be right with you,' she said.

The desk was crowded with sprawling stacks of files and paraphernalia from drug companies—pads of paper, a pen set, a calendar, a ruler—all of which had been emblazoned with the corporate logos of pharmaceutical manufacturers. A snapshot of a young woman with a child was slipped into a plastic frame imprinted with the name of a well-known decongestant. On the wall was a Norman Rockwell print of a doctor examining a freckled boy.

'I'm glad you're here,' the doctor said as he swung open the door, startling his patient. 'I've been looking into your case.'

It worried Hogue to hear his eczema described as a 'case'.

'I've found some articles on a condition very similar to yours, something called psychogenic purpura.' He held out a copy of *Archives of Internal Medicine*.

Hogue took the magazine but did not open it. 'Psychogenic what?'

'Purpura. They're spontaneous lesions—without any apparent physical cause.'

234

'Just like mine.'

'Except that your case history doesn't quite fit.' Dr Lowy paused. 'There is some other literature, though, that comes a little closer. A blood man I know lent me this.' He handed Hogue another publication, *Seminars in Haematology*. 'It's got a review of historical cases of your condition.'

'So what is my condition?'

'Have you ever heard of Therese Neumann?' the old man asked as he searched through the files on his desk.

'No, I don't think so.'

'On Good Friday in 1926, Miss Neumann, a woman about your age from the village of . . . ' Dr Lowy was distracted as he searched his cluttered desk for a particular piece of paper. 'Yes,' he said to himself, finding the sheet beneath some folders, 'Konnersreuth in Bavaria.' The doctor continued to glance at the page, looking for something. 'This woman suddenly began to bleed spontaneously from her side. At the same time, her left hand began to bleed from a spot that had been red for days. By nightfall, both hands and feet as well as the wound in her side were bleeding.' He put down the paper and looked up. 'You're luckier than she was, though. She also had drops of blood weeping from her eyes.'

'From the eyes?' Hogue repeated, unsettled.

'Yes, but these eruptions occurred in the midst of an ecstatic vision.'

'What kind of vision?'

'Of Christ's passion, of course.' The doctor looked at him as if he were missing the point. 'My boy, she was a stigmatic—like you.'

Hogue wanted to pretend the thought hadn't occurred to him. 'Why, that's ridiculous,' he objected. 'We're not living in the Middle Ages.'

Dr Lowy was searching for another piece of paper. 'Yes, here it is. I don't suppose you've heard of Padre Pio? Or the Stigmatic of Hamburg—an interesting case: the man was a Protestant. Very unusual.'

Hogue was shocked. 'You're a doctor, for Christ's sake. How can you take such superstitions seriously?'

John Biguenet

'Superstitions?' Dr Lowy put down the paper he was holding. 'Stigmata are as real as those bloody bandages on your hands.'

Hogue looked down and saw the blood soaking through the gauze.

'I thought I told you not to use bandages,' the doctor scolded.

'The wounds started bleeding again during the night.' Hogue saw the red proof spreading across his palms.

The doctor leaned back in his chair. 'Look, I'm a Jew. You think I believe that Jesus is pricking your body to make you bleed? But that doesn't mean you're not a stigmatic. The one in Hamburg, the Protestant, held only the vaguest religious beliefs. But he even carried the wounds of the Crown of Thorns on his forehead. He begged his doctors to find a cure.'

Hogue allowed himself a smile. 'What did the Catholics make of him?'

'He was quite a problem for them. You know, in all the literature, they take real pride in claiming the stigmatics as their own. One of their theologians quickly classified him among the—oh, what was the term?' The doctor shuffled through his papers. 'Here it is: the *âmes vulgaires*. The vulgar souls. It was decided that he was "spiritually mediocre" and suffered from "psychological blemishes". What a discreet expression, "psychological blemishes"! They wrote him off as a hysteric.'

'I wonder what they would have said if he had been Jewish?'

The doctor laughed. 'Now there's a thorny question.'

Hogue relaxed a bit. 'All right, let's say I'm a stigmatic. What do we do?'

'Well,' Dr Lowy said, growing serious again, 'the symptoms are physical. You know, come to think of it, that's the medical term for the characteristic signs of a disease, the stigmata. Anyway, your stigmata are physical, but the cause is clearly emotional. You're suffering from a psychosomatic disorder.'

'You mean it's stress?'

The doctor seemed uncomfortable with Hogue's interpretation. 'Sure, almost everything that goes wrong with the body has to do with stress one way or another. But this is more complicated than that.'

'Because I don't feel particularly stressed when it happens. Last night I was asleep.'

'It's not as straightforward as simple cause and effect. The body can be awfully mysterious when it wants to. We're complex machines.'

Dr Lowy gave Hogue the name of two psychiatrists. 'Talk to them both. See which one you trust.'

One question still troubled him. 'Is this going to get worse?'

'Well, the classic stigmatics exhibited two or three other symptoms, but you really don't need to worry about them. We've caught this thing in its early stages.'

Hogue persisted. 'What are the other symptoms?'

The doctor seemed annoyed. He picked up his notes again. 'Insomnia, cessation of digestion and clairvoyance.'

'What is cessation of digestion?'

'You stop eating.'

'And then you die?'

'No, not according to the literature. There was a celebrated case in the nineteenth century, a woman from Brooklyn named Mollie Fancher. According to fairly reliable witnesses, from the beginning of April until the end of October in 1866, she ate almost nothing—a piece of banana, two teaspoons of wine— basically nothing at all.'

'So what happened to her?'

'She got skinny and became a clairvoyant. And she wasn't even a stigmatic.' The doctor gave Hogue a sly look. 'Of course, she suffered from multiple personalities, so if one of them were to sneak a snack, Mollie might honestly imagine that she had consumed nothing. Like I said, it's a complicated business, this mysticism.'

Instead of going back to work after his visit to the doctor, as he had planned, Hogue drove to the park across town. It had been built at the turn of the century by a designer who must have loved small, intricate patterns. Narrow walks scrolled around elaborate plantings of delicate flowers and eddied about the feet of carved stone benches in grottoes shaded by weeping willows. In the centre of the little park, a modest fountain spilled its water into a large, shallow pool.

As he circled the fountain trying to come to grips with what the

doctor had confirmed for him, Hogue strained to see through the
shimmering water down to the mosaic arabesques that lined the
floor of the pool. He was startled when a mottled, foot-long fish
suddenly shattered the mirror-like surface of the pond as it burst
into the sunlight, devouring a mayfly that had lit upon the water.
The pool, momentarily animated, quickly regained its tranquillity;
the ripples of the extraordinary event were diluted by the stillness of
the water before they could reach the arched concrete lip that curled
back over the edge of the pool. 'Not a trace,' he almost said aloud,
but a small boy staring up at him (and watched in turn by a woman
frowning nearby) stifled his exclamation.

Hogue turned and followed one of the carefully tended paths
that spiralled away from the fountain. Finding a wrought-iron
bench encircling an oak, he sat and tried not to think. He simply
watched people—the young couples furtively embracing in the
shadows, the old retired men arguing over chessboards, the women
tending children, the swaggering guards puffing up their chests—
and felt for them all the most profound sympathy. He was surprised
by what he felt and he knew the ripples of his compassion, if he
could call it that, would fade in the spring air long before they
could interrupt the kiss of the boy and the girl closest to him, in a
little stand of trees about which the path looped back on itself and
turned once again towards the fountain.

He realized what he was doing and grew annoyed at his
sentimentality. 'I'm playing at being a saint, aren't I?' he asked a
sparrow that hopped nervously from the bench to the ground and
back again.

Hogue put off calling the psychiatrists; he was uncomfortable
with the idea. It was not long, however, before he had to
admit he needed help.

Though it was true that his appetite had diminished over the
weeks of swelling worry about his condition, the insomnia was a
more pressing problem. It had asserted itself with greater
stubbornness after his visit to Dr Lowy, but when he looked back
he remembered bouts of sleeplessness in even the first few nights
of his stigmatizing.

He took the first appointment he could get; one of the two

psychiatrists, Dr Burke, had an opening in three days. Fortunately, her free slot was in the late afternoon. He did not want to miss any more time at the office.

Hogue's work had been suffering. Taunted by inescapable worry, he pushed himself from sleepless nights to drowsy mornings to exhausted afternoons that yielded to yet more wakeful evenings. His supervisor's sympathy was souring into anger, but Hogue, of course, could not bring himself to explain. So by the time he shook hands with Dr Burke in her simple office, he was desperate for a solution.

The psychiatrist wondered if he would like coffee. As he shook his head he realized that he had stopped drinking coffee. Worried about work, he hadn't really thought about all the ways in which his life was changing. By the end of the first session, he and Dr Burke had constructed a list of the alterations, especially the inconsequential ones, that had crept into his habits. That was really all the two of them had done, except that she had asked to see his hands. He removed the gloves he had begun to wear in public. She took his hands in hers and turned them over. 'You have beautiful hands,' she said almost clinically.

'Except for my wounds,' he corrected her.

'Wounds? Is that what you call them?' she asked with surprise, and she wrote something in her notebook.

He felt better afterwards and slept for a few hours that night. The next morning he called Dr Burke's office and moved up his appointment to the following day.

The psychiatrist was surprised to see him. 'I thought we weren't going to meet again until next week.'

Hogue nodded. 'But I really felt as if we made some progress last time. And I can't go on like this. I've got to do something about my . . . ' He almost said 'wounds', but he stopped himself.

Dr Burke asked Hogue to tell her about the last year. Except for the stigmata, there wasn't much to tell.

'I live a quiet life,' he explained with some embarrassment when she asked whether he had dated anyone recently.

'What about religion?'

'Well, I'm Catholic—at least I was raised a Catholic—but of course I don't practise.'

'Why not?'

To believe in God, he patiently explained to the psychiatrist, one has to be willing to close one's eyes to a great deal. 'Isn't that what they mean by faith—refusing to accept the obvious, refusing to accept what's always been right there in front of us?'

'But that's exactly what believers say,' she countered. 'God has always been right there in front of us. We just won't open our eyes.'

'Maybe it's not so easy to see what's right in front of our eyes.'

The psychiatrist laughed. 'That's certainly true, Mr Hogue. I'd be out of business if that weren't true.'

'Not that I blame them,' he assured her. 'In fact, I sometimes wish I did believe. But I'm not going to lie to myself and pretend. It's childish.'

He had believed quite intensely as a child, he admitted. But he had outgrown religion. In college, he explained, he had realized that the wildest myths of primitive peoples weren't any more fantastic than the virgin birth or the resurrection of the dead. 'The scales,' as he put it, 'fell from my eyes.'

'But to suddenly lose everything you believe in,' Dr Burke interrupted, 'surely that must have affected you deeply.'

He smiled and shrugged. 'Not really. It all just stopped mattering.'

So he found it impossible to accept his stigmata as proof of the existence of God. 'What is a miracle, anyway,' he protested, 'except something science hasn't gotten around to explaining?' He was willing to waver in his atheism; perhaps he even hoped to be unburdened of his lack of belief. But, when he looked into himself, he insisted to the woman, he could discern not the slightest trace of faith, not even a doubt.

'I didn't say that your "stigmata", as you call them, prove that God exists,' she said, and then hesitated. 'I just wonder if, in your case, the stigmata might not be simply an extreme form of self-deception.'

Hogue was taken aback. 'Self-deception? What am I deceiving myself about?'

'I don't know. That's what we have to find out. But your body is mutilating itself. It's demanding something of you, isn't it?'

Hogue understood. 'Yes, of course it is.'

'Do you know what it wants?' Dr Burke asked almost in a whisper.

Hogue shook his head.

As his sessions with the psychiatrist progressed, the stigmata bled less frequently. Hogue was getting more sleep, and though he continued to lose weight he managed to eat something every day. He felt cautiously hopeful.

He had been visiting Dr Burke for about a month when a letter arrived from the archdiocese's chancery. A Monsignor McRae informed him that a report from an anonymous member of the laity had suggested that Hogue might carry the marks of Christ's passion on his body. 'It is the duty of Holy Mother the Church to examine all individuals claiming the stigmata of our Lord and Saviour.'

Hogue's first impulse was to deny any knowledge of the stigmata to which the monsignor referred. But he realized that was useless. Whoever had written to the archbishop—one of his co-workers, a neighbour, someone at the gas station—would continue to see the gloves on his hands, the sudden red spot staining his white shirt as he jerked his jacket closed over it. Eventually, a sceptical parish priest would be enlisted to serve as a witness. Once confirmed, the news would fill bingo halls and churches across the city. Already a ladies' guild or an altar society was no doubt spreading the gossip about the local stigmatic.

So Hogue called the monsignor and asked to meet him. The monsignor was happy to honour Hogue's plea for discretion; the Church had no wish to fan the emotional flames of 'miracle hunters', as the cleric derided them. The two men met at a rectory that had been vacated for the evening by the parish's old pastor. 'We sent him to the movies,' the monsignor explained.

After some chatting about his background (and expressions of relief that Hogue had been baptized a Catholic), the priest asked, 'May I see the manifestations?'

Hogue removed his gloves, unbuttoned his shirt and took off his shoes and socks. The monsignor gingerly touched the reddened spots. 'That's it?'

'They bleed,' Hogue told him, 'at least sometimes.'

241

'Anything else?' the priest asked, obviously unimpressed.

'No, not really.' Hogue decided to stay away from the insomnia and 'cessation of digestion'. He tried to look guilty. 'I have to tell you, Monsignor, I'm not a practising Catholic.' Then, to be safe, he added, 'Also, you probably ought to know that I'm seeing a psychiatrist.'

The monsignor was relieved. 'Good,' he said.

'So I hope we can keep this quiet,' Hogue said. 'I find it all very embarrassing.'

'Of course,' the priest agreed. 'The Church is not interested in promoting spectacles. The faithful are easily led astray.'

As he pulled away from the rectory that night, Hogue was very pleased with himself. He had portrayed himself as 'spiritually mediocre'; he had confessed to 'psychological blemishes'. He felt sure he had fended off the humiliation of publicizing his condition. He even stopped at a bar and had a beer though he found it impossible to drink more than a few sips.

His elation was punctured when he arrived home. Tacked to his door was a petition signed by five of his neighbours. Above their names, they had simply written, 'Pray for us.'

Slumped in a chair, the sheet of paper dangling from one hand, Hogue felt desolate. He understood that he could not escape. In a few days, hundreds, perhaps thousands, would know of his wounds. He lowered his head in despair and saw a trickle of blood running down the petition.

The next morning he peeked out through his drapes to see if the long, sleepless night had finally yielded to dawn. Waiting patiently in the street, ten or fifteen people jostled one another in reverent awe, apparently to catch a glimpse as he walked from the house. 'So this is how it begins,' he said aloud in the still dark room.

That evening he was visited by a representative of the Society of the Paraclete, a group with which he was unfamiliar.

'We are guided by the Holy Spirit to announce the Gospel,' said the middle-aged man. 'Despite the authorities, we believe that we continue to live in the Age of Miracles. Do you believe in miracles, Mr Hogue?'

Hogue confessed that he did not.

'Then how do you explain your stigmata?'

He knew there was no point in denying their existence. 'I'm seeing a psychiatrist. We're working on exactly what's happening to my body. It's got something to do with stress.'

'Perhaps you're right. We certainly wouldn't presume to tell you you're wrong. But have you considered the alternative?'

'I've rejected the alternative.'

The middle-aged man leaned forward. 'Mr Hogue, you are involved in something extraordinary. You can certainly choose not to participate in the miracle yourself. But do you have the right to deny others an encounter with the miraculous?'

'It's not a miracle.'

'Why not let others be the judge of that?'

The calm, indefatigable representative wore down Hogue's resolve. In the end, an agreement was reached for a single meeting with the group.

Albert Rapallo, the man with whom Hogue had spoken, picked him up the following Sunday night. 'I'm sorry for the secrecy,' Rapallo apologized, 'but the Church authorities are rather hostile to our work. We like to joke we're a little bit like the early Christians, hiding from our persecutors. Except our catacombs are just the basements of our houses.'

The group of mostly older Catholics greeted Hogue warmly. He declined the coffee that was offered and followed his host into the den. The men, women and a few children joined hands and offered a prayer that Hogue didn't recognize. Then there were readings from scripture. Finally the man who had led the service so far asked everyone to sit. 'Our good friend Bert is going to introduce our guest,' he announced.

Rapallo offered a few words of introduction and then surprised Hogue when he turned the floor over to him.

Hogue didn't know what to say. So he simply peeled off his gloves and held up his hands. He hadn't realized it, but they were bleeding.

'Please,' said a woman sitting near him, 'may we see the others?' She asked so gently and so humbly, Hogue felt he could not refuse. Removing his shoes and socks and lifting his shirt to untape the bandage he always wore now as a precaution whenever he went out, he leaned back in the chair to expose the wounds. The group dropped to their knees and began the rosary.

As they mumbled through the Our Fathers and Hail Marys, Hogue at first felt utterly ridiculous, propped up for their edification in the panelled playroom. But the intensity of their faces, the joy and awe of this moment for them, confirming their most profound desires, swayed his feelings. By the time the final prayers were recited, he felt a great sympathy for these desperate believers. He remembered the afternoon in the park but understood immediately the difference. Then he had been deluded by a kind of ambition; now, though moved by the group's innocent passion, he felt no pretence of sanctity. He did feel, however, as if he had finally resolved something within himself.

Over the next few weeks he agreed to visit other groups. Invariably meeting in secret, small bands of the laity prayed as he revealed his wounds. They rarely bled, but that did not seem to make a difference. More and more often the faithful would whisper special intentions for which they asked his intercession. Though he, of course, promised nothing, he did not refuse the woman who prayed for the remission of her husband's cancer, the man who begged for the safe return of his runaway daughter, the couple who wanted a child.

About two months later Dr Burke was awakened by a phone call just after midnight. It was Hogue.

'Did I wake you? I'm sorry. I lose track of the time at night.'

She was still half asleep. 'Mr Hogue, no, I'm glad you called. I've been leaving messages for you on your machine. I'd given up on you.'

'I'm sorry. It's been so hectic.'

'How have you been? Are you still troubled by the . . . emissions?'

She heard him laugh. 'Do you mean are my wounds still bleeding? Yes, every so often.'

'So how are you?'

'Well, I'm afraid my secret was found out. The archbishop ruled that I was not a true stigmatic, but the people, at least the older ones, were not convinced. They insist that my wounds are a miracle.'

The psychiatrist sounded worried. 'Is that what you've come to believe?'

Hogue laughed again. 'Oh, no. Not at all. I'm afraid my views on religion have not changed in the least.'

'How is your physical condition?'

He took a deep breath. 'Stable. I try to eat something every day. Not much, but something.'

'And sleep?'

'I don't know, I'm so drowsy most of the time. Perhaps I do fall asleep for a few minutes here, half an hour there. That's the worst part really, the insomnia, but at least there's no pain. I've been reading a great deal about stigmata; often there's excruciating pain.'

'What about work?'

'I had to give up my job. It got to be impossible, particularly once the premonitions began. They are so distracting.' He knew she was writing down the word 'premonitions'.

'Then how are you managing?'

'I've become a kind of religious celebrity. I display my wounds at someone's house, sometimes an elderly priest will invite me to a secret meeting in the parish hall. That's really all there is to it. And, after all, how does it hurt to encourage their belief—even if I don't share it—and to comfort them? They are so tender and innocent in their devotion, like children. You should see them.'

'You don't think it's dishonest?'

'How? I don't make any claims for myself. I let them judge with their own eyes. They believe what they want to believe.'

There was a pause, then Dr Burke asked, 'And what do you receive in return?'

'They make donations,' he admitted. 'Not much, but enough for rent. Since I stopped working and sold the car—I didn't think it was safe to keep driving—I really don't spend very much any more. And, of course, they pay my travel expenses.'

'Travel expenses?'

'I've been visiting groups in other cities.' He laughed. 'They joke that it's a reverse pilgrimage.'

'And do they come to your house, these people?'

'Yes, but not as many as you would expect. They're pretty good about respecting my privacy. Of course, I'm getting more and more mail, people asking for favours.'

The psychiatrist sounded exasperated. 'Mr Hogue, you have to stop this. It's going to get out of hand.'

'Doctor, do you remember when you told me that my body was mutilating itself, that it was demanding something of me?'

'Yes,' she said softly.

'Well, I've simply yielded to my body's demands. I don't understand what my body wants, but I do know what will satisfy it. And that's what I'm doing.'

'But what about the people you are deceiving?'

'My stigmata are real,' he insisted, losing patience. 'And I simply don't believe that the cause makes any difference.' He took a deep breath. 'Listen, if my wounds soothe a dying old man or console his widow, if a few drops of my blood help a mother and father over the loss of their baby, should I deny them that consolation? I don't see how my own lack of faith absolves me from offering comfort to those who suffer.'

There was silence. Finally Hogue said, 'I had a special reason for calling you tonight, Dr Burke. I suddenly started thinking about you. You're taking a trip somewhere this weekend, aren't you?'

The psychiatrist was surprised. 'Yes, to a conference in New York. How did you know?'

'That's not important,' he said wearily. 'But you mustn't go.'

'Why?' She glanced down at her notepad and saw where she had scribbled 'premonitions'. 'Is it the plane?'

'No, not that. All I know is that you just shouldn't go.'

'You don't actually believe that you've become clairvoyant, do you?' She was angry.

'I don't believe anything. I just know that sometimes I'm right about these things, and I wanted to warn you.'

The psychiatrist's anger was thickening into fear. 'You can't expect me to cancel my trip because you've had a vision. It's out of the question.'

'You're probably right,' Hogue said, trying to calm her. 'I just felt I shouldn't decide for you. I thought I owed it to you to call. Please, forget I said anything. I'm sorry.' He hung up.

When Dr Burke knocked at Hogue's door a month later she was greeted by an old woman who demanded to know whether she had an appointment.

'Please,' the psychiatrist insisted, 'just tell Mr Hogue that I am here.'

A few moments later Hogue himself ushered the doctor into his study. 'You must forgive Margaret,' he whispered in a weak voice. 'She can be very abrupt, I know. But she's just trying to protect me. They come at all hours now.'

The psychiatrist was shocked at Hogue's condition. He had lost a great deal of weight since the last time she had seen him. He was having trouble walking, and his face had grown so pale and sunken that his dark eyes seemed huge. He crumpled into an armchair and flicked off the lamp next to him. 'The light, you know,' he explained, touching one of his eyes.

'I'm glad to see you,' he went on. 'I wanted to call to apologize for—'

She stopped him. 'You were right.'

He winced as if he had been struck. 'What happened?'

'I'm pregnant.'

Hogue smiled. 'That's wonderful. I was afraid—'

'It's not wonderful. It was stupid what happened. What I did.'

'On your trip?'

She nodded, then took a deep breath. 'I got the test results from the lab this morning.' She slid her chair closer to Hogue's. 'I've got to decide what to do about this right away.'

'Why? You have time.'

'I'm married. This isn't my husband's child. He's going to find out.' She started to cry. 'I love him.'

There was a knock, and the door opened. 'I brought some tea for your guest, Thomas.'

Wiping her tears, the psychiatrist thanked the old woman. Margaret scowled at her. 'He needs his rest.'

'I'm almost done,' Dr Burke promised.

Hogue gestured feebly for his housekeeper to leave.

Dr Burke waited for the door to close. 'What am I going to do? Have this child and pretend it's Ted's? Live a lie for the rest of my life? Or should I have an abortion? Or tell Ted the truth?'

'But you don't expect me to tell you what to do?'

The woman took another breath. 'I want you to tell me what you saw the night you called.'

'I didn't see anything. It was a feeling.' He tried to adjust himself in his chair. 'I was thinking of you travelling—I don't know why. And I knew you shouldn't go. That's all.'

She started crying again.

'I'm sorry.' He took her hands in his. 'Dr Burke . . . Evelyn,' he said, 'don't let me confuse you. You know that what's happening to me is no miracle. It's like you said: my body is simply demanding something of me. And now your body is demanding something of you. That's all there is to it.'

She looked into his exhausted eyes and smiled. 'They take you for a saint. Maybe they'll take me for a virgin mother.'

He laughed weakly.

As she rose to leave, he whispered, 'They're wrong, you know. They've always been wrong. It's not the soul; it's the body.'

She wanted to ask him what he meant, but the old woman was already at her arm, pulling her towards the door.

It was some months later, in the heart of the winter, that Margaret first remarked on his appetite. 'Thomas, you finished your whole meal. Thank God you're finally eating.'

Hogue looked down at his plate. He was shocked to find that he had eaten everything.

That night he awoke with a start, frightened and disoriented. He put his face close to the red numerals of the clock beside his bed. It was 4.12. He tried to clear his mind. Had he really been asleep for five hours?

Hogue lay there in the dark, troubled and hungry. He had sensed changes in himself, he had to admit, small things, but changes nonetheless. The blood, when it finally came, was a mere trickle lately, each drop squeezed with enormous effort, it seemed, from the wound. He hadn't paid much attention to it—the bleeding was always irregular. But now that he thought of it, when was the last time he had bled at all?

Over the next few months he began to gain back lost weight. More and more often he slept through the night. And the bleeding diminished even further until, by summer, he could find no trace of his stigmata.

At first he tried to conceal the changes. But as obvious to those around him as had been the onset of his condition, so also was its remission. He increasingly sensed that those who, just weeks before, had crowded round to beg his intercession now regarded him as a charlatan, the agent of a counterfeit miracle. By the end of the summer, Hogue had lost his following. Even Margaret, though sympathetic, parted company with him that September, moving to Seattle to care for an ailing sister.

Like any invalid unexpectedly cured of his malady, he felt—with no little resentment—his sudden abandonment by those who had ministered to his every need. Yet he told himself he was glad to be rid of them all.

Hogue tried to pick up where he had left off. He found a job—nothing like the kind of position he had held before the stigmata, but at least in his field—and he took a cramped but cheap apartment in a different neighbourhood. Neither at work nor at home, though, could he recover the sense that things were normal.

He imagined himself, especially in dealings with his new colleagues and neighbours, to be living under an assumed identity. He, of course, dared offer no hint of the extraordinary events of his recent life. When pressed, he alluded to a rare illness that he had contracted but survived. And even if he had wanted to reveal the truth, what proof did he have? No matter how insistently the thumb of one hand worried the palm of the other, no seam of skin, no scar corroborated the existence of a healed wound.

When, having finally conceded to himself that he needed help in this readjustment, he called Dr Burke's office for an appointment, he was told that she was still on maternity leave. He declined a session with her replacement. Instead, he called her at home. She knew the little park where Hogue suggested they meet.

The woman had taken a bench near the fountain—in the sun for the baby, it occurred to him as he approached. 'It's good to see you, Dr Burke.'

She looked up from the child, squinting into the late-afternoon light. 'Mr Hogue, how are you? You look wonderful.'

'Well, I'm eating again. And sleeping.'

'Please, sit down. How have you been?'

He sighed. 'It's been strange. Like I told you on the phone, the bleeding stopped.'

'And the wounds?'

Hogue smiled. 'Is that what you call them?'

Dr Burke laughed.

'Gone,' he said, 'not a trace left.'

'I noticed you weren't wearing gloves.'

'Gloves?' He shook his head. 'I'd almost forgotten about them.'

Ever so slightly, she rocked the baby in its carriage. 'So, Mr Hogue, how are you really?'

'OK, I guess.'

'You sound disappointed. Isn't this what you wanted—to be rid of your stigmata?'

Hogue sighed. 'At first, when they began to disappear, I thought I was going to get my own life back. But that's not what happened, not exactly.' He looked away. 'You know, it's like the world you used to live in is gone, obliterated. Now all you've got is this new world, somebody else's world.'

'Mr Hogue, this is the only world there is.'

'Yeah, I guess you're right. It's just that, the whole time people were whispering, "miracle, miracle", I never once pretended at something I didn't feel, didn't believe. And now that it's all over—I know it's crazy—now I feel like I'm living some kind of lie.'

The woman shifted the carriage out of a shadow that had crawled across the path. 'You know, I've often thought about what you told me the last time I saw you.'

'About the baby?'

'No, at the end, just before I left. It's not the soul, you said, it's the body.'

He nodded. 'What else could it be? I mean, unless you believe in God and all the rest of it, what else have they been talking about? Jesus, Mohammed, Buddha—if there is no spirit, then they're talking about the body.'

'I didn't really understand what you meant until Teddy was born.'

'That's the baby's name?'

'Yes, after my husband.'

'So you didn't tell him?'

'Why? Ted would have been hurt. The baby would have grown up without a father. Where is the good in that?'

'And you don't think it's dishonest?'

She gave an exhausted laugh. 'Of course it's dishonest. And don't worry, the guilt never dulls. But I realized that to save myself from that guilt I would have to sacrifice the two people I loved most of all, my husband and my child. Why should I be the happy one?'

The woman dangled her hand above the baby, wiggling her fingers and cooing the child's name.

'You know,' she said, turning to Hogue but leaving her hand lolling over the edge of the carriage, 'maybe neither one of us is living a lie. Maybe we've just stopped deceiving ourselves. And this is what it feels like.'

The baby was growing restless. The woman lifted him and rocked him in her arms. 'He's hungry,' she explained. Discreetly adjusting a little blue blanket over her shoulder, she unbuttoned her blouse and offered the child her breast.

He could hear the infant's ravenous sucking, beneath the cloth. 'But what were we deceiving ourselves about?'

She turned her face to his, even as she continued to suckle the baby. 'Why, everything, Mr Hogue, absolutely everything.'

The woman adjusted her position, and the child, jostled, lost the nipple. Squalling, insistent, he furiously jerked a tiny fist free of the blanket, then grasping a fold in his fierce grip, tugged the blue cloth to the ground. His mother lifted her shoulder, easing her exposed breast towards the child's face. Finding the teat, but still whimpering, he nuzzled the milk from her body.

Embarrassed, Hogue looked down and saw the hands on his lap, hands that had once expressed, he knew with a certainty approaching despair, merely blood.

So Thomas Hogue carried his secret through the streets of the city, among the aisles of the corner grocery store, intent upon his role as an ordinary man. And thus he continued to live, the

quiet tenant in the next apartment, the business associate whose
name one could never quite remember, until he was recognized at
a cafeteria a few years later by a former member of the Society of
the Paraclete.

'You don't know who I am, do you?'

He looked up from his small table, crowded with a plate of
prime rib, a little bowl of mashed potatoes, another of peas, a
saucer with a piece of cornbread, a glass of iced tea and the day's
newspaper folded to the editorials. A woman stood before him,
balancing a red tray heaped with food. She was about his age,
maybe a few years older.

'I'm sorry?'

'It is you, isn't it? The bleeder?'

'I really don't know what you're—'

'I saw you at a meeting,' she interrupted, 'a prayer service.
Bert Rapallo brought you.' She wedged her tray on to the table
and sat down. 'Four or five years ago.' Her eyes narrowed. 'No,
four years ago.'

Hogue sighed. 'Yeah, I remember.'

The woman took his admission as an invitation to unload her
tray. She spread her little bowls and saucers of food among his,
even as he tried to shepherd his dinner towards his side of the table.

'You were something.' She shook her head. 'I mean really
something.'

Her hair was cropped—like fur, he thought. And there was
something coarse about her that annoyed him.

He tried to make conversation. 'Does the group still meet?'

She looked up from her slice of ham. 'I don't know. They
were friends of Frank, really.' She started to lift the fork to her
mouth, then paused. 'My ex,' she explained.

'Oh, you're divorced. I'm sorry.'

'Divorced?' she chuckled. 'No, that's not allowed. Frank got
an annulment.'

Hogue nodded.

They ate silently for a few minutes. She would take a bite
from one dish, then push it aside, trying another. Suddenly she
smiled at him slyly. 'So how did you do it? That's what I want to
know.'

'Do it?' he repeated, pretending not to grasp the question. He realized he didn't even know her name.

'The blood. What was the trick?'

Hogue was struck by the way she ate, moving from plate to plate, nibbling like a bee in a field of flowers. Now she was on to a small bowl of sweet potatoes smothered in marshmallows.

'The trick?' He thought for a moment. 'Getting it to stop, that was the trick.'

She laughed, taking his answer for a joke.

He slowly sipped his iced tea, regarding her down the long snout of brown glass. She was a worn but handsome woman. 'By the way,' he said, lowering the drink, 'my name is Thomas.'

'I'm Karen.' She smiled. 'You know, you almost saved my marriage.'

'Your marriage?'

'Frank, my ex,' she explained again, 'he eventually dumped me for Christine Aronson—do you remember her, the blonde with the big chest? Probably not. You were just there the one night. Anyway, Frank told me I wasn't committed enough to spiritual perfection, and he needed a "helpmate" who was. Can you believe that crap? That's what he actually said, "helpmate". So he dumped me and helped himself to Christine. After the annulment was in the works, of course.'

Hogue was growing uncomfortable. 'That's too bad.'

'And then,' she went on, 'right after I hear he's going to marry her once everything is legal, I get diagnosed.' She shoved her potatoes aside with her fork. 'Ovarian cancer. Advanced.' The woman slid a small cup of chocolate pudding in front of her. 'It knocked me for a loop.'

Hogue didn't know what to say. 'I can imagine,' he managed.

'Frank was right—about me, I mean. That's why I let him get away with it when we finally went to the canon lawyer. I had never really bought all that religious mumbo-jumbo, but Frank liked it, so what the hell, I thought. After a while, though, Frank could tell what I was thinking, and it made him feel small, silly, I guess. We started fighting about it all the time.'

He was confused. 'But what did I have to do with your marriage?'

'Well, when you came along, and I saw it with my own eyes—the wounds looked like they were really bleeding, I saw them—for months and months, till the next summer when Bert told us the truth about you deceiving us, I was a true believer. That whole year I was Frank's helpmate. And everything was different between us—better.'

'I wasn't trying to deceive anybody.'

'It wasn't your fault. I mean, how could it last? What do they call it, a fool's paradise? That's where I was living. But it was paradise, at least for a while.'

Hogue tried to defend himself. 'There was no trick to it. I really was bleeding.'

The woman shrugged. 'Nobody blames you. We were lying to ourselves. All of us. And to be honest, for Frank and most of them, it didn't make any difference anyway. But for me, once I knew the truth, that I'd been hoodwinked—no offence, Thomas— there was no going back. By winter we'd already signed the annulment papers, Frank and me.'

'And that's when you found out about the cancer?'

'A few months later. They pulled out all my plumbing, zapped all the cancer in sight.'

'So you're OK?'

'I was. But now it's back—in the lymph nodes. I just finished a second round of chemo last month.' She poked one of the sliced peaches with her fork. 'But it didn't do any good.'

He suddenly realized she had been forcing herself to eat.

'You know, when the doctor gave me the bad news a couple of weeks ago, I thought about you. What if there was something else? That's what I kept thinking. What if you weren't a fake? What if your hands really did bleed?' She laughed and tried the sweet potatoes again. 'Crazy, huh?'

Hogue looked at the woman. She was still smiling.

Wiping his lips, he inconspicuously slipped his steak knife under the table in a fold of his napkin. □

THE CHANNELING ZONE

American Spirituality in an Anxious Age

MICHAEL F. BROWN

"[An] artful analysis of a largely artless, anti-analytical phenomenon...Happily, *The Channeling Zone* digs beneath the fluff [of its subject]. Mr. Brown explores the ways channeling experiments with sexual identity (most channels are female, while most of the spirits they embody are male), retails religion and celebrates our post-modern fascination with multiple identities (channeling has 'elevated the protean impulse to a sacred principle'). He sees channeling, correctly, as utterly American in its individualism, commercialism and faith in progress...Mr. Brown...deals splendidly with the subtexts of channeling."
—Philip Zaleski,
New York Times Book Review
$22.00 / £14.50 cloth

ROUTES

Travel and Translation in the Late Twentieth Century

JAMES CLIFFORD

"As Clifford puts it, the museum [has] had to become 'a contact zone,' in which the collection...'become[s] part of an ongoing historical, political, moral relationship' between the culture that produced the objects and the members of another culture who...view them. The idea of a 'contact zone' relationship becomes even more startling when the objects...are located at a cultural site...[T]he observant tourist will never be able to see them in the same way again."
—Michael Kenney, *Boston Globe*

"A noted anthropologist examines the complexities of human interaction across cultures and continents in a... revelatory collection of essays...[A] fresh and well-documented perspective on human global movement."
—*Kirkus Reviews*
40 halftones
$18.95 / £12.50 paper
$39.95 / £26.50 cloth

AT HOME IN THE WORLD

Cosmopolitanism Now

TIMOTHY BRENNAN

Timothy Brennan's passionate book is a bracing critique of the critical self-indulgence that calls itself cosmopolitanism. Brennan traces his subject from George Orwell to Julia Kristeva, from "third world" writing to the Nobel Prize, with extended treatment of the Trinidadian writer C. L. R. James and the Cuban writer Alejo Carpentier. A critical call to arms, *At Home in the World* seeks to strip the false and heedless from the new cosmopolitanism in order to revitalize the idea.
Convergences: Inventories of the Present, a series edited by Edward W. Said
August
$22.00 / £14.50 paper
$39.95 / £26.50 cloth

Harvard University Press
US: 800 448 2242
UK: 0171 306 0603
www.hup.harvard.edu

NOTES ON CONTRIBUTORS

PAUL AUSTER's novels include *The New York Trilogy, Leviathan* and *Mr Vertigo*. His memoir *Hand to Mouth*, from which 'The Money Chronicles' is taken, will be published in the UK by Faber & Faber and in the United States by Henry Holt.

MANUEL BAUER was born in Zurich in 1966. His photographs of Lhasa are part of a work in progress on the Sinization of Tibet. A book of his photographs will be published by Scalo next year.

JOHN BIGUENET lives in New Orleans, where he teaches at Loyola University. His books include *Foreign Fictions, The Craft of Translation* and *Theories of Translation*.

J. M. COETZEE's novels include *Waiting for the Barbarians, The Life and Times of Michael K* and *The Master of St Petersburg*. His memoir *Boyhood* will be published in the UK by Secker & Warburg and Viking in the United States.

ISABEL HILTON is a journalist and broadcaster. She is writing a book about the Panchen Lama.

DORIS LESSING was born in Persia in 1919, spent her early life in Rhodesia and now lives in London. She is the author of more than thirty books including *The Grass is Singing, Martha Quest, The Golden Notebook* and *The Good Terrorist*. *Walking in the Shade*, from which 'The Roads of London' is taken, is the second volume of her autobiography—the sequel to *Under My Skin*—and will be published by HarperCollins in the autumn.

JOYCE CAROL OATES's most recent books are the novel *We Were the Mulvaneys* and the story collection *Will You Always Love Me?*. An opera adapted from her novel *Black Water*, for which she wrote the libretto, premiered in Philadelphia last April. She lives in Princeton, New Jersey.

IAN PARKER is a journalist in London. He has written for the *Independent on Sunday* and the *New Yorker*.

GEORGE STEINER is attached to Churchill College, Cambridge. His works include *After Babel, Real Presences* and *The Portage to San Christobal of A.H.* His memoir *Errata: a Journey Inward* will be published in the UK by Weidenfeld & Nicolson.

NELL STROUD is the ringmaster in Santus Circus which tours the south of England.

PETER WALKER is a journalist. He lives in London.